Corsica and north Sardinia

Erratum
Corsica and North Sardinia
RCC Pilotage Foundation (2001)
Plans c Imray Laurie Norie & Wilson 2001
Some of the plans of harbours and
anchorages in Sardinia have been based on
those previously published in **Italian
Waters Pilot** (5th edition) by permission
of Rod Heikell (c Rod Heikell 2001)

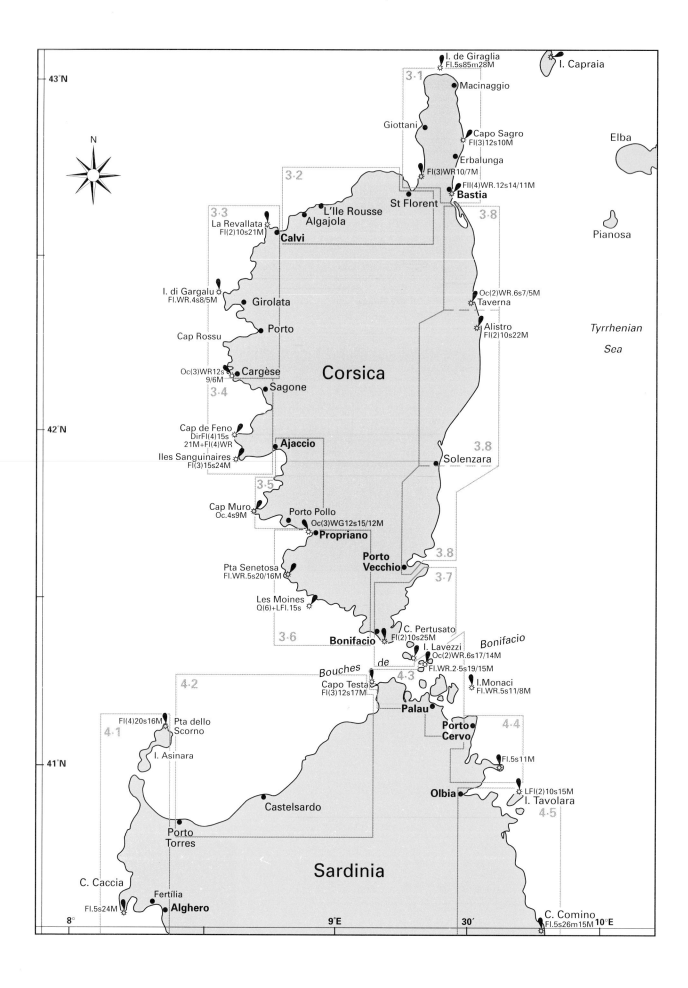

43°N

3·1

I. de Giraglia
Fl.5s85m28M

I. Capraia

Macinaggio

Elba

Giottani

Capo Sagro
Fl(3)12s10M

Erbalunga
Fl(3)WR10/7M

Pianosa

3·2

Fll(4)WR.12s14/11M
St Florent   **Bastia**

L'Ile Rousse

3·8

3·3

La Revallata
Fl(2)10s21M

Algajola

Calvi

I. di Gargalu
Fl.WR.4s8/5M

Girolata

Oc(2)WR.6s7/5M
Taverna

Tyrrhenian

Cap Rossu

Porto

Alistro
Fl(2)10s22M

Sea

Oc(3)WR12s
9/6M

Cargèse

Corsica

42°N

3·4

Sagone

Cap de Feno
DirFl(4)15s
21M+Fl(4)WR

Ajaccio

Iles Sanguinaires
Fl(3)15s24M

Solenzara

3·8

3·5

Cap Muro
Oc.4s9M

Porto Pollo

Oc(3)WG12s15/12M

Propriano

**Porto
Vecchio**

3·8

Pta Senetosa
Fl.WR.5s20/16M

3·7

Les Moines
Q(6)+LFl.15s

C. Pertusato
Fl(2)10s25M

Bonifacio

3·6

Bonifacio

I. Lavezzi
Oc(2)WR.6s17/14M

de

Fl.WR.2·5s19/15M

Bouches

4·3

I.Monaci
Fl.WR.5s11/8M

Capo Testa
Fl(3)12s17M

Palau

4·2

**Porto
Cervo**

4·4

Fl(4)20s16M

Pta dello
Scorno

4·1

I. Asinara

Fl.5s11M

41°N

Olbia

LFl(2)10s15M
I. Tavolara

Castelsardo

4·5

Porto
Torres

Sardinia

C. Caccia

Fertília

Fl.5s24M

Alghero

8°   9°E   30′

C. Comino
Fl.5s26m15M 10°E

Corsica and north Sardinia

ROYAL CRUISING CLUB
PILOTAGE FOUNDATION

Robin Brandon
Revised by John Marchment

Imray Laurie Norie & Wilson Ltd
St Ives Cambridgeshire England

Published by
Imray Laurie Norie & Wilson Ltd
Wych House St Ives
Cambridgeshire PE27 5BT England
☎ +44 (0)1480 462114, *Fax* +44 (0)1480 496109
E-mail ilnw@imray.com
www.imray.com
2001

This work has been based on *South France Pilot – La Corse.* Robin Brandon 1983.

1st edition 2001
© RCC Pilotage Foundation 2001
ISBN 0 85288 462 1

British Library Cataloguing in Publication Data.

A catalogue record for this book is available from the British Library.

This work, based on surveys over a period of many years, has been corrected to August 2001 from land-based visits to the ports and harbours of the coast, from contributions by visiting yachtsmen and from official notices. All photographs were taken during 2000.

CORRECTIONS

The RCC Pilotage Foundation would be glad to receive any corrections, information or suggestions which readers may consider would improve the book. Letters should be addressed to the Editor, *Corsica and north Sardinia*, care of the publishers.

CORRECTIONAL SUPPLEMENTS

This pilot book will be amended at intervals by the issue of correctional supplements which will be published on our website www.imray.com and may be downloaded free of charge. Printed copies are also available on request from the publishers at the above address.

Printed in Great Britain by
Imray Laurie Norie & Wilson Ltd

CAUTION

Every effort has been made to ensure the accuracy of this book. It contains selected information and thus is not definitive and does not include all known information on the subject in hand; this is particularly relevant to the plans, which should not be used for navigation. The RCC Pilotage Foundation believes that this selection represents a useful aid to prudent navigation, but the safety of a vessel depends ultimately on the judgement of the navigator, who should assess all information, published or unpublished.

PLANS

The plans in this guide are not to be used for navigation. They are designed to support the text and should always be used with navigational charts.

Where lights on the plans are identified by a number in red (the international index number, as in the *British Admiralty List of Lights*) the reader should refer to the relevant list of lights in the text for details. All bearings are from seaward and refer to true north. Symbols are based on those used by the British Admiralty – users are referred to *Symbols and Abbreviations (NP 5011).*

Contents

Foreword

Updating the 1991 edition of the late Robin Brandon's *La Corse* is long overdue. The Pilotage Foundation is fortunate to have been able to call on John Marchment's experience of these waters to carry out this work. The opportunity has been taken to extend the scope of the book by including the northern part of Sardinia. This area has many attractions for the cruising yachtsman and offers more sheltered waters than those found in the south of Corsica.

Preparation of this book has taken longer than anticipated and the Pilotage Foundation are indebted to John for his dedication to the task.

As always we will be pleased to have feedback from users of the book, be it corrections or suggestions for improving the contents. Corrections are posted on the Imray website and may be downloaded from there or supplied in paper form on request.

Francis Walker
Director
October 2001

Acknowledgements

Along with hundreds of yachtsmen I have used Robin Brandon's various pilots for many years and it was with much trepidation that I accepted the Pilotage Foundation's invitation to update the Corsica book. I was particularly interested to expand the book to include the north coast of Sardinia where I had cruised for many years.

I have found the task much harder work than I ever imagined and I owe a great debt of gratitude to all my friends, both in the UK and in Italy, who are too numerous to mention individually for their encouragement throughout the lengthy gestation of this new edition. I must also acknowledge the vast amount of help I have received from the staff at Imray, especially Julia Knight, Jill Eaton and Chris Holley, who accepted with good humour the plethora of corrections I kept on submitting.

John Marchment,
Weymouth
August 2001

 Royal Cruising Club Pilotage Foundation

In 1976 an American member of the Royal Cruising Club, Dr Fred Ellis, indicated that he wished to make a gift to the Club in memory of his father, the late Robert E. Ellis, of his friends Peter Pye and John Ives and as a mark of esteem for Roger Pinkney. An independent charity known as the RCC Pilotage Foundation was formed and Dr Ellis added his house to his already generous gift of money to form the Foundation's permanent endowment. The Foundation's charitable objective is 'to advance the education of the public in the science and practice of navigation' which is at present achieved through the writing and updating of pilot books covering many different parts of the world.

The Foundation is extremely grateful and privileged to have been given the copyrights to books written by a number of distinguished authors and yachtsmen including the late Adlard Coles, Robin Brandon and Malcolm Robson. In return the Foundation has willingly accepted the task of keeping the original books up to date and many yachtsmen and women have helped (and are helping) the Foundation fulfill this commitment. In addition to the titles donated to the Foundation, several new books have been created and developed under the auspices of the Foundation. The Foundation works in close collaboration with two publishers – Imray Laurie Norie and Wilson, and Adlard Coles Nautical – and in addition publishes in its own name short run guides and pilot books for areas where limited demand does not justify large print runs. Several of the Foundation's books have been translated into French, German and Italian.

The overall management of the Foundation is entrusted to Trustees appointed by the Royal Cruising Club, with day to day operations being controlled by the Director. All these appointments are unpaid.

In line with its charitable status, the Foundation distributes no profits, which are used to finance new books and developments and to subsidise those covering areas of low demand.

1. Introduction

Aim

This book is written with the sole intention of providing a simple and safe guide for the yachtsman who has not had a vast amount of pilotage experience in these waters. By following a series of instructions he can visit the many pleasant harbours and bays of these islands with ease and minimum risk. More experienced yachtsmen will find the obvious stated too frequently for their need, but nevertheless they should find a large amount of useful and sometimes vital information for their use.

Layout

Part 1 of this book is concerned with the general background information necessary to make a cruise in these fabulous waters as enjoyable as possible. It is always difficult to know what to include and what to omit but with so much information available in the various references listed in the bibliography the compiler has decided to keep the information to a minimum, especially that which goes out of date quickly. Part 2 is devoted to the local weather and sea conditions, weather forecasts, harbours of refuge etc. There is also a valuable planning guide which lists harbours, anchorages, headlands and passages showing the distances between important places and the direction of the winds which can make the anchorages uncomfortable and/or untenable.

It should be noted that the majority of previous guides circumnavigate Corsica anticlockwise while Sardinia is usually rounded clockwise. The compiler intends to continue with this custom. It should be noted that in the area of the Bonifacio Straits there are over 20 harbours and hundreds of anchorages within a circle of 20 miles radius and you can spend a very pleasant month or two here without spending two nights in the same place – although you should like cruising in winds of force 6 and higher on occasions!

Part 3 is the detailed pilotage section for Corsica with Part 4 the section on Sardinia.

Types of harbour

A port in this book is considered to be of large size and primarily concerned with commerce (e.g. Bastia), a harbour is small, often with a commercial or fishing quay (e.g. Port de l'Ile Rousse). A yacht harbour (⚓) is a harbour devoted to yachts, with possibly a small fishing section (e.g. San Florent). A marina is a complex of yacht harbour, shops, hotels and facilities especially designed for yachtsmen (e.g. Porto Cervo).

The pilotage notes have been written with power or sailing yachts of conventional design, drawing up to 2m, in mind. Most yacht harbours are equipped with pontoons, jetties, catwalks, landing stages and piers to which yachts can secure. There are many types of design, both floating and fixed, but in this book all have been referred to as pontoons – the words 'quay' and 'pier' are used as appropriate.

Soundings shown on the plans and mentioned in the text are in metres and are based on the local datum which is Lowest Astronomical Tide (LAT). The water level will only fall below this in extreme meteorological conditions.

Plans

The plans that are provided for each harbour are of simplified nature for the express use of yachtsmen. All irrelevant data such as depths over 5m have been excluded and extra data such as yacht clubs, harbour offices etc. have been added. They have been taken from the best information available and local visits but in view of the great changes that are taking place and are planned they should be used with care and prudence. They should only be used as a guide and not for navigation.

All bearings in this book are given in 360 degree notation, are from seaward and are true. An addition to previous editions is the addition of local waypoints normally located, and marked as 'WP' in the plans, in the harbour entrance. These may be too precise for the cruising yachtsman but, obviously, can be altered to suit individual tastes.

Note All times in the book are local time unless specifically noted. Local winter time is UT+0100 and summer time is UT+0200.

Facilities

Rather than repeat a great list of facilities at every one of the 70 or so main ports and yacht harbours in the book it is intended to list the exceptions. The majority of modern yacht harbours described in this book are well equipped and those that are new are making great efforts to come up to a good standard. Some of the extremely new ones have very limited facilities at present and these will be mentioned as appropriate.

Where the majority of the following facilities are available it will simply say 'All':

a. Fuel available at fuelling berth,
b. Water on pontoons,
c. Electricity on majority of pontoons,
d. Rubbish bins, showers and toilets available ashore,
e. Telephones available ashore,
f. Weather forecast available at office,
g. Repairs can be undertaken,
h. Crane available,
j. Restaurants and bars nearby, if not as part of the harbour,
k. Provisions and chandlery available close by,
l. Diver available.

Other facilities like post offices, banks etc. will obviously be only found in the larger towns.

Yacht and equipment

Engines A powerful and reliable engine is essential for motoring through the inevitable calms of the Mediterranean. On other occasions it will be required to motor against strong winds and a short steep sea to get into harbour. A petrol engine can be very dangerous in these waters as in the high temperatures petrol vaporises easily and the risk of explosion or fire is that much greater. Also petrol is not always available at fuelling berths.

Refrigeration A refrigerator is important in these waters and it is recommended to have one driven off the engine, like the Frigoboat. The engine is used frequently enough to keep a well-insulated fridge cool throughout the day. Ice boxes are not recommended as blocks of ice, even at commercial fishing harbours, are getting more and more difficult to obtain.

Ventilation Most British-built yachts have inadequate ventilation for Mediterranean cruising and extra skylights, vents and extra deck insulation can help mitigate the problem. Also an awning is essential to keep the hot sun from the deck/cockpit area. It should be well made with side flaps and fitted so that it can be rigged while motoring (and preferably while sailing although this is less important as if there enough wind to sail then the draught is enough to cool the deck). An air-scoop to funnel air down the forward hatch is also an excellent investment especially in marinas where the surrounding quays seem to maintain a bowl of hot, humid air even during cooler days.

Anchoring Much has been written about the difficulties of anchoring in these waters and looking at a cross section of the decorative trivia over the bow roller in marinas one can see why. There is no substitute for weight and a bower anchor of CQR or Danforth type with at least 60m of heavy chain is required. A lighter kedge with 10m of chain and a 50m line (preferably one that sinks!) is useful for lunch stops and when mooring stern-to or bow-to

quays (but do make sure there is no holding off line available before dropping your anchor). A common habit in the islands is to anchor, then go for a swim and go down and ensure the anchor is indeed well bedded in – if not it can be dug in by hand. If caught out in an exposed anchorage it is useful to have a 56lb weight available which can be lowered down the anchor cable to prevent snatching in the steep seas that quickly build up. In fifteen years of cruising in these waters the compiler has never had any problem with a dragging anchor!

Mooring The method of mooring in yacht harbours is becoming surprisingly standard, back up to the nominated berth and drop a short warp over a bollard or cleat while picking up a small line or chain which is led forward and you will arrive at a larger warp or chain which is attached to a *corpo morto* or sinker. The boat can then be positioned as required with 2 stern warps (with chain loops to prevent chafe) and appropriate tension put on the forward warp to keep the craft off the quay. The light line (or *pendillo* as Robin Brandon calls it) is quite often very dirty and in some harbours covered in small mussels, barnacles, etc. which can inflict nasty cuts to bare skin. It is advised to keep a pair of heavy leather gloves in the cockpit lockers for use during the mooring operations.

Electricity Electricity is available in most harbours and 220V 50Hz is common now. It is worth having a 25–30m coil of heavy 3-core cable to enable a trickle charger to be run at least. Note that the high harbour charges generally include electricity! There are numerous types of sockets and it is advisable to have male plug on the end of the cable to the yacht and a number of short jumpers which allow connection to any type of shoreside connector.

Water As with electricity good quality water is commonly available at the quay/pontoons in most harbours. There is usually a hose as well but it is still recommended to have a 30m length of hose on board just in case. Again there are numerous connector types but ingenuity (or borrowing the next-door neighbours hose) can make this unimportant.

Shower A shower fitted to the stern is now common in modern yachts – as are pressurised hot water systems – and they are most useful in washing off the salt after a swim. The sun-shower outfits, simply a black plastic bag with a short hose and shower rose attached, also work well but be careful the water does not get too hot.

Gang planks These *passerelle* are most useful if you are spending a fair bit of time in harbours. A plank of wood is adequate but heavy, especially if it is required to project over a long sloping stern. Consideration should be given to the purchase of a light aluminium ladder which, with a marine ply covering of the rungs, is lighter and easier to stow than a thick plank.

Mosquito nets Some people advocate fitting screens or nets to all openings. Others think this is tedious and inconvenient and use the mosquito coils and/or repellents. In 15 years of cruising these waters the compiler has never found the need for either – although he has been attacked many times when ashore for a meal – also eating a clove of garlic a day is said to be an effective repellent!!

Navigation

At the time of writing Loran is not available in the Mediterranean (and with two stations defective it probably will not come back!), shore RDF stations are slowly being abolished and most light intensities have been markedly reduced over the past 10 years (especially in Sardinia). It is with some regret that the compiler is forced to recommend the purchase of, at least, a hand-held GPS receiver so that the yacht skipper knows exactly where he is at all times.

A VHF set is required for talking to marinas and harbour masters – it is essential to know if there is room in a harbour you are bound for!

A good SSB receiver is also useful if full use is to be made of the excellent weather forecasts broadcast regularly from both French and Italian shore stations. Do not make the mistake of buying a radio capable of receiving only AM transmissions broadcast by national radio stations or assume that SSB is only applicable to transceivers. Most coast radio stations broadcast on SSB, whether USB (Upper Side Band) or LSB (Lower Side Band) is easily determined. Digital tuning is very desirable and the set should be capable of tuning to 0·1kHz. Several makes of SSB receivers are presently available in high street retailers and marine outlets.

Italians have taken to the mobile phone – a *cellulare* or *telefonino* – in a big way and they use them everywhere – including on yachts (and often in restaurants unfortunately) – and many places which do not have VHF now give phone numbers to contact the mooring authorities. Obviously it is not a vital piece of equipment but if you have an international mobile for your own use it may be useful on occasions to help you decide which yacht harbour to use.

Place names

Names of places on charts of these islands vary considerably, with the age of chart and who published it. The official language of Corsica is French but there is also a Corsican language with dialects, while Sardinia is Italian speaking with their own language and dialects also. This can cause a certain amount of confusion but when it is realised that features, usually miles apart but sometimes quite close, can have identical names further confusion is likely.

As the compiler is better at Italian than French he has used the Italian and/or common spelling in all cases. Local variations abound and this is a further excellent reason for the recommendation of a GPS system as although most of the navigation is

'eyeball' it is often necessary to double-check your actual position on the ground!

Charges

There is a law in Italy that mooring at a pier for 24 hours is free but, like most laws in Italy, the locals can find a way round a new law before it is ratified and this one has been on the statute books since before Caesar probably so there has been plenty of time to sort it out! What usually happens is the local 'Commune' or council rent out sections of the quay to individuals who are allowed to charge (usually a modest sum actually) for assisting you to moor and will look after the vessel. If you refuse to pay this man you may occasionally find a few small items disappear but much more likely is the water/fuel charges are inflated to a point where you pay anyway. Play this one by ear but even if you do not think the man that approaches you is genuine it is prudent to smile and pay up to keep on the right side of him. Naturally in the yacht harbours where you moor to a pontoon there will be charges and these charges depend on size, season (and who you know).

In 2001 a 'tax' was instituted in all Italian national parks which includes Isola Asinara and all the islands of the Maddalena group which all visiting craft have to pay. Buoys have been laid in many bays and use of these, (and, note, even if one anchors in the area of the park) costs 30,000 lire (15·5 euros or £10) a night. The fee is collected by official boatmen but note that there is a monthly fee of 180,000 lire (93 euros or £60) which makes stays of more than 6 days relatively cheaper. Areas prohibiting the use of anchors, fishing and diving gear have also been set up and visiting craft can make themselves aware of the details by visiting www.parks.it.

Local habits

The compiler started sailing in 1946 from Falmouth and has, since then, sailed in most oceans of the world but particularly in the Channel Isles/Brittany coast area which are easily accessible from his home in Weymouth for most of his life. In 1984 he was fortunate to find a job in La Spezia where he spent 8 happy years sailing in the Mediterranean (when not working!). The first thing he noticed was that although the average Italian sailor was happy to anchor off a beach or in a bay for lunch, swim, tea etc. around 1700 he wanted to get home to his mooring or to a more secure place for the night. It is true that conditions do change more rapidly than in the Channel (and the compiler has been caught out a couple of times) but usually the forecasting is as accurate as in UK and he has never been really able to obtain an explanation of this need for a really secure berth for the night. It may be due to the Italians' love of food and the disruption of a meal to shift is more than they can bear – or maybe they like a guaranteed night's sleep?

Again during the compiler's visit to Sardinia for the preparation of this book, everyone that he talked to was warning him not to sail at night around the coast. There are many unlit rocks but so there are in the Channel Isles for example, and the Mediterranean does not have tides to worry about, but I still cannot get to the bottom of this habit. It appears to be a combination of:

a. You miss all the beautiful scenery sailing at night.
b. Secure anchoring is becoming a lost art – see comments on anchoring above.
c. All the lights may not be functioning.
d. You miss the best meal of the day when sailing in the evening.
e. There is absolutely no chance of getting a reasonable (any) berth after 1700 or before 0900 in the months of July and August.

Seriously though with a GPS, an experienced navigator and reasonable crew there is no real difficulty in sailing at night in these waters. However, it is also true that some harbours close at night and one or two prohibit all movement during the hours of darkness.

Another custom, very common in Sardinia, is that many yachts leave their berths about 0900–1100, motor a few miles and anchor off a beach for lunch etc. but will return around 1700 or 1800 having reserved their berth with the *capitaneria* for as long as a week or two. This enables the family to come over from the mainland by car (Italian wives are similar to the English in this respect!) and have a one or two-centre holiday without a long sea cruise each way! This habit does create problems because if you enter the relatively empty harbour at midday, say, and tie up to a berth you nearly always have to shift when the (temporary) owner returns. A yacht harbour at 1700–1800 on an August day is not a place to be as the battle for berths can become quite acrimonious.

There is one very useful (and most friendly) facility which is common in Corsican yacht harbours (but rarer in Sardinian ones) which is allowing a visitor to berth free for 2 or 3 hours. This enables one to shop, fuel and water and then leave for a chosen anchorage without having to check in to the bureau and pay money (which can sometimes be a lengthy procedure).

Like the mobile phone or *cellulare*, another modern convenience the Italians have taken to in a big way is the rigid inflatable boat (rib) or *gommone*. These are trailed to the islands in their thousands during the summer season and used for fishing, swimming etc. As they cannot easily be brought ashore this has resulted in an explosion of pontoons appearing in all sorts of shallow water areas, especially around La Maddalena, and a crowd of RIB's tied to a pontoon should be viewed with extreme caution by a yacht with a normal 2m draught.

Further reading

The Granite Island by Dorothy Carrington (Longman)
This Corsica by Dorothy Carrington (Hammond)
Unknown Corsica by G. Pillement (Johnson) which describes, in outline, the country, places of interest and towns and villages.
Corsica by Ian Thomson (David and Charles).
Les Guides Seuil No. 20, Corse (in French). A useful guide to the towns, villages and places of interest in Corsica.
Regions of France No. 24, Corsica. Issued gratis by the French Tourist Office giving general information.
Corsica Today by Jean Hureau (Editions j.a.). Interesting guide with good photos.
Green Guide Michelin – Corse. Useful detail but not up to the usual standard.
Mediterranean Island Hopping. Diana Facanos and Michael Pauls. Only 63 pages on Corsica but containing a lot of data.

2. Technical information

Climate and weather

The islands, although appearing quite large when sailing around their coasts, are small in meteorological terms. Their general weather patterns are similar and, in general, are controlled by the larger land masses that surround them. Local land and sea breeze effects are common in summer and can blow at surprising force, especially off deep valleys that abound round the islands' coasts. The Straits of Bonifacio are another very special area where there can be strong westerly (or easterly) winds blowing for days on end sometimes while 20–30 miles north or south there is no wind at all! This will be brought up again later in the book.

The Italian (and Corsican) habit of referring to the direction of the wind by name is initially confusing to strangers as not only do they use names for winds but they use the same names for compass points (see figure). Officially *grecale* is northeast, as shown, but of course the *grecale* wind rarely blows from exactly northeast so you can see there is plenty of scope for error. The *maestrale*, for example, often blows westerly in northern Corsica and it is quite obvious a *maestrale* from the temperature and strength. A *ponente* pressure wind is quite different and will blow from the west as well. You must be clear whether the person you are speaking to is referring to a direction or the wind itself!

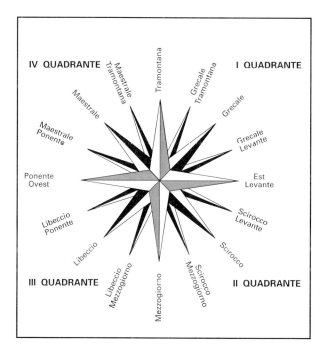

The radio weather forecasts usually use the quadrantal system for wind direction. Wind from the first quadrant, for example, and this means a wind in the 90 degree quadrant from north to east, with the other 3 quadrants to south, to west and to north usually numbered in Roman numerals (I, II, III, IV).

The major wind to affect the islands is the *maestrale* the cold wind that blows down the Rhone valley and fans out over the Golfe du Lion arriving at the islands normally as a northwesterly air stream but it can be westerly or even southwesterly at times. It can be very strong (force 6–8) in winter at Cap Corse in the north (usually less in the summer) but rarely gets more than force 4–5 at the south end of the west coast of Sardinia. This can be a dangerous wind on the west coast of the islands as the longer fetch can build in a much bigger sea than occurs near the French coast. Also the effect of the *maestrale* on the nominally leeward east coast can be dramatic as the wind is accelerated over the high mountains and comes down the valleys at force 8 to 9 sometimes, causing chaos in normally sedate marinas! Weather forecasts give up to 12 hours notice of a strong *maestrale*.

The *tramontana* is the cold northerly air stream that comes from the Alps and the Apuane mountains. Again the fetch can build up a large sea but the wind rarely gets above force 5 and it is generally a short lived blow – in fact the sea may build up without wind arriving at all and it is generally a winter/spring phenomenon.

The *libeccio* is a southwest to west pressure wind which blows fairly frequently throughout the year. It is a warmer and more humid wind than the *mistral* but it can blow up to gale force in winter and the fetch allows a nasty sea to build up. Again it can be dangerous to be in an exposed bay on the west coasts but as this wind originates from a depression moving through the Mediterranean the forecasts usually give 12 or more hours notice.

The *scirocco* is a very warm south to southeast wind that blows off the deserts of Africa and can reach gale force in the winter months and can blow fairly strongly in the summer especially on the south and east coasts of Sardinia. It picks up sand from the desert and water from the sea and can bring the 'red rain' up as far as Genova sometimes.

The *grecale* is the northeast wind which can be dangerous in the central Mediterranean (Malta) but rarely blows above force 6 in the northern part of the islands. If in an exposed anchorage it is wise to move, however, if a *grecale* is forecast

You may also hear of *ponente* and *levante* which are west and east, normal pressure winds, respectively, but these usually get subsumed into one of the more exotic names above.

Clouds and precipitation

The islands are relatively free from cloud cover with a summer average of 2/8 and a winter average of 4/8. In spite of this lack of cloud cover the islands do receive some 400 to 1200mm of rain each year, except on the north coast of Corsica which is virtually a desert. However when it does rain it is very heavy (50mm in one hour is not uncommon!) and can seriously reduce the visibility. The main rainy season is around October but rain can occur in any month with thunder storms being prevalent in the summer months. These storms normally take place near the coast or over the nearby mountains and can be absolutely spectacular with almost constant thunder and lightning with torrential rain. The winds can increase from nothing to force 5 to 6 in minutes and blow all round the compass which makes for excitement in crowded anchorages but usually the locals know the conditions and make sure they are tied up in a secure place. The one consolation is that they usually last for only an hour or so. Fog is rare and any dawn radiation fog quickly clears by mid-morning. Mirages can also form on calm days.

The sea

The temperature of the waters around the islands varies considerably due to local wind effects but is about 12°C (54°F) in winter and 24°C (76°F) in summer. Currents in the Mediterranean around the islands are generally weak and tend to flow in a southerly direction at about half a knot or less. However the sea is much saltier than the Atlantic Ocean, which increases the surface tension and the wind effect is much more apparent than in the large oceans. Surface currents of up to 3 knots to the west have been reported in the Straits of Bonifacio after an easterly blow of 3 days, and similarly for westerly winds. It is true to say that if the winds have been blowing in one direction for 2 days or more there will be a surface current in the direction of the wind.

This surface tension effect also helps to account for the incredibly swift build up of seas around the islands. Where there is enough fetch for the sea to develop a force 5 to 6 wind will build up a metre trough to crest sea, with crests only tens of metres apart in less than two hours. These seas should not be underestimated and a powerful engine is required to motor against them. Swell is not such a problem as in the channel as the fetches are much reduced but the swell that remains after a blow can be uncomfortable for up to a couple of days. The swells seem to get everywhere, including quite sheltered

marinas where there can create a nasty surge or *risacca*. For this reason berthing lines should be heavy, preferably with a chain loop around the bollard or ring ashore, and some form of spring or stout rubber snubber is advisable. Needless to say deck cleats must be capable of taking the extra strains imposed.

Tidal range can be 0·25m at springs which can be ignored for all practical purposes as the atmospheric effects of barometric pressure and onshore/offshore wind effects can exceed this range by a factor of 4.

Waterspouts have been witnessed off the north and west coasts of Corsica but the compiler has never heard of any damage to yachts being caused by these spectacular occurrences.

Magnetic variation

As of 2001, the lines of magnetic variation run virtually north/south over the two islands with the west coasts experiencing 0°25'E variation and the east coasts 0°35'E variation both increasing by some 5'E per year.

In practice, for the next few years, this can be ignored due to the lack of accurate data on the exact current set and rate and the difficulty of steering to better than 2° or 3°. There are also some areas of magnetic perturbations which are mentioned in the text.

Lights

The numbering system for lights shown in lists and on the harbour plans is taken from the *Admiralty List of Lights*, where possible. However, many of the smaller lights are not covered by the UK light list and in these cases the number is taken from the equivalent French or Italian publication and indicated with a bracketed (F) or (I), as appropriate.

Weather forecasts

Both the Italian and French forecasts for the areas around the islands are extremely accurate, considering the complexities of the meteorological situation. The main stations are given below but times and frequencies are prone to change and an up-to-date almanac or the RYA *Weather Forecasts* handbook (G5) should be carried to ensure details given below are correct. The RYA booklet *G5* is updated each year and contains all the information required together with a very comprehensive multi-language vocabulary.

Weather forecasts in French and English
Monaco (43°43'N 07°43'E)
On 4363kHz SSB (Ch 403) at 0903, 1403 and 1915 LT in French and English for Lion, Provence, Ligure, Corse, Elbe, Baleares, Minorque, Sardaigne, Maddalena and Est Cabrera.
On 8728, 8806kHz (Ch 804, 830) SSB at 0715 and 1830 UTC in French and English for all western Mediterranean areas.

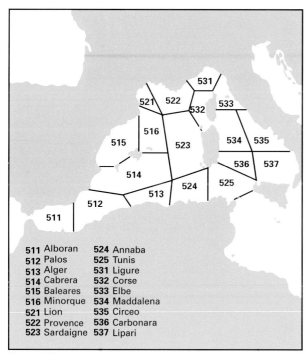

511 Alboran   524 Annaba
512 Palos   525 Tunis
513 Alger   531 Ligure
514 Cabrera   532 Corse
515 Baleares   533 Elbe
516 Minorque   534 Maddalena
521 Lion   535 Circeo
522 Provence   536 Carbonara
523 Sardaigne   537 Lipari

France. Forecast areas

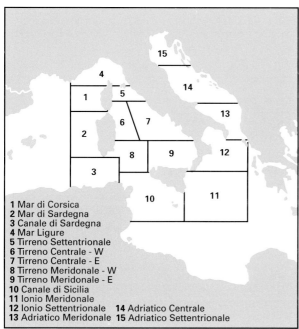

1 Mar di Corsica
2 Mar di Sardegna
3 Canale di Sardegna
4 Mar Ligure
5 Tirreno Settentrionale
6 Tirreno Centrale - W
7 Tirreno Centrale - E
8 Tirreno Meridonale - W
9 Tirreno Meridonale - E
10 Canale di Sicilia
11 Ionio Meridonale
12 Ionio Settentrionale   14 Adriatico Centrale
13 Adriatico Meridonale   15 Adriatico Settentrionale

Italy. Forecast areas

Weather forecasts in French and Italian

Bulletin Inter-Servicer-Mer on 162kHz Sat, Sun 0654, 2003 LT

Radio France-Internationale 1184kHz at 1140

Radio Bleue from Bastia 1494kHz at 0655 LT

La Garde CROSS on 1696, 2677kHz SSB after call on 2182kHz at 0650, 1433 and 1850 LT for same areas as Monaco (1) above.

However Radio Italia (Radiouno) broadcast a Bollettino del Mare at 0554, 1408 and 2249 Monday to Friday, with the 1408 broadcast being omitted during the weekend, in Italian for all Italian sea areas. Porto Cervo gives local waters forecast on

VHF Ch 26, 28 or 85 at 0150, 0750, 1350 and 1950 (in English and Italian) as does Ajaccio on VHF Ch 24 (Grasse on VHF Ch 2) at 0733 and 1233 (in French) all with a call on VHF 16 beforehand.

A new forecast from the Italian Aeronautical Service was launched in 1998 and is broadcast continuously on VHF Ch 68 in Italian and English at dictation speeds. Gale warnings (*burrasca*) are broadcast as they are received and the whole message is updated two or three times a day.

Coastal radio stations

Most European countries are radically reducing the number of manned radio stations and concentrating the service on a (small) number of centres with remotely controlled outstations.

Marine radio direction finding (RDF) stations are being taken out of service, generally through lack of funds to maintain them but the aeronautical beacons are being kept in service due, mainly, to the increased air traffic to the islands.

VHF	*Ch*	*Ch*
Cagliari	*(manual)*	*(automatic)*
Campu Spina	82	83
Monte Serpeddi	04	78
Porto Cervo	26	88
Monte Moro	28	66
Margine Rosso	62	63
Monte Limbara	85	86
Osilo	26	61

Local weather forecasts are broadcast at UTC 0135, 0735, 1335 and 1935 with a call on Ch 16 beforehand. Traffic lists are supposed to be transmitted at each hour +15 minutes (with a call on Ch 16 beforehand) but this seems to be going out of fashion and is being transferred to SSB frequencies.

SSB

Cagliari 2182kHz (call), 2680kHz work, Ch 268 (automatic).

Porto Torres 2182kHz (call), 2719kHz (work)

Traffic lists, navigational warnings and weather forecasts are broadcast 4 or 5 times a day with a call on 2182kHz beforehand.

Radiobeacons

At the time of going to press there were but 2 marine RDF stations remaining in service and 10 aeronautical RDF stations. Care should be exercised as the 2 marine stations could vanish at any time in the future.

Marine

Capo Ferro 41°09'N 09°31'E *CF* (−·−·/·−−·) 291kHz 100M

Capo Sandalo 39°09'N 08°13'E *IP* (··/·−−·) 310kHz 100M

Harbours of refuge

The following harbours can be entered under storm conditions although in some cases with difficulty

Corsica

Bastia – use the commercial port if the gale is from NE or E

Calvi – use the yacht harbour for a NW gale but there are problems with the swell

7

NAVTEX (N4) TRANSMITTERS

Country	Transmitter identification character	Freq kHz	Times	Language used	Range NM	Status of implementation
France						
La Garde (CROSS)	(W) (S)[1]	518	0340, 0740, 1140, 1540, 1940, 2340	French	250	Operational
Italy						
Roma – Remotely controlled stations						
Augusta (Sicilia)	(V)	518	On receipt. 0330, 0730, 1130, 1530, 1930, 2330	English and Italian	320	Operational
Cagliari (Sardinia)	(T)	518	On receipt. 0310, 0710, 1110, 1510, 1910, 2310	English and Italian	320	Operational
Roma		518	On receipt. 0250, 0650, 1050, 1450, 1850, 2250	English and Italian	320	Operational
Trieste	(U)	518	On receipt. 0320, 0720, 1120, 1520, 1920, 2320	English and Italian	320	Operational

1. French bcst 490kHz

Ajaccio – swell enters when gale is from S
Bonifacio – strong gusts in east or west winds
Porto Vecchio – swell enters during NE gales with a confused sea at entrance

Sardinia

San Teresa di Gallura – tricky entrance in N gales
Olbia – some swell can enter in E gales
Alghero – difficult approach in W and NW winds

Note The section of 42 miles of coast from San Teresa di Gallura to Olbia has literally hundreds of anchorages, small harbours and marinas and a secure mooring can be found in all weathers with judicious use of large-scale charts. Note that it is a very crowded area in July and August and this may be the time to explore the east and west coasts!

Berthing

Due to the vast numbers of yachts and limited space available, berthing stern-to the quays and pontoons is the normal method used in the Mediterranean. For greater privacy or because the design of the yacht prevents berthing stern-to, it may be desirable to berth bow-to the quay or pontoon.

The manoeuvres to bring a yacht stern first into a narrow berth between two other yachts sometimes with a cross wind blowing is a skill which has to be acquired and it is most advisable that some practise at manoeuvring astern should be undertaken in advance. The only advice offered is:

- Have plenty of fenders out especially near the stern.
- Approach the berth slowly from some distance off.
- If not fully satisfied with the approach draw off and try again.
- Warping the yacht or pulling her in by hand when close in is better than using the engine.

It is better to make several attempts in slow time and to berth quietly in a seamanlike manner than to go rushing around with engines roaring and endangering nearby yachts.

The yacht is usually secured to the quay or pontoon by two stern lines leading from the quarters. In order to hold the yacht away from the quay or pontoon, a bow mooring of some kind will have to be picked up. These take several different forms as follows:

- A small buoy with line or light chain attached to it which leads to a heavier chain which must be pulled in, brought aboard and secured.
- A line or light chain that has one end attached to the quay or pontoon and the other to the heavy mooring chain. This light chain has to be picked up from near the quay or pontoon and followed along to the heavy mooring chain which has to be pulled in, taken on board and secured.
- Finally there are the mooring posts or piles located either side of the berth which sometimes have chains running out to them from the quay or pontoon. In this case it is necessary to secure the bow lines to the posts.

In many cases the chains are heavy and dirty and gloves are advisable when handling them because they are often covered with small sharp barnacles. Where no mooring chains are provided yachts have to use their own anchors which should be dropped at least 50m from the berth and should have an unbuoyed sinking type of anchor trip line attached to facilitate recovery should they become foul.

In winter and stormy weather these securing lines will have to be doubled and extra lines such as quarter lines, cross-stern lines and bow lines laid out. Extra fenders may be necessary especially where the stern (or bow) could ride up to and touch the quay or pontoon.

Winds of gale force can arise with great speed and if the yacht has to be left unattended even for a short period it is wise to lay out extra lines. In the few places where it is possible to lie alongside, holding-off lines are usually employed especially by fishing boats and can present an unexpected obstruction when approaching a berth. Harbours in the Mediterranean are subject, during gales, to exceptionally strong surges of water much more powerful than encountered in British harbours and berthing lines should be stronger than those usually used at home.

Moorings

Virtually all moorings are privately owned and if one is used it will have to be vacated should the owner return. There are often no markings to give any indication as to the weight and strength of the mooring so they should be used with caution.

Documentation

Again it is not proposed to go into great detail here as details, especially in Italy, change frequently even though we are all in the EU. The handbook from the RYA *Planning a Foreign Cruise – Volume 2 – The Mediterranean and the Black Sea* is worth having as it is kept up to date on a yearly basis. However as a minimum one should carry:

a. Ship's registration papers
b. Proof of yacht's VAT status
c. A certificate of insurance with a translation in Italian.

In Italy there are numerous organisations which appear to have authority to board any vessel, even at sea, and check the ships papers etc. These include the *guardia di finanza* (finance people); *guardia di costiera* (type of coastguard); *capitaneria di porto* (harbour officials); *dogana* (customs), *carabiniere* (one of the many types of police) all of whom have smart high-speed powerboats. It is recommended that they should all be treated politely and it helps to have a printed list of the following items ready for such an occasion:

Name of yacht	*Nome della barca*
Country of registration	*Paese di registro*
Registration Number	*numero di matricola*
Registered Tonnage	*stazza netta di registro*
Length (overall)	*lunghezza fuori tutto*
Beam	*traverso*
Draught	*pescaggio*
Type of vessel	*tipo di barca*
Owner's name	*nome di armatore*
Owners address	*indirizzo*
Passport Number	*numero di passaporto*
Time and date of arrival in port	*ora e data d'arrivo*
Last Port of call	*porto precedente*
Next Port of call	*porto prossimo*
Crew list with Surname	*cognome*
Christian name	*(Nome)*
Date and place of birth for each crew member	*(data e paese di nascita)*
Passport number	*numero di passaporto*
Nationality	*nazionalità*

However following a series of complaints from irate (Italian) yachtsmen, some of whom had been boarded up to three times in one day, the government is now looking into ways of reducing this harassment by appointing just one of the above authorities as the boarding authority. Discussions are likely to go on for years but a yacht with a foreign flag that is obeying the international rules (an inverted cone hoisted when motor sailing for example) is now unlikely to be boarded too often.

Planning guide

Note This guide is listed in an anticlockwise direction from Ports de Bastia.

Distance	Headlands	Ports & anchorages	Open to winds
CORSICA			
		Bastia page 19	NE
		⚓ **Vieux Port** page 19	NE
		⚓ **Port de Toga** page 21	NE
	Pointe de la Vasina		
		⚓ *Marine de Erbalunga*	NE–E–SE
		⚓ *Port de Erbalunga*	E
16.5M	Capo Sagro		
		⚓ *Marine de Sisco*	NE–E–SE
	Ancien Couvent de Ste Catalina		
		⚓ *Marine de Pietracorbara*	NE–E–SE
	Punta a i Ghiunchi		
		⚓ *Marine de Portocciolo*	NE–E–SE
		⚓ **Port de Luri** page 23	E–SE
		⚓ **Port de Macinaggio** page 23	NE
		⚓ *Baie de Macinaggio*	NE–E–SE
	Punta di a Coscia		
	Iles Finocchiarola		
		⚓ *Rade de Santa Maria*	NW–N–E
	Pointe d'Agnello		
		⚓ *Pointe d'Agnello NW*	N–NE
		⚓ *Marine de Barcaggio*	NW–N–NE
	Ile de la Giraglia		
	Cap Corse		
28M	Capo Grosso		
		⚓ **Port de Centuri** page 26	W–NW–N
		⚓ *Baie de Centuri*	
	Ile de Centuri		
		⚓ *Marine de Morsiglia*	SW–W–NW
	Punta di Stintinu		
		⚓ *Marine de Giottani*	SW–W–NW
	Punta di Canelle		
	Amianto asbestos mine and works		
		⚓ *Marine d'Albo*	SW–W–N
	Punta Vecchiaia		
		⚓ **Saint Florent** page 28	
	Cap de Fornali		
		⚓ *Anse de Fornali*	N–E–SE
		⚓ *Anse de Fiume Santu*	N–NE–E
	Punta Mortella		
	Punta Cavallata		
		⚓ *Plage du Loto*	N–NE–E
	Punta di Curza		
		⚓ *Plage de Saleccia*	NW–N–NE
		⚓ *Anse de Malfalcu*	NW–N
	Punta di Solche		
		⚓ *Baie de l'Acciolu*	NW–N–NE
	Punta di l'Acciolu		
		⚓ *Anse de Peraiola*	SW–W–N
		⚓ *Anse de Lozari*	W–N–NE
26M	Punta Saleccia		
		Port de L'Ile Rousse page 33	NE–E
	Passage between Le Grande Ile Rousse and Isula dei Brucciu		
	Punta di Vallitone		
		⚓ *Anse d'Algajola*	W–NW–N
		⚓ *Port d'Algajola*	N–NE
	Punta San Damiano		
	Danger d'Algajola		
		⚓ **Port de Sant'Ambrogio** page 35	E
	Punta Spano		
	(with Ile de Spano off)		
		⚓ *Baie Agajo*	NW–W–SW
		⚓ *Portu Agajo*	W–NW–N

Distance	Headlands	Ports & anchorages	Open to winds
		⚓ *Golfe de Calvi*	
		⛵ **Port de Calvi** page 38	NE
	Punta San Francesco		
		⚓ *Golfe de la Revellata*	N–NE
	Station de Recherches Océanographique		
	Passage Ile de la Revallata		
	Punta Revellata		
		⚓ *Porto Vecchiu*	S–SW–W
		⚓ *Port d'Agro*	S–W–NW
	Punta Caprara		
		⚓ *Baie de Nichiareto*	W–NW
	Capo Cavallo		
	Capo Mursetta		
	L'Ile Mursetta and passage		
		⚓ *Baie de Crovani*	SW–W–NW
	Punta di Ciuttone		
		⚓ *Golfe de Galéria*	W–NW–N
	Iles Scuglietti and passage		
	Punta Rossa		
	Punta Bianca		
		⚓ *Anse d'Elpa Nera (de la Foata)*	SW–W–NW
		⚓ *Anse de Focolara*	W–NW–N
	Punta Scandola		
	Écueils de Porri and passage		
		⚓ *Anse Pori*	W–NW–N
	Punta Nera		
		⚓ *Baie d'Elbo*	NW–N–NE
	Punta Palazzu		
	Ilot Palazzu and passage		
	Ile di Gargalu and passage		
		⚓ *Baie di Solana*	S–SW–W
	'Dog Leg' Passage		
32M		⚓ *Anse de Gattaghia*	S–SW–W
	Punta Muchillina		
		⚓ *Cala Muretta*	SE –SW
		⚓ *La Girolata*	S–SW
		⚓ *Cala di Tuara*	S–SW–W
	Capo Senino		
	Punta à Scoppa		
	Golfe de Porto		
		⚓ *Anse Gradelle*	S–SW–W
	Punta Bianca		
		⚓ *Marine de Bussagghia*	S–SW–W
		⛵ **Porto Marina** page 45	SW–W–NW
		⚓ *Anse de la Castagna*	N–NE
		⚓ *Anse de Ficajola*	NW–N–NE
	Punta di Ficajola		
	Ilot Vardiola		
		⚓ *Sbiro*	N
	Cap Rossu		
	Cap Rossu Passage		
		⚓ *Cala Genovese*	S–W
		⚓ *Cala di Palu*	S–SW
		⚓ *Portu â Leccia*	SW–W–NW
	Punta a i Tuselli		
		⚓ *Porto d'Arone*	S–SW–W
		⚓ *Golfe de Topidi*	W–NW–N
	Punta d'Orchina		
		⚓ *Anse de Chiuni*	SW–W–NW
	Punta d'Omigna		
		⚓ *Golfe de Peru*	S–SW–W
	Punta di u Puntiglione		
		⛵ **Port de Cargèse** page 48	SE–S
		⚓ *Baie de Cargèse*	SE–S–W
	Punta di Molendinu		
	Rocher Marifaja	⚓ *Baie de Menasina*	SE–S–W
	Pointe de Triu		

Distance	Headlands	Ports & anchorages	Open to winds
	Pointe de la Batterie		
		⚓ **Port de Sagone** page 50	S–SW–W
		⚓ *Baie de Sagone*	SE–S–SW
	Pointe de St-Joseph		
	Recif de St-Joseph and passage		
	Pointe Capigliolu		
		⚓ *Baie de Liscia*	SW–W–NW
	Pointe Palmentoju		
	Iles de Pointe Palmentoju and passage		
		⚓ *Anse d'Ancone*	SW–W–NW
	Pointe Paliagi		
21M	Recif de Paliagi and passage		
	Pointe Parragiola and Pointe Pellusella		
		⚓ *Portu Provençale*	SW–W–NW
	Pétra Piombata and passage		
	Cap de Feno		
	Écueil de Fica		
		⚓ *Anse de Fica*	S–SW–W
	La Botte		
		⚓ *Anse de Minaccia*	S–SW–W
		⚓ *Anse d'Alta*	SW–W–NW
	Pointe de la Corba		
	Pointe de la Parata and		
	Iles Sanguinaires and passages		
		⚓ *La Grande Sanguinaire*	E–SE–S
	La Botte de Canicciu		
	Écueil de la Guardiola		
		⚓ *Anse Maestrellu*	E–S–SW
	Rocher Citadelle		
		Ajaccio page 56	
		⚓ **Port Tino Rossi** page 57	
		⚓ **Port Charles Ornano** page 57	
	Pointe d'Aspretto		
	Pointe de Porticcio		
	Écueil Dorbera		
		⚓ *Pointe de Porticcio*	SW–W–NW
		⚓ *Anse de Ste Barbe*	W–NW–N
	Pointe de Sette Nave		
	La Campanina beacon		
		⚓ *Anse Medea*	S–SW
		⚓ *Anse Ottoni*	SW–W–NW
		⚓ *Port de Chiavari*	W–NW–N
		⚓ *Ile Piana*	NE or SW
		⚓ *Anse de Portigliolo*	W–NW–N
23M		⚓ *Pointe de la Castagna NE*	NW–N–NE
	Pointe de la Castagna		
		⚓ *Pointe de la Castagna SE*	S–SW–W
		⚓ *Anse de Cacalu*	N–NE–E
	Pointe Guardiola and passage		
	Cap Muro		
		⚓ *Cala di Muru*	SE–S–SW
		⚓ *Cala d'Orzu*	S–SW–W
	Capu Neru		
		⚓ *Baie de Cupabia*	S–SW–W
	Pointe de Porto Pollo		
		⚓ **Port de Porto Pollo** page 64	E–SE–S
		⚓ *Plage de Baraci*	
		⚓ **Port de Propriano** page 64	W–NW
		⚓ *Portigliolo*	W–NW–N
		⚓ *Campomoro*	NW–N–NE
	Pointe de Campomoro		
		⚓ *Cala d'Agulia*	W–NW
	Punta d'Eccica		
	Ile d'Eccica reef and passage		
		⚓ *Anse de Ferru*	S–SW–W
		⚓ *Anse d'Arana*	S–SW–W
		⚓ *Cala di Conca*	SW–W–NW

Distance	Headlands	Ports & anchorages	Open to winds
	Pointe de Sénétosa and Pointe d'Acula		
		⚓ *Cala Longa*	S–SW–W
		⚓ *Port de Tizzano*	S–SW
	Pointe de Lattoniccia		
	La Botte de Tizzano and passage		
		⚓ *Cala di Brija*	E–S–SW
		⚓ *Golfe de Murtoli*	SE–S–W
	Pointe de Murtoli		
		⚓ *Golfe de Roccapina*	SE–S–W
	Pointe de Roccapina		
		⚓ *Anse de Roccapina*	SE–S–SW
	Les Moines (islets and reefs and passage)		
30M	Punta di Caniscione		
	Écueils d'Olmeto and Le Prêtre and passages		
		⚓ *Cala di Furnellu*	SE–S–SW
		⚓ *Anse d'Arbitru*	S–SW
	Iles Bruzzi		
		⚓ *Anse de Chevanu*	SE–S–SW
	Punta di Capuneru		
		⚓ *Baie de Figari*	SE–S–SW
		⛵ **Port de Pianottoli-Caldarello** page 73	SW
	Punta di Ventilegne		
		⚓ *Anse de Pesciucane*	S–SW
		⚓ *Golfe de Ventilegne*	SW–W
		⚓ *Iles de la Tonnara*	NW–N
		⚓ *Port de Stagnolu*	SW–W–NW
		⚓ *Cala Grande*	S–SW
	Cap de Feno		
		⚓ *Cala de Paraganu*	S–SW
		⚓ *Iles and Anse de Fazziolu*	S–SW
		⛵ **Port de Bonifacio** page 75	
	Cap Pertusato		
	Ile St Antoine and passage		
	Le Prêtre beacon		
	Punta de Sperono		
		⚓ *Anse Piantarella*	NE–E–S
		⚓ *Cala Longa*	E–SE–S
		Les Bouches de Bonifacio page 77	
		Iles Lavezzi page 80	
		Ile Cavallo page 83	
30M	Punta di u Capicciolu	⛵ **Port de Cavallo** page 83	
		⚓ *Golfe de Sant'Amanza*	NE–E
		⚓ *Anse de Balistra*	NE–E–SE
	Punta di Rondinara		
		⚓ *Golfe de Rondinara*	NE–E–SE
	Pointe de Sponsaglia		
		⚓ *Golfe de Porto Novo*	N–NE–E
		⚓ *Golfe de Santa Giulia*	NE–E–SE
	Ile du Toro		
		⚓ *Plage de Palombaggia*	NE–E–S
	Pointe Cerbicale		
	Iles Cerbicales		
		⚓ *Anse de Carataggio*	NE–E–S
	Punta di a Chiappa		
	Roches de Chiappino (and beacon)		
		Porto Vecchio page 87	NE
		⛵ **Port de Plaisance** page 87	
	Tourelle Pecorella and beacon		
		⚓ *Baie de San Ciprianu*	E–S
	Punta d'Arasu		
		⚓ *Punta Capicciola W*	SE–S
	Punta Capicciola		
	Ile de Pinarellu		
		⚓ *Golfe de Pinarellu*	NE–E–SE
14.5M		⚓ *Pointe de Fautéa SW*	E–SE–S
	Ile et Pointe de Fautéa		
		⚓ *Anse de Fautéa*	NE–E–SE

Distance	Headlands	Ports & anchorages	Open to winds
		⚓ *Anse de Tarcu*	NE–E–SE
		⚓ *Anse de Favone*	N–NE–E
		⚓ *Anse de Cannella*	NE–E–SE
		⚓ *Marine de Cala d'Oru*	NE–E–SE
		⚓ **Port de Solenzara** page 92	E–SE
	Aérodrome de Solenzara		
	Offshore Fuel Terminal, Solenzara		
	Foce di u Fium Orbu (mouth of the river Fium Orbu) (Calzarello) and wreck		
32M	Foce de Tavignano Fleuve (mouth of river Tavignano)		
	Phare d'Alistru (lighthouse)		
		⚓ **Port de Taverna** page 93	NE–E
	Résidence des Iles, Dome and Aero RC		
23M	Lucciana Offshore Fuel Terminal –		
	Aérodrome de Bastia Poretta		
	Offshore Fuel Terminal – Bastia		
		⚓ *Anse de Porto Vecchio*	NE–E–S

SARDINIA (Anticlockwise from Alghero)

Distance	Headlands	Ports & anchorages	Open to winds
		⚓ **Alghero** page 98	
		⚓ **Fertilia** page 99	S–SW
		⚓ *Cala Galera*	E
	Capo Galera		
		⚓ **Base Nautica Porto Conte** page 99	NW
		⚓ **Cala Tramariglio** page 99	E
		⚓ *Cala del Bollo*	E
	Capo Caccia (Neptune's Cave)		
41M		⚓ *Porto Ferro*	S–NW
	Capo Argentiera		
		⚓ *Porto San Nicolo*	SW–N
	Capo Falcone		
	Fornelli Passage		
	Isola Asinara		
	Isola Piana		
		⚓ **Yacht Club l'Ancora** page 101	W–NW
	Punta Negra		
		Stintino page 101	E
		⚓ **Porto Mannu** page 101	
		⚓ **Porto Minore** page 102	
		Porto Torres page 102	
		⚓ **Porto Commerciale** page 103	
		⚓ **Castelsardo** page 104	
	Punta Vignola	⚓ *Isola Rossa*	
	Capo Testa	⚓ *Portobello di Gallura*	
		⚓ *Baia la Colba*	W–S–SE
		⚓ *Cala Spinosa*	W–N–E
45M		⚓ *Baia S Reparata*	N–E
	Isola Municca		
		⚓ *Cala*	N–W–SW
		S. Teresa di Gallura page 106	
		⚓ **Porto Longosardo** page 106	N
		⚓ *Porto Quadro*	N–NW
	Punta Falcone		
	Isole Marmorata		
		⚓ *S of Marmorata*	NE–E
	Punta Monterosso (with Scoglio		
	Pagenetto 4 cables off)	⚓ *Porto Pozzo*	N
12M		⚓ **Conca Verde** page 108	N
	Punta delle Vacche		
		⚓ *Porto Liscia*	N–NE
	Punta Cavalli (with rock 1.5 cables off)		
		⚓ *Porto Pollo (Puddu)*	N
	Punta Sardinia		
		⚓ **Yacht Club Porto Rafael** page 109	NE–E–SE
	Punta Palau		
		⚓ **Palau** page 109	NW–N–NE

Distance	Headlands	Ports & anchorages	Open to winds
		La Maddalena archipelago page 111	
	Bocche di Bonifacio passages		
	The Northern Group		
	Isola Razzoli, Budelli, S. Maria.		
		⚓ *Cala Lunga*	W–SW
		⚓ *Cala Giorgio Marino*	W–S–SE
		⚓ *Cala S Maria*	E–S
		⚓ *Cala Muro*	SW–NW
		⚓ *Cala Rosa (Pink Beach)*	NE–S
	Southern Group		
	Spargi		
		⚓ *Cala d'Alga*	S–W
		⚓ *Cala Corsara*	E–S
		⚓ *Cala Ferrigno (rocky)*	NE–E
	La Maddalena		
10M		⛵ **Cala Gavetta (Porto Mercantile)** page 115	S
		⛵ **Cala Mangiavolpe** page 115	S
		⛵ **Marina del Ponte** page 115	
		⚓ *Cala Nido d'Aquila*	S–W
		⚓ *Cala Francese*	W
		⚓ *Stagno Torto*	N
		⛵ **Porto Massimo** page 116	E
		⚓ *Cala Spalmatore*	E
		⚓ *Cala di Villamarina (Santa Stefano)*	S
	Caprera		
		⚓ *Cala Stagnali*	W
		⚓ *Porto Palma*	S
		⚓ *Cala Portese*	NE–E
		⚓ *Cala Brigantino*	NE–SE
		⚓ *Cala Coticcio*	S
		⚓ *Porto Garibaldi*	N
	Capo d'Orso		
		⚓ *Golfo di Saline*	
	Golfo di Arzachena		
		⚓ *Cala Porteddu*	E
		⚓ *La Conia*	E
		⛵ **Cannigione** page 118	N
		⛵ **Cala Bitta** page 119	W
		⚓ *North Bay*	
		⚓ *Cala south of Capo Tre Monti*	W–NW
	Capo Tre Monti (rocks off point)		
	Tre Monti		
	Punta Battistone		
		⛵ **Marina dell'Orso (Poltu Quatu)** page 120	
		⚓ *Liscia di Vacca*	N
	Isola Cappucini		
	Capo Ferro (with Isola delle Bisce 3 cables off)		
		⚓ *Cala Granu*	NE–SE
		Porto Cervo page 121	
		⚓ *Golfo Pevero*	
	Isole di li Nibani & Passo delle Galera		
		⚓ *Porto Liccia*	N–E
	Punta Capaccia		
	Isole Poveri and Isole Mortorio and Soffi		
		⚓ *Mortorio*	E
	Punta Capriccioli		
		⚓ *Cala di Volpe*	S
	Punta Ligata		
	Isola Portisco		
		⛵ **Marina di Portisco** page 123	E
20M		⚓ *Golfo di Cugnana*	N
	Punta Nuraghe		
		⛵ **Porto Rotondo** page 123	
	Punta Volpe (Rocks off)		
		⛵ **Porto Oro (Palumbalza)** (private) page 124	E

Distance	Headlands	Ports & anchorages	Open to winds
		⚓ **Punta Marana** page 124	
		⚓ *Marinella (private)*	N
	Punta Cannigione (Rocks off)		
	Capo Figari		
		Golfo Aranci page 125	W
		⚓ **Baia Caddinas** page 126	SE
		⚓ *SW of Isola Porri*	E
		Olbia page 126	E
		⚓ *Liscia delle Saline*	N
	Capo Ceraso		
		⚓ *Porto Istana*	E
	Isola Piana	⚓ *Porto Spurlatta*	NE
		⚓ *Porto San Paolo*	N
		⚓ *Porto Taverna*	NE
	Tavolara	⚓ *Off SW Beach*	SE–S
	Isola Molara		
30M		⚓ *Cala Coda Cavallo*	N
	Capo Coda Cavallo (Isola Proratora off)		
		⚓ *Porto Brandinchi* (very rocky)	E–S
		⚓ **Marina di Puntaldia** page 130	NE
	Punta Sabbatino		
		⚓ **La Cinta** page 130	SE
	Punta d'Ottiolu		
		⚓ **Porto Ottiolu** page 130	SE
	Isolotto d'Ottiolu		
	Isolotti dei Pedrami (keep to seaward)		
		⚓ **La Caletta** page 131	SE
	Capo Comino (keep 1 mile offshore S of here!)		

Key to symbols

	English	French	Italian
⚓	Harbourmaster	*Capitainerie*	*Ufficio Marittimo*
	Fuel	*Carburant*	*Carburante*
WC	WC	*Toilettes*	*Gabinetto*
	Showers	*Douche*	*Doccia*
	Yacht yard	*Carénage*	*Cantiere Navale*
	Travel lift/Crane	*Cale de Halage/Grue*	*Travel-lift/Gru*
	Yacht Club	*Club Nautique*	*Club Nautico*
Ⓥ	Holding berth	*Accueil*	*Ormeggio Transito*
	Telephone	*Telephone*	*Telefono*
	Water	*Eau*	*Acqua*
	Electricity	*Électricité*	*Elettricità*
	Slipway	*Cale*	*Scalo d'Alaggio*
⚓	Anchorage	*Mouillage*	*Ancoraggio*
Ⓐ	Yacht Chandler	*Chandler*	*Negozio di Nautico*
⊕	Waypoint		

3. Corsica

General description

The island of Corsica lies 100 miles off the French Riviera and from 50 to 120 miles from the Italian coast. To the north is the Gulf of Genoa and the Ligurian Sea. To the east are the Tuscan Archipelago islands and the Tyrrhenian Sea, to the south is Sardinia only 7 miles away, while to the west lie the Balearic Islands and Spain some 220 miles away.

The island itself is 100 miles long and 45 miles wide at its maximum but it has a coastline of nearly 600 miles due to the many bays and penninsulas that it has. Many illustrious writers have tried to describe this indescribable island in a concise way and to paraphrase some of these efforts, from a yachtsman's point of view, the island could be said to be 'a scented granite mountain surrounded by anchorages'. No short description of this sort can do justice to what is one of the finest cruising areas in the western Mediterranean and, moreover, it has not suffered too badly from the hands of the developers. The island is sparsely populated with only some 300,000 people with nearly half living in the two largest towns of Bastia and Ajaccio.

Except the bare mountain peaks (highest is Mt Cinto at 2,710m (8,900ft)) and a few small cultivated areas the island is covered in the Mediterranean *maquis* – a mixture of low shrubs, most of them aromatic which give off a characteristic scent, mainly in spring, which can be smelt many miles offshore.

History

It is impossible to give more than a bare outline of the long and complex history of Corsica but those interested in the subject should refer to *History of Corsica* by Paul Arighi, 1966, or *The tragic history of the Corsicans* by Dom JB Gai, 1951.

Around 3000 BC the first megalithic civilisation inhabited the SW of the island and left many dolmens and menhirs and by 1600 BC these people were building statue-menhirs to honour the dead. Another group, the Toreens, was established in the SE around 2000 BC and left a series of large domed buildings *Torris* – not unlike the Nuraghs of Sardinia. The Toreens vanished about 1200 BC and may have moved to Sardinia.

The Phoenicians were probably the next to establish themselves although little evidence remains of them. Alalia (Aliera on the east coast) was founded in 560 BC by them and the Greeks and, in spite of invasions and occupations by the Cathaginians and Eutruscans around 280 to 260 BC, they remained at Alalia until driven out by the Romans when they invaded in 259 BC. The Romans colonised the island, established several towns (Mariana for one) and ruled for 700 years. They were driven out by the Vandals in AD 450, followed by the Ostrogoths, Byzantines, Lombards and the Saracens. In 1077 the Pope, who had been given titular control by Pippen the Short in 758 when he drove the Lombards out, assigned the administration of the island to the Bishop of Pisa. This was disputed by the Genovese who seized Bonifacio (1187) and Calvi (1278) and they finally defeated the Pisans in the naval battle of Meloria. Anarchy still reigned, however, and another pope assigned the islands to the Dukes of Aragon. Unrest continued as the people supported Genoa while the nobles supported Aragon. In 1420 a large force from Aragon seized the island and ruled it until 1434 when the Viceroy was captured and executed by the Genovese. The Genovese then gave the island to the Bank of St George to look after until 1553 when the French took the island but gave it back in 1559 and the Genovese ruled it until 1729. During this period the Genovese built the fortified citadels of Calvi and Bonifacio, imposing forts at Aleria, Girolata and Tizzano and a series of watch towers around the island.

In 1729 a rebellion broke out against the Genovese but it was Paoli in 1755 who proclaimed himself as General of the Corsican Nation and got things organised. In 1768 Genoa sold the rights of the island to France who defeated Paoli who took refuge in England. (Napoleon Bonaparte was born in Ajaccio in August 1769). In 1790 after the French Revolution and Paoli's amnesty, he returned and occupied a controlling post in the island's government. In 1792 an expedition to take Sardinia failed, Paoli was blamed and he appealed to England for assistance while his partisans drove the Bonaparte's from the island. The British put Sir Gilbert Eliot in as Viceroy of the Anglo-Corsican kingdom (Nelson lost his eye in the battle for Calvi in 1794). In 1796 the British evacuated the island and France repossessed it and it has remained with France ever since. The Germans and Italians held it during the Second World War and the Corsicans liberated themselves in 1943. Tourism is on the increase and the depopulation of the island has been halted but although France is giving the island more autonomy the Corsicans still believe they should govern their own island.

Data and warnings

Restricted areas

There have been several nature reserves established near the following places:

Bastia
Saint Florent
Ile Rousse
Calvi
Ile Gargalu
Porto Piana
Propriano
Bonifacio
Iles Cavallo- Lavezzi
Porto Vecchio

Details are given in the section dealing with the harbour concerned. Note that there are plans to make the whole of the Bouches de Bonifacio a restricted area. No anchoring, fishing or subaqua diving is allowed in the areas.

There are a number of underwater cables linking the islands and anchoring and fishing is prohibited in areas (shown on the appropriate chartlets):

S of Bastia
N of Saint Florent
W of Ile Rousse
S of Bonifacio
N & S of Iles Lavezzi

There are offshore oil terminals in the following areas where fishing and anchoring is forbidden:

S of Bastia
Near Bastia-Poretta Airfield
Near Solenzara Airfield

The underwater and air training area east of Ajaccio harbour near Pointe d'Aspretto must not be entered if a blue flag is flying on the point. There is also a large area south of Campoloro which is a bombing range.

The French authorities use large seaplanes to fight forest fires which plague the islands during the summer season. These Canadair planes scoop up water into body tanks while taxiing at high speed on the water. They then take off, drop the water on the fire and come back for more. Depending on the size of the fire there may be up to 10 or so planes involved in the exercise. The first plane to arrive flies down the flight path at low level and all yachts must leave the area as quickly as possible and stay well clear. Areas commonly used are:

Golfe de Saint Florent
Golfe de Calvi
Golfe de Girolata
Golfe de Porto
Golfe de Sagone
Golfe de Liscia
Golfe d'Ajaccio
Golfe de Valinco
Golfe de Figari
Golfe de Ventilegne
Golfe de Sant'Amanza
Golfe de Porto Vecchio

On the east coast the planes may use the open sea if calm.

Major lights

0856 Jetée du Dragon (Bastia) 42°41'·6N 9°27'·3E
Fl(4)WR.12s16m14/11M White tower, red top 6m

0855 Capo Sagro 42°47'·7N 9°29'·5E Fl(3)12s10M
White tower, green top 4m

0852 Ile de la Giraglia 43°01'·6N 9°24'·4E
Fl.5s85m28M White tower black top

0926 La Pietra (Ile Rousse) 42°38'·6N 8°56'·0E
Fl(3)WG.12s64m14/11M White square tower,
green top 13m

0918 Punta Revellata 42°35'·0N 8°43'·5E
Fl(2)10s97m21M White square tower, black top 7m

0916 Ile di Gargalu 42°22'·3N 8°32'·2E
Fl.WR.4s37m8/5M White column, black top 7m

0902 Iles Sanguinaires 41°52'·7N 8°35'·7E
Fl(3)15s98m24M White square tower, black top
18m

0894 Pointe de Sénétosa 41°33'·5N 8°47'·9E
Fl.WR.5s54m20/16M 2 White towers, black tops,
15m

0888 Cap de Feno 41°23'·6N 9°05'·8E
DirFl(4)15s21m21M White tower black top 11m
Fl(4)WR.15s23m7/4M On same structure

0876 Capo Pertusato 41°22'·0N 9°11'·2E
Fl(2)10s100m25M White square tower, black top
21m

0872 Capu di u Beccu (Ile Lavezzi) 41°20'·1N
9°15'·6E Oc(2)WR.6s27m17/14M Square tower,
red and white stripe 12m

0866 Punta di a Chiappa 41°35'·7N 9°22'·0E
Fl(3+1)15s65m23M White square tower, red top
21m

0864 Alistru 42°15'·6N 9°32'·5E Fl(2)10s93m22M
Grey octagonal tower, black top 27m

3·1 – Bastia to Saint Florent

This section is probably unique in that it is in effect a peninsula 20M long by only 5M wide lying in a N–S direction with a high mountain range as its backbone reaching to 1,305m (4,280ft) at its highest point. There are several natural harbours and many anchorages in the bays and creeks around the peninsula. The coast is of steep rocky cliffs sloping sharply up to the mountains behind. At the heads of the many bays and estuaries lie beaches, most of which are of stone and sand. The coast is steep-to and except for the Ile Finocchiarola, a shallow area just to NW of it and the large Ile de la Giraglia, there are no off-lying dangers. In general the W side is more rugged than the E and the slope of the hills much steeper.

A corniche-type road follows the coast around the peninsula and there are several roads that cross the mountains. There are no towns and only a few small villages in this area and between these villages the country is almost deserted.

Particular attention should be paid to the dangers of the strong westerly winds which cause heavy gusts of wind to sweep down the valleys on the eastern side.

Winds from an easterly or *levante* direction bring in heavy seas and they make all anchorages on the east coast dangerous and even entrance to ports and harbours becomes difficult if not impossible.

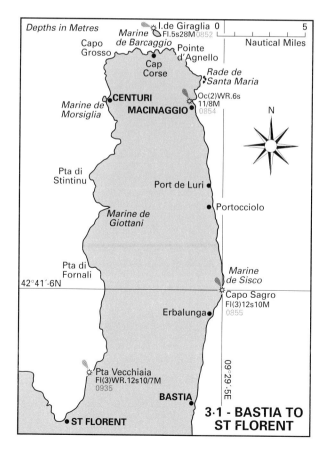

Bastia

General

Bastia has three ports, the delightful picturesque old fishing harbour, the Vieux Port at the south end of the town has good facilities but only limited space for yachts and becomes very crowded in the season. The commercial and ferry harbour, Port St Nicolas which is in the centre and pleasure craft are forbidden to use it without prior permission or in the event of an emergency. The modern yacht harbour Port Toga, with 350 berths, is at the north of the town and has all facilities. The attractive old town surrounds the Vieux Port in the true Mediterranean style. Approach and entrance are easy and protection is offered once inside though heavy swell from the NE–E makes the old harbour very uncomfortable and sometimes untenable. The town, which is the largest in Corsica, has very smart and excellent shops which can supply most requirements. Port Saint Nicolas, the commercial ferry port and the airfield to the south provide excellent communications for the exchange of crews. A road tunnel passes under the harbour.

⚓ Vieux Port or Port du Plaisance

⊕1 42°41'·75N 09°27'·4E
Depth 7–1m
Number of berths 267

Charts

Admiralty *1425, 1999*
French *6822, 6823, 6856*

Port radio

VHF channels 16 and 9.

Weather forecast

Posted at *capitaneria* daily.

Lights

0856 Jetée du Dragon head 42°41'·6N 9°27'·5E
Fl(4)WR.12s16m14/11M Grey tower red lantern, 000°-W-326°-R-342°-W-000°
0858 Môle Génois head Oc(2)G.6s13m8M Light grey tower, dark green top
0859 Vieux Port Q.G
0860 Jetée Saint Nicolas head Fl.G.4s9m11M White tower, dark green band
0861 Car ferry berth head Q.R.2m5M White tower, red top
TV tower Pigno 2·45M to west F.Rs

Warnings

If there is a strong gale from NE–E it may be necessary to seek shelter in Port St Nicolas due to the swell. Heavy gusts of wind can also be experienced when the wind is blowing from the SW (*libeccio*) direction. If an anchor has to be used in the Vieux Port it is essential to use an anchor tripping line because the bottom is foul. Pay attention to rocks at the foot of quays. Commercial craft and ferries have right of way in the port area and must not be obstructed.

Corsica and north Sardinia

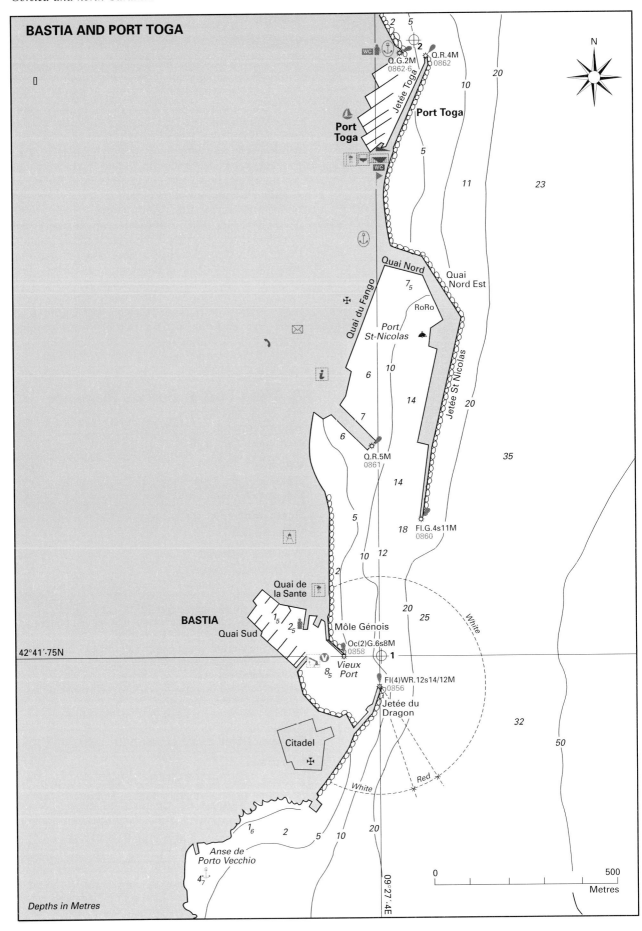

BASTIA AND PORT TOGA

N

Q.G.2M
0862·6

2

Q.R.4M
0862

5

2

10

20

Jetée Toga

Port Toga

Port
Toga

11

23

5

WC

Quai Nord

7₅

Quai
Nord Est

Quai du Fango

RoRo

Port
St-Nicolas

6

10

14

20

Jetée St Nicolas

35

7

6

Q.R.5M
0861

14

18

Fl.G.4s11M
0860

5

10   12

20   25

White

Quai de
la Sante

BASTIA

1₅

2₅

Môle Génois

Oc(2)G.6s8M
0858

1

Quai Sud

2

8₅

*Vieux
Port*

Fl(4)WR.12s14/12M
0856

Jetée du
Dragon

42°41′·75N

Citadel

White

Red

32

50

1₆

2

5   10

20

*Anse de
Porto Vecchio*

4₇

09°27′·4E

0   500
Metres

Depths in Metres

Restricted areas

An area to the north of Bastia between the Tour de Miomo and Port Toga extending 1·5M seawards is a nature reserve. Fishing, sub-aqua diving and anchoring is forbidden within this area. See plan page 22.

Approach

Due mainly to the physical properties of the site (mountains behind, sea in front) Bastia has developed into a classic 'ribbon development' town with buildings lining the main north/south road for up to 10 miles or more, especially to the south. At night it is extremely difficult to make out the harbour lights against the background of street, shop and house lights.

By day From the south the coast is low, flat and sandy with only a few recognisable features. The building with a large white dome and some other large buildings near the mouth of the Fiume Alto where there are some training walls, can be identified as can the Lucciana E cardinal light buoy (VQ(3)5s) which is located outside a series of mooring buoys at the oil pipe terminal for the airport. There are some black painted tanks on shore here. The houses of Bastia will be seen from afar and in the closer approach the walled Citadelle which has a tall square church tower rising above the buildings. The harbour is just to the north of this Citadelle. The red and white TV tower on Pigno (961m) 2·5M to the west of Bastia (F.Rs) is conspicuous as are the ferries if in harbour.

From the north The coast is of rocky cliffs with many small indentations and bays mostly with sandy beaches. The following may be recognised:

The breakwater at Luri, the village of Porticciolo which has two small breakwaters, Sisco village which has a training wall at the mouth of a river and a statue ¼M to the north standing on the cliff by a convent. The tower and village of Erbalunga with a small harbour is unmistakable. The TV tower (see above) is also conspicuous from this direction.

The houses of Bastia will be seen from afar and in the closer approach the Jetée St Nicolas will be seen usually with ferry ships behind it.

By night The following lights allow a night approach though in the close approach only the lights from Bastia will be seen:

0852 Cap Corse, Ile de la Giraglia 43°01'·6N
9°24'·4E Fl.5s85m28M White tower, black top, signal station
0854 Macinaggio, Jetée Est head
Oc(2)WR.6s8m11/8M White tower, red top
Radio tower F.Rs, 2·45M to west of Bastia
0864 Alistru 42°15'·6N 9°32'·5E Fl(2)10s93m22M
Grey 8-sided tower, red house, black lantern

Entrance

By day Approach the entrance on a W–SW course and enter between the head of Jetée du Dragon to port and the head of the Môle Génois to starboard. Do not obstruct commercial vessels entering and leaving Port St Nicolas which lies to the north of the Vieux Port.

By night Approach the Fl(4)WR.12s on a W–SW course in the white sector. Leave it 20m to port and then the Oc(2)G.6s 20m to starboard. The many lights along the shore are confusing at night.

Berth

There are 30 places for visitors, 20 on Môle Genois, 10 on Jetée du Dragon stern to the quays. It is essential to have a trip line on the anchor as the bottom is foul but only use the anchor in emergency as anchoring is prohibited in the port area.

Formalities

All authorities available.

Facilities

All.

⚓ Port Toga
⊕2 42°42'·65N 09°27'·45E
Depth 5m at entrance 2·5–4m inside
Number of berths 357 of which 150 are for visitors

Charts

Admiralty *1425, 1999*
French *6822, 6823, 6856*

Port radio

VHF Ch 16 and 9 (☎ 04 95 32 79 79).

Weather forecast

Posted daily at *capitaneria*.

Lights

0862 Jetée Est Q.R.1·2s10m4M
0862·6 Contro-jetée Q.G.1·2s2M (not visible until in entrance channel)

General

Port Toga is difficult to make out from seaward but it is situated some 500m to the north of the commercial harbour.

Approach

As stated above it is difficult to make out the entrance by day or night but use either the waypoint WP2 or identify the commercial harbour with its ferries and move 500m north.

By day Identify a white 10m high tower with a red band at the top with Port Toga written on it at the end of Jetée Est with a square 3-storey block behind it (the *capitaneria*).

By night Again it is difficult to identify the occulting red light until very close – make for the commercial harbour and track north until the red light is obvious. Keep close (20m) around the end of the jetty and the green light will become visible.

Entrance

Only 30m wide – try and keep to the middle of the channel in some 4m of water steering just east of south.

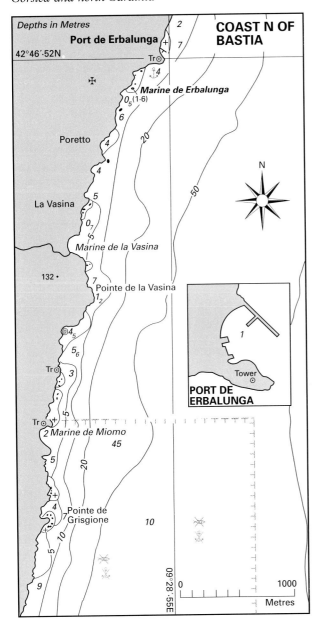

Berth

Turn sharply to starboard at the entrance channel end and you are alongside the *capitaneria* where berthing instructions will be given.

Formalities

All authorities available.

Facilities

All.

⚓ Marine de Erbalunga

A pleasant anchorage just south of the most attractive little harbour of Erbalunga. Open to NE–E–SE. Some inshore rocks, small rocky beach. Anchor in 3–4m, shingle and sand. Supplies from the small village.

⚓ Port de Erbalunga

42°46'·52N 09°28'·55E

A beautiful little harbour for small fishing boats and dinghies drawing less than 1·5m. 23 berths for local boats. Open to the east. A useful landing place for yachts' tenders. A shingle hard and concrete slip are at the west end of the harbour. Cafés and restaurants, an unclassified hotel, some shops and an engineer. The ruined tower at the entrance is conspicuous.

Capo Sagro

A headland with conspicuous signal station on top, rocky cliffs and coast road at bottom. Light Fl(3)12s10M.

⚓ Marine de Sisco

A wide open bay with a wide deep valley behind with a few houses around it and a small boat harbour at the mouth of the river for craft drawing less than 1m. Anchor off the harbour in 3m sand. The bay is open to NE–E–SE and entrance to the harbour is not possible in strong easterly winds. There is a slip and hard in the harbour, a 3-tonne crane, water point, petrol pump and the Club Nautique de Sisco (CNS) which has showers at the clubhouse. A motor mechanic, a garage, some shops, an unclassified hotel and a beach of shingle. There is a conspicuous TV tower to the south.

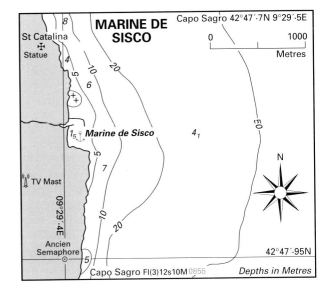

Ancien Couvent de Ste Catalina

Has a statue close to the rocky cliffs with a large church behind it, which has a tower like a clover leaf.

⚓ Marine de Pietracorbara

A wide bay with the road running behind the sand and stone beach and a few houses scattered around. One-star hotel and a restaurant in the small village. Anchor near the moorings at the south side of the bay in 3m, sand and shingle. Open to NE–E–SE. The village has a small jetty where landing is possible. A few dinghies are kept in the river mouth in the south side of the bay. The river has a training wall. A ruined square fort Tour d'Aquila on top of a peaked hill (134m) to the south of this area is conspicuous.

⚓ Marine de Portocciolo
⊕ 42°52'·6N 09°28'·4E

A very small fishing harbour and anchorage open to NE–E–SE with a T-shaped breakwater. Anchor off in 4m stone and sand. The village has a three-star hotel, small shingle beach at head of cove with the coast road behind.

⚓ Port de Luri
⊕ 42°53'·3N 09°28'·6E

A harbour built for a number of small yachts and dinghies, there are 130 berths with 20 for visitors up to 12m in overall length. The basin has depths of 2–3m on the east side, is shallower on the west side and is open to E–SE. The entrance is on the southwestern side, secure and report to the harbour officer for allocation of a berth. Water and electricity on pontoons and fuel is available on the road nearby. There is a slip on the north side of the harbour. It is possible to anchor in 3m of sand in the bay south of the entrance.

⚓ Port de Macinaggio

General

This yacht harbour, which was constructed in 1971, is based on an old fishing harbour and it has managed to maintain some of the attractiveness of the original. The surrounding area is beautiful and the small village pleasant in an unsophisticated way but inevitably the tourist industry development is spoiling the old charm. Approach and entry are easy but would be hazardous in heavy seas from NE–E. Protection within is good though a heavy swell from the NE–E makes it uncomfortable. Facilities good and everyday requirements can be met. The harbour becomes very crowded in the summer as it is usually the first stop of Italians coming from the Ligurian or Tuscan coasts.

⊕ 42°57'·65N 09°27'·5E
Depth 1·5m to 3·5m
Number of berths 585 with 200 for visitors
Maximum length 40m

Charts
Admiralty *1425*
French *6822, 6850*

Port radio
VHF Ch 9 (or ☎ 04 95 35 42 57).

Weather forecast
Posted twice a day (0800 & 1400) at *capitaneria*.

Lights
0854 Jetée Est head 42°57'·7N 9°27'·3E
　　Oc(2)WR.6s8m11/8M White tower, red top 120°-
　　R-218°-W-331°-R-120°
0854·4 Jetée Nord head Fl.G.2s4m2M White tower, green top
0903(I) Finocchiarola 49°59'·5N 9°28'·7E
　　Q(3)5s4m6M E card BYB light buoy located 2M
　　NNE of port and 0·5M NE of Iles Finocchiarola

Warnings
Heavy swell from the NE–E will break near the entrance and make it dangerous to enter. Heavy gusts of wind from SW–W sometimes occur. Depths in the harbour may be different to the plan due to periodic dredging. No anchoring is allowed in the port.

Approach
By day From the south the coastline is broken by many small bays but it lacks any conspicuous landmarks. The houses, tower and small harbour at Erbalunga, the villages of Sisco and Portocciolo,

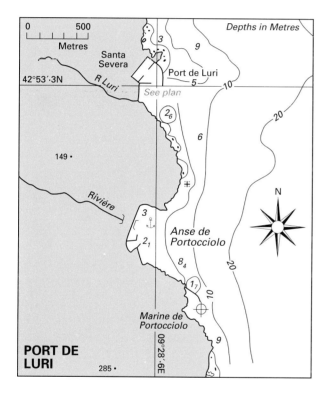

Santa Severa
42°53'·3N
R Luri
Port de Luri
See plan
149 •
Riviére
Anse de Portocciolo
Marine de Portocciolo
285 •
PORT DE LURI
09°28'·6E
Depths in Metres
0　500 Metres

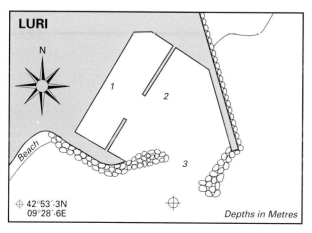

LURI
N
Beach
⊕ 42°53'·3N
　09°28'·6E
Depths in Metres

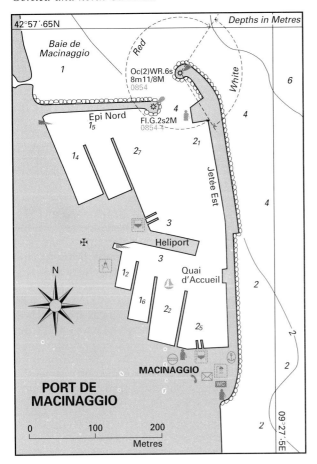

PORT DE MACINAGGIO

both of which have training walls at the mouths of their rivers, and the small harbour at Luri may be identified. In the closer approach the village of Macinaggio will be seen but not until the bay opens up. A conspicuous radar and TV tower and dome are located 3M to the west on the skyline.

From the north or rounding Cap Corse either inside or outside the Ile de la Giraglia which is conspicuous and has a lighthouse and signal station on its top. Follow the coast round and in bad weather give it a 1·5M berth to avoid the Banc de Santa Maria (9·5m). Pass outside the light buoy listed above and round the Iles Finocchiarola which extend 0·5M from the coast and has a tower on the top of the outer island. The houses of Macinaggio will be seen from here.

By night Using the following lights, the approach to the area may be made:

0852 Cap Corse, Ile de la Giraglia 43°01'·6N
  9°24'·4E Fl.5s85m28M White tower, black top
1404 Punta del Trattoio 43°01'·3N 9°47'·5E
  Fl.8s150m9M White house (this is on Capraia, an island 15M west of Giraglia)

Then use the Jetée Est light to approach the entrance.

Entrance

By day Approach the head of the Jetée Est which has a conspicuous white light tower, red top, on a course between NW and SW and round it leaving it 20m to port onto a course of south.

24

By night approach the Oc(2)WR.6s light on course between NW and SW in the white sector. Divert in the close approach towards N into the red sector and round the light at 20m leaving it to port and onto a southerly course. Leave Fl.G.2s 20m to starboard.

Berth

On arrival secure to the holding berth well inside the entrance on the port hand and report to the *bureau de port* for berthing instructions. Secure stern-to the pontoon or quay berth allocated with the mooring chain from the bow. This chain is connected to the pontoon by a lighter chain or rope.

Formalities

The *bureau de port* (☎ 95 35 42 57) is at the SE corner of the harbour open in summer 0600–1200, 1300–2030, in winter 0700–1200, 1400–1800. The customs office (☎ 95 35 43 03) is on the S side of the small square. The *affaires maritimes* (☎ 95 35 43 20) is in a house south of the village.

Facilities

All.

⚓ Baie de Macinaggio

A wide bay with the Port of Macinaggio at the south end and the conspicuous Pointe de Corsica at the other. A long sandy beach stretches along the coast with gently sloping ground behind. Open to NE–E–SE. Anchor in 3m sand.

Punta di a Coscia

A conspicuous pyramid-shaped point (60m) with a TV tower and the round stone base of an old windmill on top. The point is steep-to.

Iles Finocchiarola

There are three rocky islands with some islets and rocky heads extending 700m offshore. These islands are a nature reserve and landing is not permitted. The outer island (27m) is the largest and has a conspicuous ruined tower and small hut. The middle island (12m) is separated from the outer island by a narrow gap partially blocked by two rocks and a wreck of a small coaster. The inner island (5m) is of irregular shape and has many rocks to SE–S–SW including a small islet, there are also rocks along the Corsican coast to the west. Note the E cardinal BYB buoy Finocchiarola Q(3)5s lying 0·5M NE of this group of islands.

It is not recommended to pass through any of the narrow passages between the islands or the inner island and the shore.

⚓ Rade de Santa Maria

A wide open bay with a conspicuous ruined tower on its NW point and Chapelle Ste Maria standing inland. Open to NW–N–NE–E. Several shingle beaches with rocks between. Track to beach but otherwise deserted. Anchor in 4m on rock and sand in the centre of the bay, paying attention to off-lying rocks to SE. Another anchorage is available in 10m, sand and weed, 350m NNE of the tower.

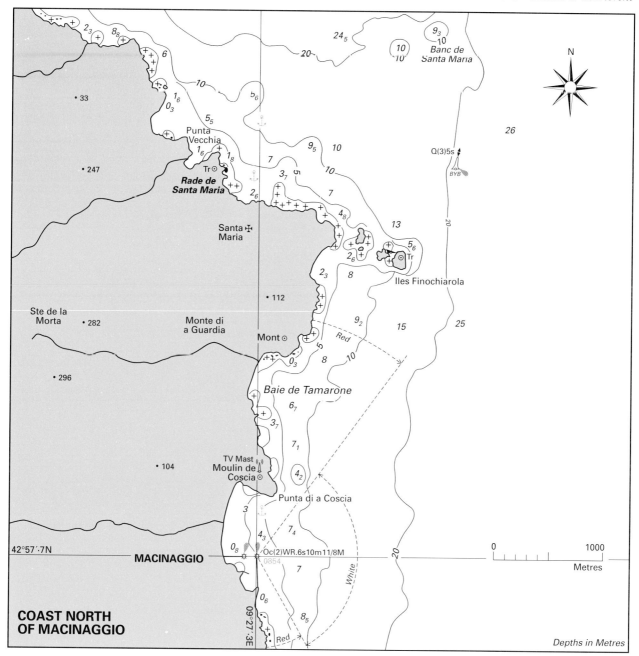

Pointe d'Agnello

A conspicuous promontory of green-grey rocks in two parts, it has a ruined tower on its NE point. The land behind the point is round and high (141m). Rocky dangers extend 100m towards the northeast. The point is split into two parts by a narrow creek. The northwestern part of the promontory is lower with whitish coloured cliffs.

⚓ Pointe d'Agnello NW

An attractive small anchorage open to N–NE and deserted, it has three small coves with rocky sides. Anchor in 4m, sand. The Tour d'Agnello is a good landmark.

⚓ Marine de Barcaggio

A large bay open to NW–N–NE with a small harbour for fishing boats and dinghies in the western corner where there is a small fishing village with church, shop and road inland. A long sand and shingle beach divided by a group of rocks often used by nudists. Anchor in 3m sand to the north of the harbour. A deep water (16m) anchorage is available 300m to the north of the village on sand and weed.

Ile de la Giraglia

1M to N of Barcaggio lies the Ile de la Giraglia which is 1200m long, 300m wide and 65m high with whitish rocky cliffs. There is an old square stone fort at the NW end of the island with a white lighthouse tower black top (22m) alongside (Fl.5s85m28M) a

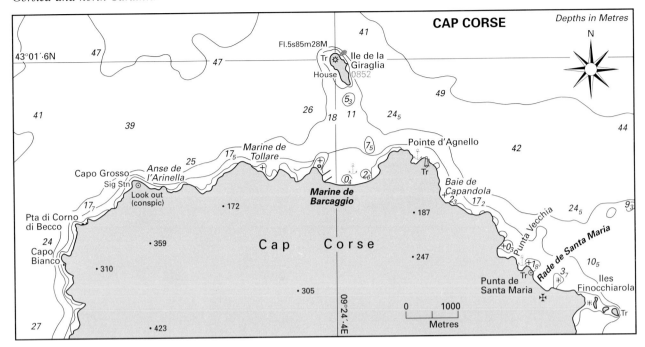

low flat white house is near the centre of the island. There are landings on the NE side of the island where there is a small hut and a road cut into the rock.

Cap Corse

This is the general term for the whole of the N section of Haute-Corse and it covers the coast from Iles Finocchiarola to Capo Bianco including the Ile de la Giraglia.

Capo Grosso

A pointed headland with a conspicuous signal station on its top. Steep cliffs and one small rock close into the point otherwise steep-to. The land slopes up to 364m inland.

⚓ Port de Centuri

⊕ 42°58'·0N 09°21'·02E

Some 2·5 miles south of Capo Grosso is the Baie de Centuri with a very new yacht harbour at its south end. It is well protected from the SW by the Ile de Centuri but it is open to the NW which makes it of doubtful tenure during strong northwesterlies. There are 2–3m depths in the harbour with space for 125 craft (25 for visitors). All facilities were due to be ready for the 2000 season but delays have been caused by bombers who blew up the breakwater in 1998! The *capitaneria* can be reached on ☎ 04 95 35 60 06 and note there are no lights planned at present and entering and leaving are only permitted during daylight hours. Approach the head of the jetty on an ESE course and pass close to the end of the jetty coming round to a course of south inside the jetty.

⚓ Baie de Centuri

A large bay open to W–NW–N with Port de Centuri in the SE corner and the Ile de Centuri in the SW corner. Anchor in the southern part in 5m, rock and sand, but note that the holding is not good.

Ile de Centuri

An island 300m by 200m which is 43m high. It has foul ground to the east and to the northwest extending to 200m. A dangerous unmarked rock covered 0·4m lies 200m north of the island.

⚓ Marine de Morsiglia N

A fair weather anchorage off a stony beach in a small bay, off-lying rocks, open to SW–W–NW. It lies about 200m to the north of the village of Mute. Anchor with care in 3m, rock and weed, near to the centre of the bay between a group of four islets and a single islet. Road ashore.

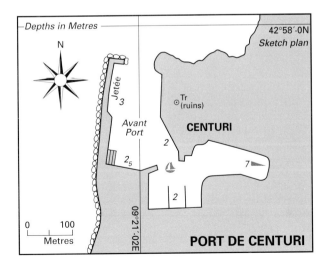

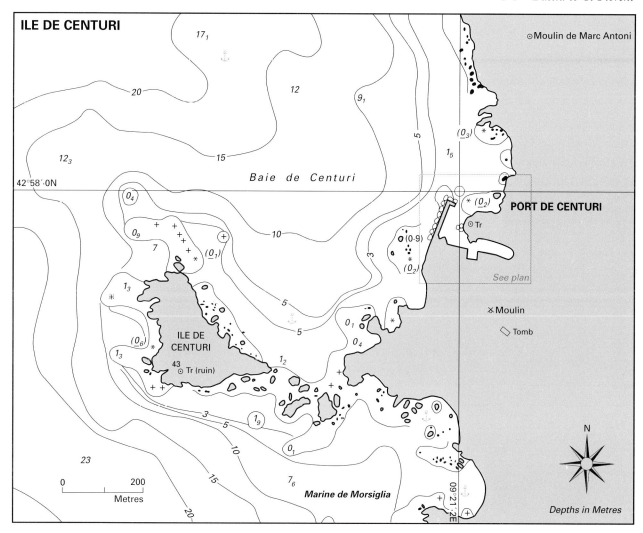

ILE DE CENTURI

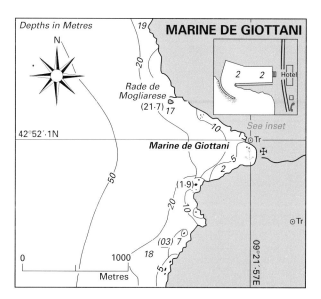

⚓ Marine de Morsiglia S

A more open bay than that described above with the rocks confined to the sides, open to the SW–W–NW. A small group of houses ashore behind a stony beach and a road. Anchor in 3m, rock, stone and weed, near the centre of the bay.

Between Centuri and the next reasonable harbour of Saint Florent there are 19 miles of high rocky coastline with a few small villages on the winding coast road. A good offing should be maintained in all but the most settled weather. In ideal conditions it is possible to anchor for lunch or a swim at a couple of places. Just south of Punta di Stintinu there is a small inlet of Marine de Giottani with a small basin, 2m deep for *gommones*. South again is the Punta di Canelle and the Amianto asbestos works.

⚓ Marine de Giottani

A deep bay with white rocky cliffs and a rocky beach at its head where there is also a small fishing boat and dinghy harbour with 2m depth. A tower stands on the hill behind the harbour while the bay is open to SW–W–NW. Anchor near the centre of the bay in 6m, sand. A few houses and a hotel/restaurant stand

behind the beach while the coast road runs further inland. There is a conspicuous church with a tall steeple up the valley behind, and a village further inland.

Amianto asbestos mine and works

The hills above the Roches d'Albo and Punta Bianca have been extensively mined for asbestos and the white scar that has been left on the sloping hillside can be seen from afar. In the closer approach the huge processing buildings will be seen. The works were closed in 1965 but the debris which was discharged into the sea is still washing along the coast partially filling the bays and indentations.

⚓ Marine d'Albo

A wide bay partially filled by the grey debris from the asbestos works, in fact the original pier and beach have been totally covered by the debris. The northwest side has a few rocks close inshore, a small village and restaurant stands behind the beach of grey stones and a conspicuous tower marks the south side of the bay. The coast road loops behind the head of the beach. Anchor in 4m, sand and stone, in the middle of the bay, open SW–W–NW–N.

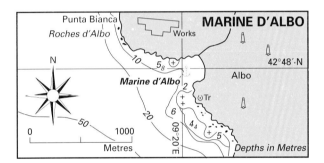

3·2 – Saint Florent to Calvi

The first part of the coast, running west from the wide and indented Golfe de Saint Florent, follows the mainly low-lying shore of the Desert des Agriates. It is a totally uninhabited section of bare rock and shrub with many deserted anchorages off delightful sandy beaches. The next stretch includes the harbours of Ile Rousse and Sant'Ambrogio and is rather more rocky with some off-lying dangers. The coast is backed by a relatively flat, fertile region, La Balagne, and is well populated. This entire section is very open to the prevailing NW winds and shelter should be sought in either Saint Florent or Calvi if a *maestrale* is forecast.

⚓ Saint Florent

General

This fishing and yacht harbour is situated at the head of the wide Golfe de Saint Florent at the edge of a flat delta of the Rivière Aliso with high ranges of mountains in the background. Approach and entrance are easy but in heavy weather from the northwest could become difficult and perhaps dangerous. There is good shelter once inside the harbour though heavy gusts of wind off the mountains can be experienced from an E–SE direction. The old and attractive town has a number of shops which can provide everyday requirements. The town and harbour are very crowded in the season.

⊕1 (west of Écueil de Tignosu) 42°41'N 09°17'·5E
⊕2 (entrance) 42°40'·8N 09°17'·9E

Depth 5m to 1·5m
Number of berths 790 with 270 for visitors

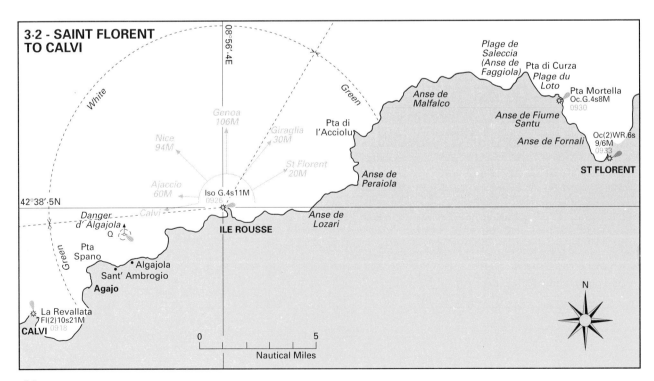

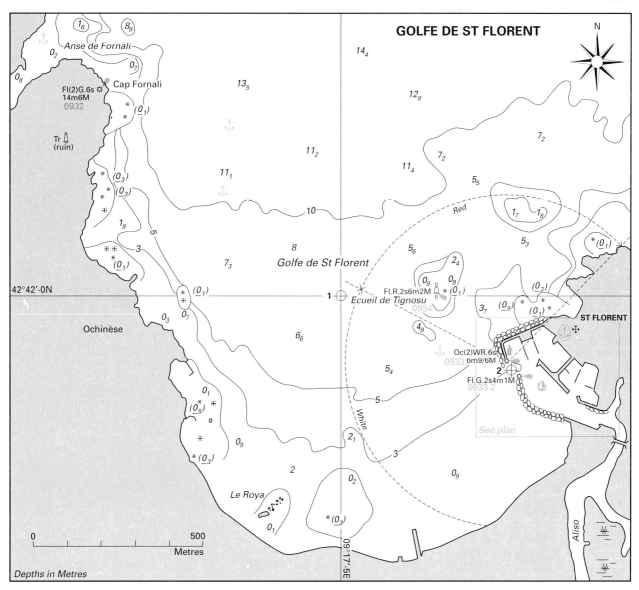

GOLFE DE ST FLORENT

Charts

Admiralty *1999*
French *6850, 6969*

Port radio

VHF Ch 9 or ☎ 04 95 37 00 79.

Weather forecast

Posted daily at *capitaneria*.

Lights

0935 Pointe Vecchiaja 42°42'·9N 9°19'·5E
Fl(3)WR.12s35m10/7M Round white tower, red
top
0932 Cap de Fornali 42°41'·3N 9°16'·9E
Fl(2)G.6s14m6M White square tower, green top
and corners
0930 Punta Mortella 42°43'·0N 9°15'·4E
Oc.G.4s43m8M White square tower, green top
0934 Écueil de Tignosu 42°40'·9N 9°17'·7E
Fl.R.2s6m2M Red tower on rocks 350m NW of
port

0933 Jetée Nord 42°40'·8N 9°17'·9E
Oc(2)WR.6s6m9/6M White column red top 116°-
R-227°-W-116°
0933·2 Jetée Sud Fl.G.2s4m1M

Warnings

The shores of the Golfe de Saint Florent are fronted
by shallow banks and rocky patches. Two isolated
rocky patches lie near the entrance of the harbour:
the Écueil de Tignosu, 0·1m deep, some 500m to
NW of the entrance and another rocky patch, 1·7m
deep, some 600m to N of the entrance. The area S
of the harbour entrance shallows quickly.

Important warning

Fire fighting flying boats may use the Golfe de Saint
Florent to pick up water.

Restricted area

A nature reserve where fishing, subaqua diving and
anchoring are forbidden lies to the N of this
harbour, it stretches from the tower de Farinole to
the tower de Nonza and extends 2M seawards.

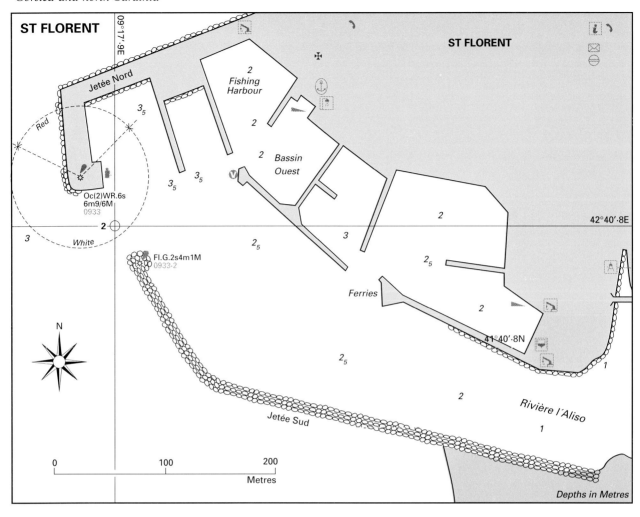

ST FLORENT

09°17'·9E

Jetée Nord

Red

Oc(2)WR.6s
6m9/6M
0933

White

3₅

3₅

3₅

3₅

3

2

Fishing
Harbour

2

2 Bassin
Ouest

2₅

Fl.G.2s4m1M
0933·2

2₅

ST FLORENT

2

3

2₅

2

Ferries

2

41°40'·8N

2₅

2

42°40'·8E

1

Rivière l'Aliso

1

Jetée Sud

N

0   100   200
Metres

Depths in Metres

Approach

By day From the north follow the rocky, mountainous and broken coast southwards. The white cliffs and disused quarry and asbestos factory at Marine d'Albo, the town of Nonza perched on a steep rocky hill and the lower rounded Punta Vecchiaia with a very small lighthouse will all be easily identified. The town of Saint Florent will be seen in the closer approach. Proceed down the centre of the gulf on a southerly course leaving the beacon tower La Tignosu 200m to port. When this beacon is in line with Saint Florent church tower, course may be altered towards the harbour entrance.

From the west follow the broken rocky coast with white sandy beaches of the Désert des Agriates around into the Golfe de Saint Florent. Punta Mortella which has a disused signal station and lighthouse, Pointe de Cepo which has an old fort and Cap Fornali with its small lighthouse are all easily recognised. Keep to the centre of the gulf on a southerly course and proceed as detailed in the approach above.

By night Using the lights on Punta Vecchiaia, Cap Fornali and Punta Mortella it is easy to arrive at the ⊕1 off the Écueil de Tignosu. Leave the beacon 200m to port and approach the entrance in the white sector of the light on an ESE'ly course and steer to go between the red and green lights on the pier ends.

Entrance

The entrance is 30m wide and is simple by day or night.

Berths

Secure to the holding berth immediately ahead of you on entering and obtain berthing instructions. Secure stern-to pontoon or quay allotted, with mooring chain from the bow. This is connected to the pontoon or quay by a light pick-up rope/chain. Note that anchoring is not permitted inside the harbour.

Formalities

All authorities available

Facilities

All.

History

The original village, dating from Roman times, was at Nebbio 1M inland; this developed considerably in the 12th century on becoming the seat of a bishop and when the cathedral of Sainte Marie was built. The village with its cathedral was abandoned in the 16th century owing to an outbreak of malaria and a new town, Saint Florent, was built beside the round Genoese fort which had been erected some 100 years earlier on a low hill overlooking the harbour.

General Gentile, one of Paoli's companions was born in Saint Florent and buried in the cathedral at Nebbio. In 1794 when Lord Hood and the British fleet attempted to reduce the town and nearby fortifications by bombardment, the defenders of the tower on Punta Mortella, now in ruins, refused to surrender and a strong shore party had to be landed to capture it.

The ability of these Genoese towers and forts to resist heavy bombardment so impressed the British that the design and details were sent back to England and used as a basis for the 100 Martello towers that were subsequently built on the south coast of England as a defence against the threatened attack of the Corsican, Napoleon Bonaparte.

Cap Fornali

An easily recognised headland with an old square fort on the top of the hill behind the point and a white square lighthouse on the point with green top and corners, white house alongside (Fl(2)G.6s 14m6M).

⚓ Anse de Fornali

An old harbour once used by large sailing vessels, over the years it has silted up, old guns are embedded along the coast for mooring and warping purposes. A private landing stage and house stand on the south side of the Anse. Sound carefully as there is a 1·6m shallow patch in the mouth of the Anse and a lone rock is in mid-channel further in. Anchor north of the landing stage in 2m sand and mud open to N–NE–E–SE. Road on the southeast coast.

⚓ Anse de Fiume Santu

A good anchorage open to N–NE–E in 3m sand in a bay at the mouth of a river which once had a large sand and shingle beach to the northwest of its mouth. One hut and track on both sides of the bay,

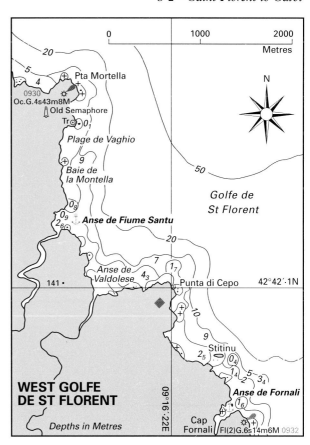

deserted. Some years ago, the beach was swept away after a cloud burst in the hills behind.

Punta Mortella

A very prominent point with a lighthouse on a higher hill behind. A coast road. Rocky dangers extend 200m. A conspicuous ruined tower stands on a small point 300m to the south. This is the famous tower that Lord Hood's force failed to destroy in the 1794. See Port de Saint Florent history page 30.

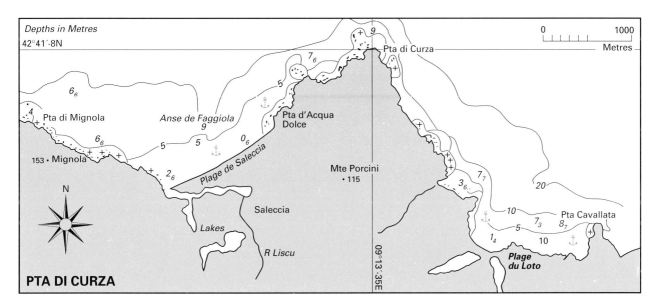

Punta Cavallata

A narrow pointed headland sloping up inland and then falling away, sheer-to with a small anchorage on its W side.

⚓ Plage du Loto

A wide white sandy bay open to N–NE–E. Anchor in 3m sand off sandy beach. Low ground with lagoons behind beach. Deserted, wreck at the west end of the bay.

Punta di Curza

A prominent headland of whitish rock sloping up to 115m with a stony pyramid on top. Rocky off-liers extend 200m.

⚓ Plage de Saleccia

A very large bay backed by a long white sandy beach. Anchor in 3m of sand off the beach, open to NW–N–NE. Sand dunes and track along back of the beach. There is a camping ground behind the beach in season and a river at southwest end of beach. This is a very popular spot for lunching and swimming during the season as it is only an hours trip from Saint Florent and it gets very crowded.

⚓ Anse de Malfalcu

An attractive narrow *calanque*-type anchorage with hills around it and low cliffs with some close inshore rocks. Sound carefully while approaching due to shallows. Anchor and moor with 2nd anchor in 3m, sand inside the entrance, open to NW–N. Small white sand and shingle beach at head. Ruined house to SW. Tracks along coast and inland. Deserted.

⚓ Baie de l'Acciolu

A small white sand and shingle beach in the centre of a wide bay with Mont Orlando (107m) towering over it. The sides of the bay are rocky. Enter on a southerly course and anchor off the beach in 3m, sand, open to NW–N–NE. Track inland. Deserted.

Punta di l'Acciolu

A conspicuous headland with a narrow jutting rocky point, sheer-to. The W side resembles a beak. Mont Orlando (107m) stands behind this point.

⚓ Anse de Peraiola

A wide bay open to SW–W–NW–N with a long white sandy beach with dunes behind, it has a river mouth at the south end. Some houses and a café on the road that is above the river. There is a tower 500m to the north of the north end of the beach. Anchor in 3m, sand, off the beach.

⚓ Anse de Lozari

A wide bay open to W–NW–N–NE with a long sand and shingle beach. Camping site and houses behind the northeast end of the beach, a large apartment block in the middle and the village of Lozari at the southwest end. There are some beach cafés ashore and a small river mouth at the west end of the beach. Note that there is a 4 x 1·5 cable area off the river mouth, in a 010° direction, where fishing and anchoring are prohibited. Anchor to the east of this area in 3 to 5m on sand.

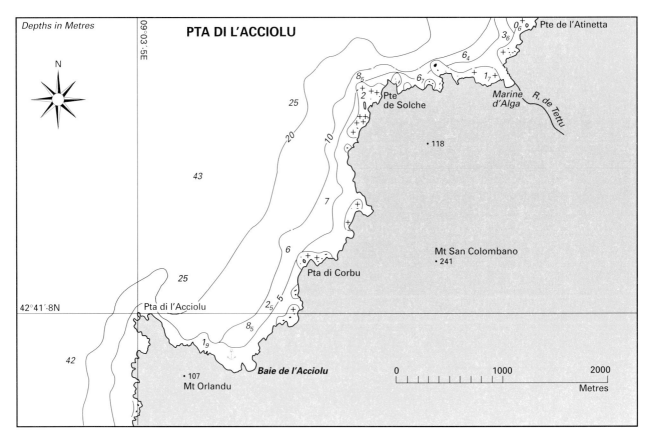

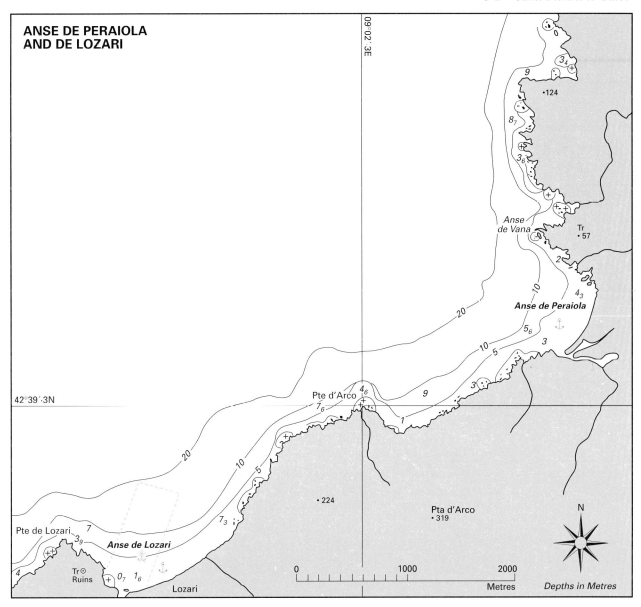

ANSE DE PERAIOLA AND DE LOZARI

Punta Saleccia

A small headland with a tower on its point, the coast road and railway behind.

Port de L'Ile Rousse

This harbour has been classified as a commercial harbour although it has recently been extended with a brand new marina, Port Abri, with 250 berths (85 for visitors). It is clear the marina will offer reasonable protection from the prevailing southwest to northwest winds but the strong northeasterlies (*tramontana*) may still make the berths somewhat uncomfortable and the approach, to the harbour itself, difficult.

Lights
0926 Phare de la Pietra 42°38'·6N 8°56'·0E Fl(3)WG.12s64m14/11M White tower, green top and white house 13m 000°-G-079°-W-234°-G-000°
0928 Jetee head 42°38'·5N 8°56'·4E Iso.G.4s12m11M White tower, green top 12m

0927 Quai du Commerce Oc.R.4s2m4M Red pedestal 1m
0926·5 Jetee du Large head Fl.G.4s2m (300°-vis-218°)
0927·2 Buoy 42°38'·4N 8°56'·3E VQ(3)5s5m3M E card BYB in centre of harbour some 250m east of 0926·5.

Approach

Ile Pietra is an unmistakable large reddish island connected to the mainland by a causeway. Approaching from any direction steer to arrive about 1 mile north of the jetty keeping well clear of the island and its outliers. Then steer a course between 160° and 180° towards the end of the jetty passing between the Haut-fond de Naso and the Danger de l'Ile Rousse. Leave the jetty well to starboard, taking care to keep well clear of any commercial traffic that may be manoeuvring in the harbour, and proceed to the marina entrance on a westerly course. Again watch for fishing boats entering and leaving the entrance and proceed on a

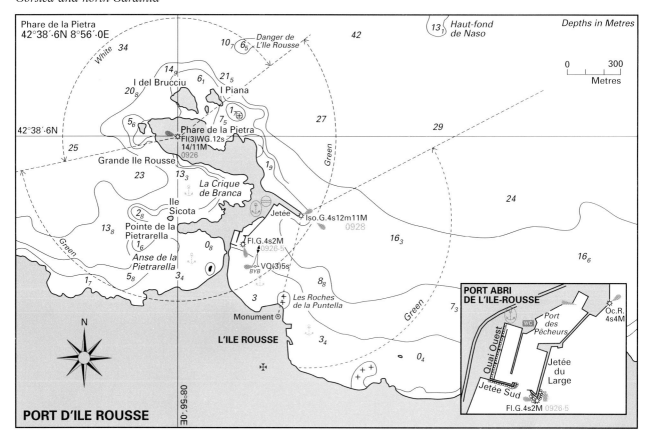

PORT D'ILE ROUSSE

northerly course through the pier heads and turn immediately to port to enter the marina.

Berths

Either pick up a vacant berth and report to the *capitainerie* for a berth or call ahead to the *capitainerie* on Ch 9 or ☎/Fax 04 95 60 26 51 and instructions will be given. Note that anchoring in the harbour area is still under the jurisdiction of the *capitainerie* who must be contacted before dropping an anchor.

Facilities

Most facilities for the yacht are available at the port but for stores one should go to the attractive town some 0·5 mile to the south of the marina, where there is a good range of shops.

Passage between Le Grande Ile Rousse and Isula dei Brucciu

A passage exists between Isula dei Brucciu and Grande Ile Rousse 50m wide, 250m long and 2·5m deep which can be used by an experienced navigator in good weather. It is spectacular because the red rocky sides are high and steep and the water is a dark blue colour.

From the west there is no problem because depths are in excess of 18m and the entrance wide, enter on an ESE course and cross the mouth of the Crique de Fontanacci close in.

From the east more care is necessary, as there is a small isolated rock 120m southeast of the small

Isula Piana. Keep close in to the Grande Ile, cross the Crique de Fontanacci and enter the channel on a WNW course.

Passage

The actual passage is 8·5–18m deep and is steep-to, the only problem a 2·5m rock lying in the approach from the eastern side.

Punta di Vallitone

A prominent point with off-lying dangers extending 300m to northwest and north. It is low and has a tower near the point, houses have been built over this area.

⚓ Anse d'Algajola

A wide bay with a long white sand beach. Punta di Varcale is at the north end of this beach and the town of Algajola which has a conspicuous church tower and fortress is on a point at the southwest end. There are sand dunes behind the beach, a railway line and a road. A number of apartment blocks and houses have been built and there are several beach cafés. Anchor in 3m, sand, off the beach open to W–NW–N. Everyday supplies obtainable from the town where there is a mechanic and chandlers.

⚓ Port d'Algajola

About 800m to the west of the beach a small harbour for fishing boats and dinghies has been built. There is 6m in the entrance and 3m in the centre of the harbour but the sides are very shallow. On the northwest side is a slip and a small jetty, a road leading to the main road lies behind the jetty.

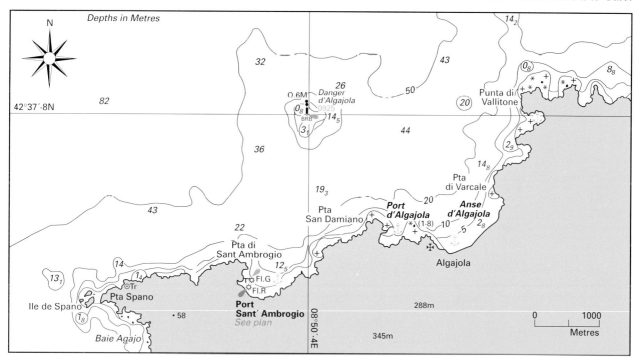

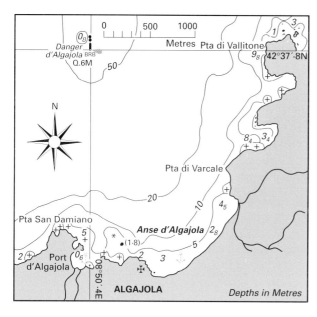

topmark located at the centre of this shoal which extends about 200m around it. The balls are occasionally missing and the pole is very difficult to see, especially in poor conditions. Just to the north of the danger is a buoy which is Danger d'Algajola 42°37'·8N 8°50'·4E Q.6M N cardinal buoy. A 1500m passage exists between this danger and the shore. The lighthouse on Grande Ile Rousse on 068° leads through the inner passage. The white sector of this lighthouse leads outside this danger and, unfortunately, the green sector covers it. In rough weather the seas break over the shallows.

⚓ Sant'Ambrogio

⊕ 42°36'·15N 08°49'·8E

A modern, private yacht harbour which is a part of a large holiday housing complex, and therefore it becomes very crowded in season. There are 150 berths with 20 for visitors in 1–2·5m. Approach and entrance are not difficult in good weather but as the entrance lies in shallow water close to the beach it is potentially dangerous in heavy weather from the N or NE as you have to turn beam-on to the swell to effect an entrance. The shelter inside the harbour is good though some swell enters with strong NE–E winds. In season, adequate supplies of provisions are available from shops beside the harbour but out of season the nearest shops are at Algajola over 1M away. The entrance tends to silt up during storms.

Although the ends of the jetties are lit Fl.G.2s7m2M and Fl.R.2s7m2M the lights are difficult to see against the background of shop, house and street lights so a night approach is not recommended for the first visit! Once inside berth near the fuelling point and await instructions – all normal facilities are available.

The area is surrounded by a housing estate and the railway passes behind. A small islet (1·8m) lies 300m to the northwest of the town. Anchor in 3m, sand and rock, just inside the harbour, open to N–NE.

Punta San Damiano

A small point west of the Port d'Algajola which slopes gently inland and is covered by a housing estate. This point is virtually steep-to.

Danger d'Algajola

⊕ 42°37'·8N 08°50'·4E

A shallow group of rocks submerged and awash, minimum depth 0·8m lies 1M NNW of Pointe St Damiano and 2M west of Pointe Vallitone. A beacon consisting of a BRB iron pole with two balls

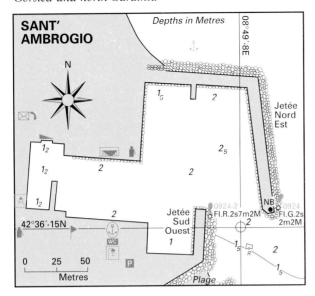

SANT' AMBROGIO

Depths in Metres

N

Jetée Nord Est

42°36'·15N

Jetée Sud Ouest

08·49·8E

0924·2 FI.R.2s7m2M NB 0924 FI.G.2s 2m2M

Plage

0   25   50
Metres

Punta Spano

A low but prominent point (29m) sloping gently upward and inland, with several islets and covered and exposed rocks off its point. A ruined tower stands 400m to the northeast.

Ile de Spano

One large islet 200m long 90m wide and 14m high, a small islet 5·9m high and many small exposed rocks. Fishing craft and dinghies can use the passage between these islets with care in calm weather.

⚓ Baie Agajo

An open bay, south of Punta Spano, with rocky shore and some small sandy beaches. Camping site on shore, houses in the northeast corner with a road. Anchor in 5m, sand, open to SW–W–NW–N.

⚓ Portu Agajo

A small creek in the southeast corner of the Baie Agajo with white sandy beaches. Sound carefully because it is shallow. Anchor in sand off beach, open to W–NW–N.

⚓ Golfe de Calvi

A 2M wide gulf which is 1M deep and has depths of up to 36m. It is backed by a very long sandy beach and pine woods. La Figarella and Fiume Seccu Rau rivers enter the gulf on the southeast side. The bottom is mostly of sand and weed with a few patches of mud and one of rocks. It is open to NW–N–NE but somewhat protected from NW and NE by Punta Revellata and Punta Spano. There is a nature reserve area, see chart page 37. The usual anchorage is to the south and southeast of Calvi's Citadelle in 5–6m, sand and weed, well clear of the harbour entrance but the holding ground is reported to be poor.

3·3 – Calvi to Cargèse

This next section is certainly the most impressive of the whole island as it is extremely rugged, mountainous and, in places, is of awe-inspiring beauty. It is, however, a dangerous coast in bad weather and there are virtually no harbours of refuge except Calvi. Again with the exception of Calvi and Cargese and a few villages the land is virtually deserted. There is a very tortuous coast road running along the foot of the mountains that reach up to nearly 3000m and these lie only 22M inland.

The coast itself is of red rocky cliffs, with deep steep-sided bays and gulfs some of which offer anchorages; Girolata is the only one with any pretence of security for a small number (10?) of craft. The incredible Golfe de Porto, though a dangerous place, is well worth a visit in order to see the fantastic mountains that surround it.

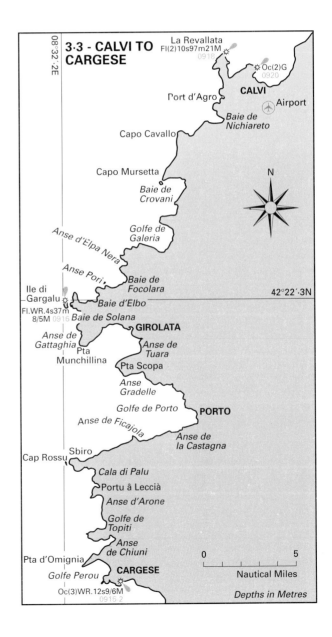

3·3 - CALVI TO CARGESE

08·32'·2E

La Revallata
FI(2)10s97m21M 0918

Oc(2)G 0920

CALVI

Port d'Agro

Airport

Baie de Nichiareto

Capo Cavallo

N

Capo Mursetta

Baie de Crovani

Golfe de Galeria

42°22'·3N

Anse d'Elpa Nera

Anse Pori

Baie de Focolara

Ile di Gargalu
FI.WR.4s37m 8/5M 0916

Baie d'Elbo

Baie de Solana

GIROLATA

Anse de Gattaghia

Pta Munchillina

Anse de Tuara

Pta Scopa

Anse Gradelle

Golfe de Porto

PORTO

Anse de Ficajola

Anse de la Castagna

Cap Rossu

Sbiro

Cala di Palu

Portu â Leccià

Anse d'Arone

Golfe de Topiti

Anse de Chiuni

Pta d'Omignia

CARGESE

Golfe Perou

Oc(3)WR.12s9/6M
0916·2

0   5
Nautical Miles

Depths in Metres

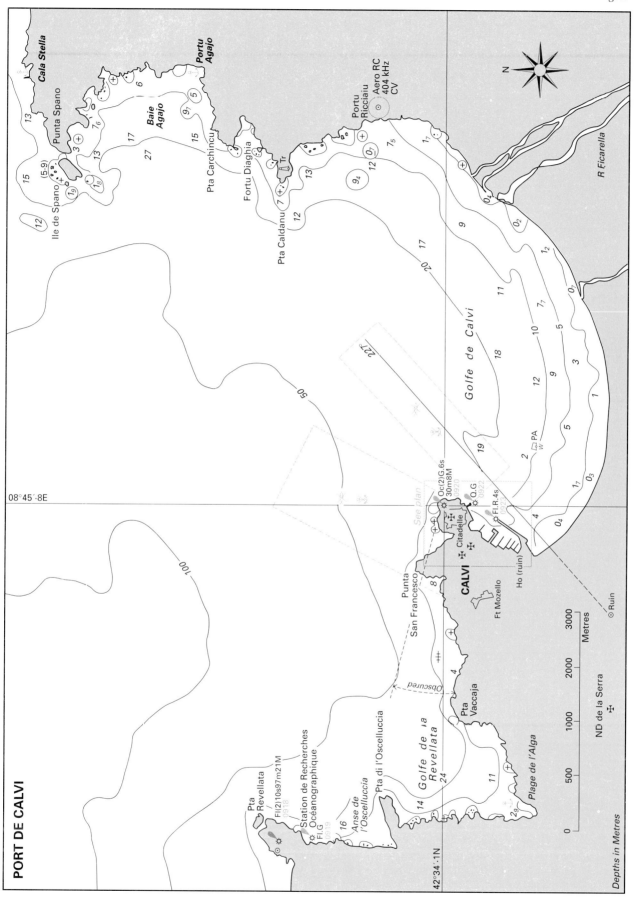

PORT DE CALVI

08°45′·8E

Cala Stella

Punta Spano

Ile de Spano

Portu Agajo

Baie Agajo

Pta Carchincu

Fortu Diaghia

Pta Caldanu

Portu Ricciaiu

Aero RC
404 kHz
CV

Golfe de Calvi

R Ficarella

N

See plan

Punta
San Francesco

Oc(2)G.6s
30m8M
09920

Q.G
09922

Fl.R.4s
09?2?

Citadelle

CALVI

Ft Mozello

Ho (ruin)

Obscured

Pta
Vaccaja

Plage de l'Alga

N⃝ de la Serra

⊙ Ruin

Pta
Revellata

Fl(2)10s97m21M
09?8

Station de Recherches
Océanographique
Fl.G
09?9

Anse de
l'Oscelluccia

Pta di l'Oscelluccia

*Golfe de la
Revellata*

42°34′·1N

0   500   1000   2000   3000

Metres

Depths in Metres

37

⚓ Port de Calvi

General

One of the most beautiful harbours on the island which is easy to enter under almost any conditions and which provides adequate shelter, though with strong winds from NW–N–NE the anchorage can become uncomfortable from the swell. Berths in the yacht harbour are well protected but there is some swell from NE gales. The harbour is very crowded in the season. Yachts from the French mainland usually make this harbour their first port of call. The Citadelle and the town are most picturesque and everyday requirements can be obtained from the shops. Parts of the harbour are reserved for commercial and fishing vessels.

⊕ 42°34'·00N 08°45'·70E

Depth 5·5–1·5m
Number of berths 380 with 160 for visitors
Maximum length 50m

Charts

Admiralty *1425*
French *6980, 6970*

Port radio

VHF Ch 9 or ☎ 04 95 65 10 60.

Weather forecast

Posted twice a day (0800 & 2000) with 5-day forecasts

Lights

0918 Punta Revellata 42°35'·0N 8°43'·5E
   Fl(2)10s97m21M White square tower, black top 19m
0920 Citadelle NE side 42°34'·2N 8°45'·8E
   Oc(2)G.6s30m8M White metal framework tower, green top 6m
0922 Pier head Q.G.10m8M White metal column, dark green top
0923 Digue du Large head Fl.R.4s6m7M White structure, red top
0981·02(I) Porte de Péche left side Fl(2)R.6s2M
0981·03(I) Porte de Péche right side Fl(2)G.6s2M
From 1 June to 30 September there may be a buoy at 42°33'·9N 8°45'·9E marking the anchorage area with a Q light.

Warnings

Anchoring is prohibited within 300m of the harbour but there is a mooring area for some 230 yachts laid from June through September about 300m east-southeast of the breakwater. The commercial harbour including Quai Landry are forbidden to yachts without prior permission of the *capitainerie*.

Restricted areas

A nature reserve lies to NNW of the coast between Punta Revellata and Punta Rossa, it is 1M wide and extends 3M to seaward. Another area 400m wide and 1500m long stretches from Calvi in a NE direction, a similar area stretches from Calvi to NNE. Fishing, subaqua diving and anchoring is forbidden in these areas. See chart page 37.

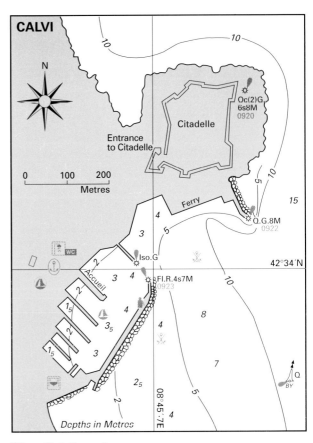

Fire-fighting planes

Large Canadair flying boats may use the Golfe de Calvi to load water for nearby fires.

Approach

The approach is easy by day or night, simply make for the high land in the centre of the gulf and the Citadelle (and/or its light) becomes obvious. Keep the Citadelle to starboard and pass outside the pier head, keeping well clear of any commercial traffic. Make for the entrance of the yacht harbour.

Entrance

A 50-metre wide unobstructed entrance.

Berths

On arrival moor to the visitors pontoon opposite the fuel berth, at the fuel berth or in any vacant berth. Report to the *bureau* for berth allocation. All berths are stern-to with chain/rope forward with a *pendillo* from the pontoon.

Formalities

All authorities available.

Facilities

All.

History

Calvi has been a small fishing harbour since before recorded history. The Romans had a small garrison here and in AD 225 beheaded Ste Restitute. In 1268 the little village on the site of the Lower Town was rebuilt and the Genoese colonised it building the Citadelle to defend the place.

Calvi remained faithful to Genoa and the Citadelle held despite the two attacks by the French and Turks in 1553. This is recalled by a plaque over the gateway with the inscription *Civitas Calvi semper fidelis*. In 1795 the English fleet under Lord Nelson attacked and, after its surrender, entered Calvi. Over 4,000 shells were fired into the town and the marks of them can still be seen on the dome of the church of St Jean-Baptiste. Nelson lost an eye during an opposed landing and a tablet to commemorate this event inscribed *Ici Nelson dirigeant le feu des batteries contre Calvi perdit un oeil, 12 Juillet 1794,* is to be found on a large rock at Macarona about 1M to the west. His battery of two 26-pounders and a 12-inch mortar from HMS *Agamemnon* were landed at Port Agro 3M to the southwest. Even the patriot Pascal Paoli was unable to shake the inhabitants' faith in Genoa and he was forced to found and develop l'Ile Rousse in 1795 as an alternative to the 'Citadelle of the North'.

Christopher Columbus is reputed to have been born in this town and in 1793 Napoleon took refuge in the Citadelle when he was obliged to flee from Ajaccio. Plaques in the Citadelle commemorate these events.

In more recent years there has been a steady development of the tourist industry. Holiday camps and hostels are to be found all around the bay while at the same time cultivation and farming of the fertile area, the Balagne, inland has decreased. Since 1963 the French Foreign Legion have occupied the barracks in the Citadelle.

⚓ Golfe de la Revellata

A small deep gulf, just to the west of Calvi, with a bottom of sand, shell and weed. A small stony beach Plage de l'Alga lies in the SW corner of this gulf. Anchor off this beach in 3m, sand and weed, open to N–NE. Track to road inland.

Station de Recherches Oceanographique

A very small harbour with light tower white and green (Fl.G.4s5m6M) on the head of the jetty. A road leads inland. Entrance into and anchorage off this harbour is not permitted.

Passage Ile de la Revellata

Ile de la Revellata is a pointed rock (27m) lying just off Punta Revellata. A passage only 15m wide and 2m deep lies between them. This passage should only be used by experienced navigators in calm conditions with great care and a careful lookout.

Punta Revellata

A conspicuous and prominent headland with a large white square tower on a house with corners and top picked out in black and a radio mast on top. The light is Fl(2)10s97m21M. The light is obscured when bearing less than 060°. The point and island are steep-to.

⚓ Porto Vecchio

A narrow V-shaped bay offering good protection but open to S–SW–W. Anchor in 5m to 3m, sand and

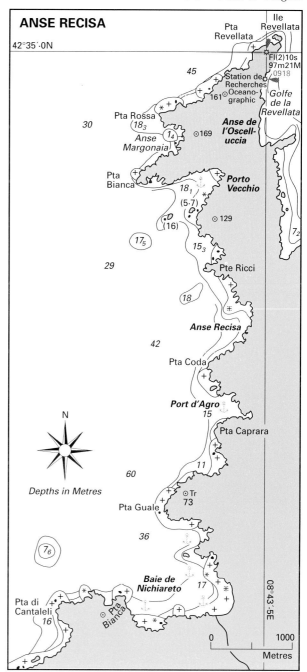

rock, near its head in front of small stony beach. There is a rocky island (16m) in the mouth of the bay. Deserted.

⚓ Port d'Agro

A narrow creek-type inlet with a stony beach at its head, high sloping rocks on each side and track to coast road above. Anchor in 6m, sand and rock, open to S–SW–W–NW. Deserted. It was here that Nelson landed his guns for the attack on Calvi in 1794.

Punta Caprara

A round rocky-cliffed point sloping up inland to the coast road. It is steep-to.

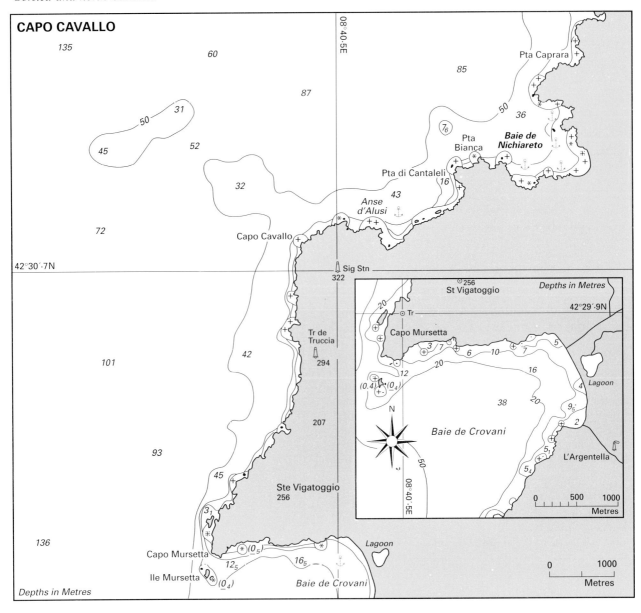

⚓ Baie de Nichiareto

Anchorage in a large bay with four small sub bays and a long white sand and stone beach. Anchor off the beach in 4m, sand and rock, or in one of the sub bays in 6m, rock. Open to W–NW. A track to coast road.

Capo Cavallo

A major headland with rocky cliffs and a round shape. Although appearing steep-to it has a shallowish (30m) reef running some 2 miles to the northwest which in strong northwest or west winds kicks up a very nasty breaking steep sea. In strong onshore winds both this headland and Capo Mursetta, 2·5 miles to the south (qv), should be given a wide berth. It has a conspicuous disused signal station (322m) on the summit.

Capo Mursetta

About 2·5M south of Capo Cavallo and a part of the same extended coastline, this cape, though similar, has a more irregular outline and has a group of islets extending 500m to the south. Halfway between these capes is the conspicuous ruined Tour de Truccia (294m).

L'Ile Mursetta and passage

This islet lies 300m to the S of Capo Mursetta and is 16m high and 150m long, has awash and just covered rocks on E–SE and N–NW sides. An easy passage 100m wide with a least depth 17m lies between the isle and the cape. This passage should be taken in ESE or WNW directions equidistant between the two sides.

⚓ Baie de Crovani

A spacious anchorage in a wide bay with a long white sandy beach, with beach restaurants. It is surrounded by high mountains in the background. Anchor off the beach in 4m, sand and stone. It is open to SW–W–NW. Deserted. At the south end of the bay is a small landing stage with an overhead

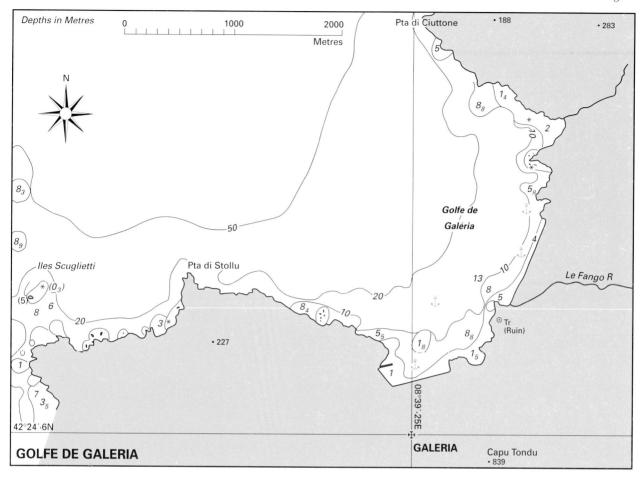

GOLFE DE GALERIA

GALERIA   Capu Tondu • 839

railway (disused) running via a small village and a factory at L'Argentella (1km inland) to the old silver and lead mines inland. The coast road runs through this valley. Another factory lies inland off the north end of the beach.

Punta di Ciuttone

A high prominent headland with red rocky cliffs, and one close inshore islet otherwise steep-to. Inland the point rises to 200m with a stony pyramid half way up the slope.

⚓ Golfe de Galéria

This wide deep gulf has one long, one medium and several small sandy beaches. The northern anchorage is off the north end of the long beach, Le Plage de Fango, in 4m sand open to W–NW–N. The area is backed by a wide river valley and The Tour de Galéria stands on a hillock at the south end of this beach and close to the river mouth. There is a conspicuous cemetery and caravan site inland and track to the beach.

To the southeast of the tower there is another beach and the village of Galéria itself, which has an hotel, some shops and many houses standing behind the beach. There is also a caravan site. Road runs to the main coast road and a fuel station is 3M inland. Anchor in 3m, sand, mud and rock, off the beach and clear of moorings and paying attention in the approach to a 1·8m shallow patch off the centre of

the beach. Open to W–NW–N. At the west end of the beach there is a new pier with 6 or 7 berths for shallow draught craft only. There is a bar, restaurant and telephone 300m to the south of the pier.

Iles Scuglietti and passage

Iles Scuglietti is a dangerous shoal area of islets, awash and covered rocks stretching up to 600m to NNW of Punta Rossa. The Ile Scuglietti is 5m high. A passage 200m wide and 8m deep exists between a group of islets lying off the north side of Punta Rossa and a second group lying near Ile Scuglietti. Take the passage in NE–SW directions.

Punta Rossa

A broken rocky-cliffed point with off-lying dangers – see above, sloping up to 100m high inland.

Punta Bianca

A headland similar to Punta Rossa, steep-to but sloping up to 408m.

⚓ Anse d'Elpa Nera

A small rocky-cliffed bay just south of the point. Anchor in 6m rock near head of bay, high land behind. Deserted. Fishing and subaqua diving forbidden. Open to SW–W–NW.

⚓ Baie de Focolara

A wide deep bay surrounded by high rocky cliffs and a range of high tree covered hills. It is most

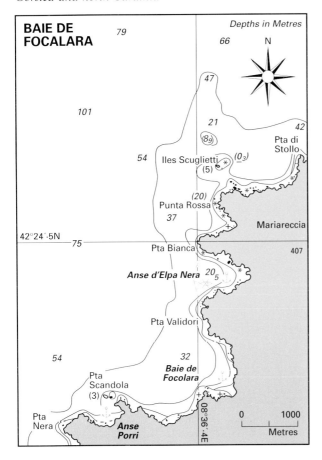

attractive. Anchor near the centre of the bay just north of a projecting rock in 4m, rocks, open to W–NW–N. Deserted. Small stream.

Punta Scandola

A narrow rocky projecting point with Ecueils de Porri (31m) lying 200m to NW of the point.

Écueils de Porri and passage

Écueils de Porri (31m) lies 200m northwest of Punta Scandola and it has a small exposed rock 100m to its east. Punta Scandola has two exposed rocks close inshore. A passage 50m wide lies between the rocks close to Punta Scandola and the rock off Écueils de Porri with a minimum depth of 16m. Take the passage in NE–SW directions with great care and in calm conditions.

⚓ Anse Porri

A small rocky bay with an anchorage in 6m, rocks at its head, open to W–NW–N. Deserted.

Punta Nera

A square-shaped rocky headland with an islet close inshore, the land behind slopes up to 303m.

⚓ Baie d'Elbo

Probably the most fantastic and beautiful area in the very attractive section of coast that stretches from here as far south as Cap Rossu. The cliffs, islands and islets are of dark red rock and their shapes are most extraordinary. The sea is clear dark blue and most of the land is covered with light and dark green vegetation. The area is a nature reserve and fishing, subaqua diving and camping are forbidden; also landing on the islands or mainland is not permitted and no boat may stay longer than 24 hours in the area. See page 43 for the boundaries of the area. In addition to the anchorage in the Marine d'Elbo there are many creeks, caves and fissures to explore in the area, some have vertical sides, an ideal place for fantastic photographs. Open to NW–N–NE.

Marine d'Elbo is a small creek with a sand and stone beach used by fishermen. A line of rocky islets and awash rocks terminate at the rocky Ile d'Elbo to the north. The Tour d'Elbo on the east side of the harbour is conspicuous. A lone awash rock lies 200m northwest of the western side of the entrance. Anchor in 4m, sand and weed, in the centre of the creek, open to NW–N–NE, mooring to two anchors (fore and aft) is advised. Track inland and a ruined hut near the beach. Deserted. Winds from SE–S–SW sometimes funnel down the valley behind the anchorage.

Punta Palazzu

A high steep-sided point of very jagged aspect and with vertical striations. Steep-to with Ilot Palazzu (58m) off its NW corner and a smaller *ilot* off its northern side.

Ilot Palazzu and passage

A simple little passage 45m wide and 22m deep between an almost vertical red rocky point and a steep-sided *ilot* 58m high. Take it in NE–SW directions in calm conditions. There is a smaller nameless *ilot* to the east of Ilot Palazzu with a narrow passage which can be used with great care by experienced navigators.

Ile di Gargalu and passage

The largish red rocky Ile di Gargalu is 75m long and 45m wide, the highest point where there is a tower at 127m. There is an inconspicuous lighthouse on a neck of rocks that stretches out to the northwest (Fl.WR.4s37m8/5M white column black top). There is a 40m long passage 10m wide and 2·5m deep to be taken in N–S directions; this passage should only be attempted in good conditions. The approach from the N is easy and 16m can be carried into the passage. From the south it is necessary to approach the entrance on a NW course carrying 16m into the passage. However three large rocks in mid-passage reduce the depth to 2·5m and the width to 10m, care is necessary here and a good forward lookout is advised, the water is clear and the bottom can be seen, proceed slowly.

⚓ Baie di Solana

A deep anchorage in a small rocky-cliffed bay in 16m rock open to S–SW–W. Use only in good conditions. Deserted.

'Dog Leg' passage

A passage with fantastic scenery around a small unnamed island in a creek, both the sides of the creek and the island have very nearly vertical red

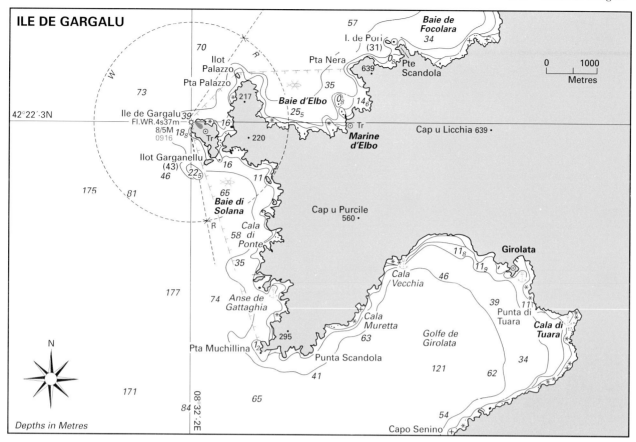

ILE DE GARGALU

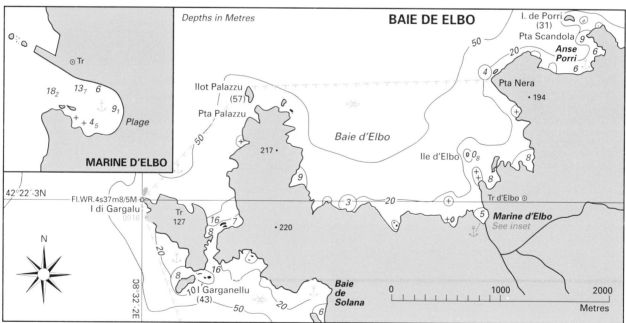

BAIE DE ELBO

rock cliffs. The water is very deep 11–27m. This passage is just to the north of the Anse de Gattaghia and there is a pyramid-shaped rocky islet on the south side of the southern entrance. Keep a look out for tourist boats from Calvi. A second passage has been reported to the south of Dog Leg and there are several small anchorages in this vicinity (in settled weather only).

Punta Muchillina

A red rocky-cliffed point which is very prominent. There are awash and covered rocks extending 100m off shore. Proceeding east from the point, en route for Girolata, you pass an unnamed point and then Punta Scandola. Some 1,000m northeast of the point there is a small islet and just beyond this there are a number of small bays, which offer reasonable shelter with the wind in the north or northwest quadrant and are a possible alternative to Girolata, if the latter is full. The first one past the islet is Cala Muretta with rocks off the western side of the entrance. On the beach there is a smoke-blackened barbecue chimney, anchor in 3–4m off the beach. There are two rings let into the rocks to the east of the beach to which a shore line can be taken, if required.

⚓ La Girolata

⊕ 42°20'·1N 08°37'·0E

Girolata is a superb anchorage in a beautiful setting and is the only anchorage that gives reasonable shelter to the prevailing winds between Calvi and Ajaccio for a small number (10?) of yachts drawing less than 2m. The shelter for deeper draught craft is not good because they must anchor near the entrance and might have to leave in heavy SW winds. Approach and entrance are easy as there is a conspicuous ruined fort with tower on the pyramidal-shaped headland at the west end of the anchorage. Round this point at some 50m and steer north into the bay. There are a number of pontoons off the beach which are solely for the use of ferries that run to and from the major towns. Unfortunately this anchorage becomes dangerously crowded in the season. Yachtsmen are advised not to use it during the months of July and August when there can be over 100 yachts at anchor each evening and only the first 10 or so yachts will find good shelter. Late arrivals have to anchor at the mouth of the *cala* fully exposed to S–SW–W. Motor boats run daily trips from Calvi, Porto and Ajaccio and other harbours for tourists to this anchorage. The only facilities are several restaurants, cafés and bars with a small shop ashore in summer season only – note that it is forbidden to take garbage ashore here.

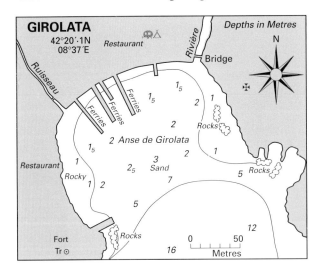

⚓ Cala di Tuara

A small bay at the foot of a valley at the mouth of a small river with a beach of sand and stone at its head just south of Girolata. Anchor in 5m, sand and weed, off the beach which is open to S–SW–W with some rocks on the south side of the entrance. Track to Girolata and also to coast road. A useful alternative to Girolata in settled weather.

Capo Senino

A red rocky headland rounded and facing NW, steep-to backed by the high pyramid-shaped Mont Senino (618m).

Punta à Scoppa

A similar feature to Capo Senino. There is a shallow area northwest of this point.

Golfe de Porto

A wide-mouthed deep bay surrounded by high hills and mountains mostly of red rock. Some of the cliffs on the south side of the gulf are especially spectacular. There are anchorages on both sides of the gulf and one at its head. These anchorages should be used with caution because the gulf is funnel-shaped with high sides, and this configuration is carried on inland up a valley at the head of the gulf. Because of this shape any SW–W–NW wind is speeded up as it passes up the gulf and the seas become very rough. Yachts will find it very difficult to leave the area and are, on occasions, driven ashore. With strong or gale force winds from the IV quadrant yachts should never attempt to enter this gulf but should keep well clear of the coast and eventually seek shelter in Calvi (20M) or Ajaccio (25M). In poor visibility or at a distance it is easy to mistake the Golfe de Porto for the Golfe de Girolata, careful navigation is advised.

⚓ Anse Gradelle

A small bay with rocky cliffs and a beach of sand and stone at its head. A track leads up the valley, some houses behind the beach. Anchor off the beach in 5m, sand, avoiding an awash rock on the eastern side. Open to SE–S–SW. Another little beach to the east can also be used to anchor off and there are two restaurants ashore in season.

Punta Bianca

A high rocky-cliffed point with rocky dangers extending 150m offshore. The land behind slopes up to 262m and a coast road runs across it.

⚓ Marine de Bussagghia

A large bay with a long sand and stone beach. A river valley runs inland where there are a number of houses, small hotels and restaurants, a road joins the main coast road. There are beach restaurants and cafés. An awash rock is located just offshore in the middle of the beach. Anchor in the north corner in 5m on sand. Open to S–SW–W.

Porto

This beautiful fishing village in magnificent surroundings is being rapidly spoiled by the construction of low cost apartment blocks and hotels for holidaymakers and by the daily arrival of hundreds of cars and coaches disgorging day-

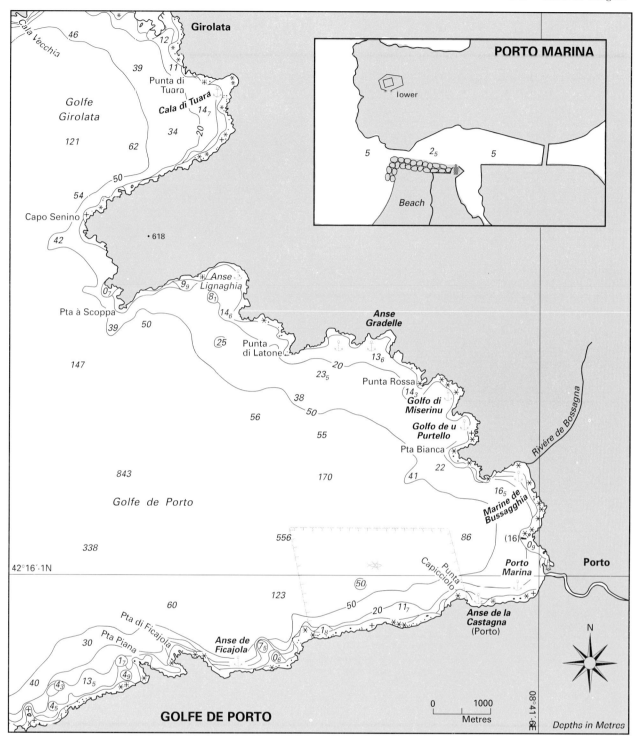

PORTO MARINA

tower

Beach

Girolata

Cala Vecchia

46

12

39

11

Punta di
Tuara

*Golfe
Girolata*

Cala di Tuara

14₇

20

121

34

62

50

54

Capo Senino

42

• 618

0₇

Pta à Scoppa

9₉

*Anse
Lignaghia*

8₁

14₆

39

50

25

Punta
di Latone

*Anse
Gradelle*

147

13₆

23₅

20

Punta Rossa

14₃

38

50

*Golfo di
Miserinu*

56

55

*Golfo de u
Purtello*

Pta Bianca

Rivère de Bossagna

843

170

41

22

Golfe de Porto

16₅

*Marine de
Bussagghia*

338

556

86

(16)

0₉

Porto

42°16'·1N

50

*Porto
Marina*

123

50

20

11₇

*Anse de la
Castagna*
(Porto)

Pta di Ficajola

60

N

Pta Piana

30

*Anse de
Ficajola*

1₈

1₇

7₅

0₆

40

4₃

13₅

4₉

4₅

GOLFE DE PORTO

0   1000
Metres

Depths in Metres

---

trippers. There is a quay with 1·5m alongside on the north side of a pinnacle rock with a small square fort on top. This is in frequent use by tourist boats from Calvi and sometimes by local fishermen. There are many restaurants and cafés. Everyday requirements can be obtained from the village. Marine engineer and chandlers. A restricted area lies to west of Porto between Punta Capicciolo and an unnamed headland 1·5M to the west where subaqua fishing is forbidden. (See chart above.)

⚓ Porto Marina

⊕ 42°16'·1N 08°41'·6E

A small yacht harbour has been constructed at the mouth of the river south of the village. It has 5m depth at the entrance but only 2·5–1m inside. There are 120 berths with 49 for visitors (maximum length 14m). Contact the *capitaneria* on VHF Ch 9 or ☎ 04 95 26 19 90. There are some facilities (fuel, showers (300m), water and electricity)

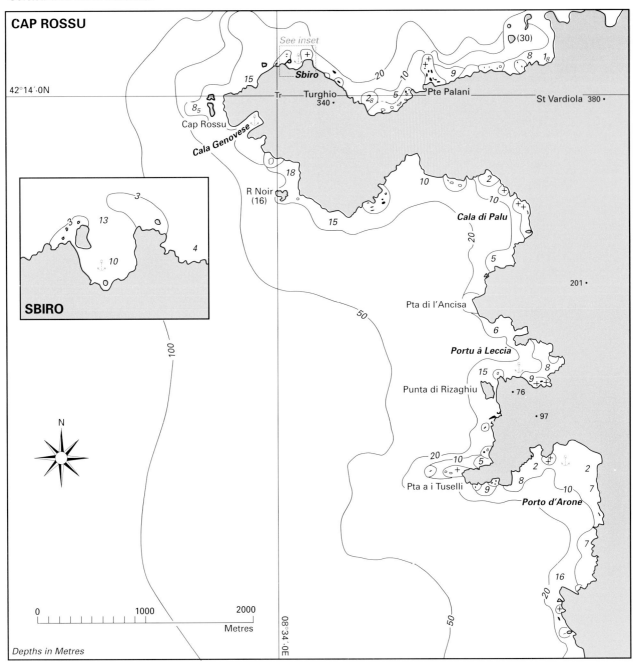

CAP ROSSU

42°14′·0N

Sbiro

15

Cap Rossu

Cala Genovese

8₅

Tr — Turghio
340 •

Pte Palani

2₈   5

20   10   9

(30)

8   1₈

St Vardiola 380 •

18

R Noir
(16)

10   2

+

10

+ +

Cala di Palu

15   20   5

Pta di l'Ancisa

201 •

6

Portu â Leccia

15   8
9 + +

Punta di Rizaghiu   • 76

• 97

20   10   5
-      + 2   2
+

Pta a i Tuselli   9   8   10   7

Porto d'Arone

7

16

20

50

50

100

SBIRO

3

3   13

10   4

N

0   1000   2000
Metres

Depths in Metres

08°34′·0E

♈ **Anse de la Castagna**

A minute deserted anchorage in 5m sand tucked away behind Pointe Capicciolo open to N–NE and where some protection from the NW–W may be found. Two anchors are advised due to the wind swirling around the point and down the steep hills. The bay has steep sides and there is a small quay (2m) alongside with a road to Porto.

♈ **Anse de Ficajola**

Another small anchorage in beautiful surroundings at the foot of the Côte des Calanques. Anchorages and moorings are to the south of a small beach in 10m sand. A restaurant 400m up a rocky path is open in the season, there are fishermen's huts on the beach. The anchorage is open to NW–N–NE but is still subject to a swell from the west. At the top of the hill after a tremendous climb to the northwest lies the town of Piana where everyday supplies can be bought.

Punta di Ficajola

A red rocky-cliffed promontory lying at 45° to the coast pointing NW. There is a 2·8m shallow patch to the north of the point, otherwise steep-to.

Ilot Vardiola

A conspicuous islet 32m high of red rock which stands 200m off the coast.

♈ **Sbiro**

500m to the east of Cap Rossu there is the Sbiro rock and you can anchor to the southeast of this rock in 10m depth on rock and sand. It is quite a tricky entrance but slow speed and a good lookout at the bow should enable you to anchor in this tiny landlocked bay. If you are put off by the narrowness of the entrance you can anchor in 4m off an un-named beach some 500m to the southeast. The approach is straightforward but a careful lookout is required as there are numerous isolated rocks close in.

Cap Rossu

A prominent peninsular headland with the conspicuous Tour de Turghio on top of a pointed hill (342m). The point is of high broken reddish rocky cliffs with an islet 100m to W and some rocky heads and shallows 200m to the northeast.

Cap Rossu passage

A passage 250m long, 3m deep and 75m wide at the N end between the 18m high and 200m long islet off the W point of Cap Rossu. Use from S to N for the first time because the entrance is obvious from the southern end. Navigate with care at slow speed with a bow lookout, in calm weather.

⚓ Cala Genovese

Another spectacular anchorage for the experienced navigator in calm weather. The entrance is close to the west side of Cap Rossu and is 200m south of its off-lying islet. It has high steep red cliffs and is narrow, there is a small white sand and stone beach at the head of the bay, anchor off this beach in 5m, sand and rock, open to S–SW–W. Deserted.

⚓ Cala di Palu

An anchorage in a large bay surrounded by rocky cliffs above which are high hills. Anchor in the northern corner in 5m sand with care because of rocky heads close inshore. Open to S–SW. Another

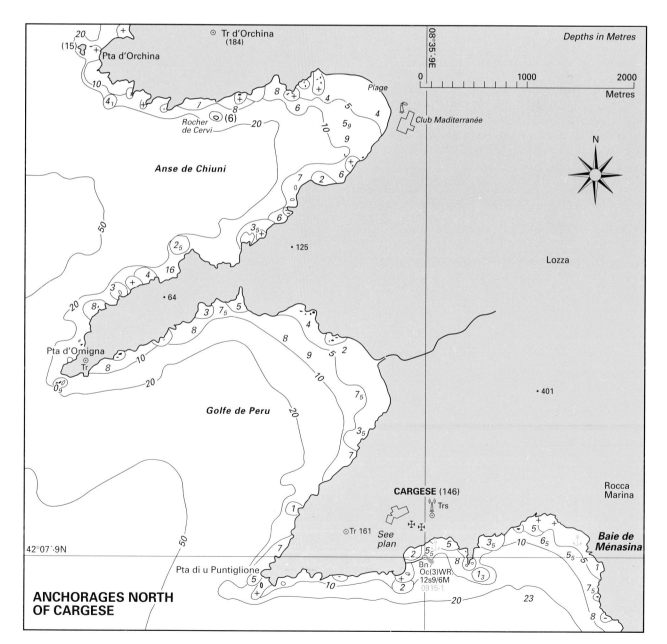

ANCHORAGES NORTH OF CARGESE

anchorage in 5m on sand and weed lies 700m to the southeast of the above anchorage. Deserted.

⚓ Portu â Leccia

A small anchorage in 6m to 10m, rock and sand, open to SW–W–NW. Road inland.

Punta a i Tuselli

A hooked point with rocky cliffs and rocky dangers extending 400m westward from the point, a hill (97m) stands behind the point.

⚓ Porto d'Arone

A large bay with black rocky-cliffed sides and a large sandy beach at the head. Some houses, a caravan site and a road inland stand behind the beach. The anchorage is off the beach in 4m, sand, it is open to S–SW–W.

⚓ Golfe de Topidi

A deep bay sheltered from the south and southwest by the mass of Punta d'Orchina, its rocky cliffs around it. At its head are some small sand and stone beaches and an open valley. Anchor at the head of the bay in 5m, sand, open to W–NW–N. Pay attention to some rocky heads near the shore.

Punta d'Orchina

A large prominent point 184m high inland where there is a conspicuous tower. A rounded point with an islet and rocky dangers extending west some 200m.

⚓ Anse de Chiuni

A wide deep bay with sandy beach at its head and behind it a conspicuous Club Mediterranée site with buildings that look like sails. Coast road inland. Anchor off beach in 5m, sand, open to SW–W–NW. A small bay on the south side of the bay provides a useful alternative calm weather anchorage in 6m rock.

Punta d'Omigna

A long narrow low rocky promontory with a conspicuous tower near its point. A small rock and 0·9m shallows 75m off its point.

⚓ Golfe de Peru

A wide deep bay with sandy beach behind which are sand dunes and the houses of Cargèse. There is also a housing estate in the N corner. Anchor off beach in 4m, sand. Open to S–SW–W.

Punta di u Puntiglione

A pointed promontory with rocky cliffs and a conspicuous tower standing on a hill behind the point 162m high. The houses of Cargèse to NE of the tower are easily seen.

3·4 – Cargèse to Ajaccio

Although the coast of this section is less spectacular than the last, it is still quite impressive consisting of the very wide and deep Golfe de Sagone, the northeast side of which is populated to a limited extent but the southeast side and the relatively high coast south to the Iles Sanguinaires is again virtually deserted. From this extraordinary chain of islands the coast becomes more and more populated as Ajaccio is approached.

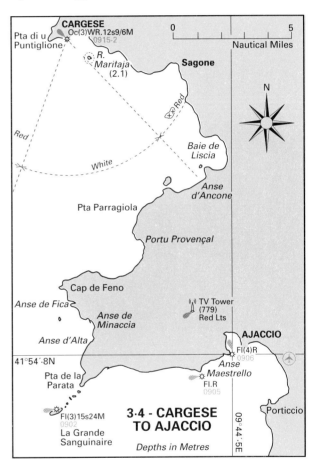

⚓ Port de Cargèse

General

Cargèse has a fairly new small yacht harbour with a 200m long jetty pointing northeastwards which gives good shelter in almost any conditions. Although the jetties are lit it is only permitted to enter and leave in daylight hours and the *capitaneria* operates only from May to October.

⊕ 42°07'·73N 08°35'·9E

Depth 2–5m
Number of berths 170 of which 35 are allocated to visitors

Charts

Admiralty *1985*
French *7050*

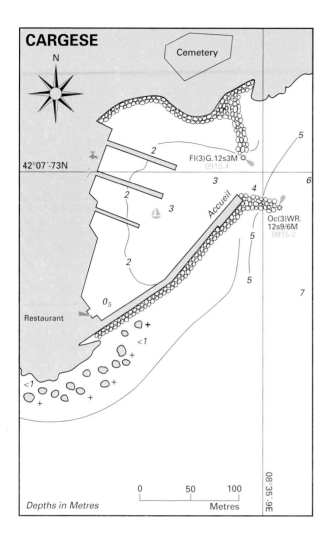

CARGESE

N

42°07'·73N

2

Fl(3)G.12s3M
0915·4

5

3

2

3

2

0₅

Accueil

4

Oc(3)WR.
12s9/6M
0915·2

5

5

6

7

Restaurant

<1

+

<1

+

+

+

+

+

Cemetery

0   50   100

Metres

Depths in Metres

08°35'·9E

Port radio

VHF Ch 9 (May–October) or ☎ 04 95 26 47 24.

Lights

0915·2 Jetée Sud head 42°07'·9N 8°35'·9E
Oc(3)WR.12s7m9/6M 025°-R-325°-W-025° White
tower, red top, 7m

0915·4 Jetée Nord head Fl(3)G.12s4m3M White pole
green top 4m

Warnings

There is a dangerous rocky shallow patch to the SW
of the heel of the south jetty which should be
avoided when approaching from the west, whilst the
Rocher Marifaja (2·9M 140° from jetty head) must
be avoided when coming from the south. Remember
that the harbour should be approached in daylight
hours and when full, a *Complet* notice is shown at
the jetty head.

Approach

By day From the north the sloping, reddish, rocky
promontory of Cap Rossu and the four points to its
south, Puntas Tuselli, Orchino, d'Omigna (which
has a conspicuous tower) and Puntiglione, also with
a conspicuous tower, are easily identified. Punta di
u Puntiglione has the town of Cargèse on a saddle
just to the northeast of the tower. All of these points

have off-lying islands and rocks and should be given
a 300m berth. An easterly course for 1M from Punta
di u Puntiglione brings this harbour abeam and the
rocky breakwater will be seen.

From the south cross the wide and deep Golfe de
Sagone on a northerly course from Cap de Feno, a
low rocky-cliffed point with a ruined tower towards
the far side of the gulf where the points listed above
will be seen with Cap Rossu in the far distance. The
nearer, Punta di u Puntiglione has a tower on its
summit and the town of Cargèse shows on the
skyline just to the east of it. Below the town lies the
harbour. The two church towers are conspicuous.

By night Although lights are in place it is not
permitted to enter at night.

Entrance

Round the south jetty end at 20m and proceed at
very slow speed on a course of west. When past the
north jetty head turn to port and berth near the fuel
station to get berthing instructions.

Berths

Berth only on the instructions of the *capitaneria*.

Formalities

Capitaneria only between May and October.

Facilities

All.

History

The history of this harbour is of particular interest in
view of the present disharmony between the French
Algerian settlers and the native Corsicans. In 1676 a
group of Greeks from the Gulf of Colokythia in the
Peloponnesus appealed to Genoa because they were
being tyrannised by the Turks. The Genoese senate
who were having difficulties themselves in crushing
the Corsican resistance to their occupation of
Corsica offered them the territories of Paomia,
Reonda and Salogno located inland from Cargèse.
In March 1676 some 730 Greeks arrived, settled in,
and within a few years, due to their hard work, were
becoming prosperous. Troubles commenced about
three years later in 1679 when the Corsicans of Vice
and Niolo, knowing the Greeks to be allies of Genoa
and envying them their prosperity, murdered one of
the Greeks. From this time on there was constant
friction between the two groups ending in 1731 with
the Greeks being driven out to take refuge in
Ajaccio, and their villages being burnt to the
ground. In 1768 when France annexed Corsica a
new village, Cargèse, was built for the Greeks
complete with their own church. The 110 remaining
families who spoke only Greek and had kept their
own religion, costume and customs, moved in and
have remained there ever since. Over the ages they
have intermarried with the native Corsicans and
except for their religion and capacity for hard work,
there is little to distinguish them from the native
Corsican.

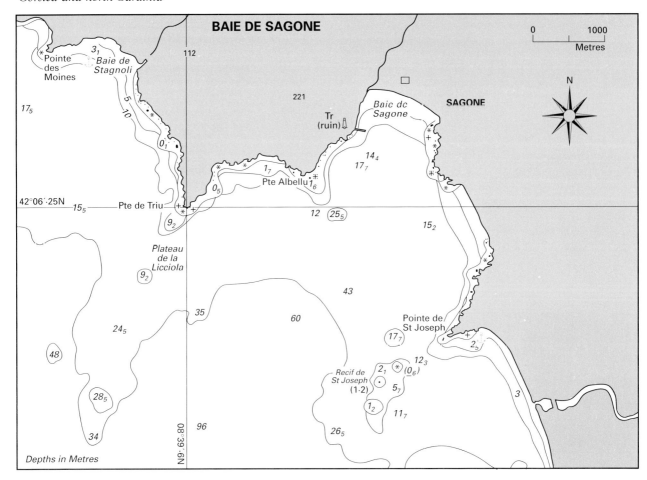

⚓ Baie de Cargèse

Two bays with a small rocky point and an off-lying 1·8m shallows dividing them. Anchor in the northeast corner of either bay in 4m, sand and rock, open to SE–S–SW–W. Road runs above low rocky cliffs, a few houses. Landing very difficult due to rocks.

⚓ Baie de Menasina

A large open bay with a big sandy beach at its head and low rocky cliffs at each side with off-lying rocks. A single awash rock is 100m off the north end of the beach. Anchor off the centre of the beach in 3m, sand, open to SE–S–SW–W. The coast road runs behind the beach, with a few houses.

Punta di Molendinu

A small rocky-cliffed point with three small islets off the point otherwise steep-to.

Rocher Marifaja

A small 1·8m isolated rock with a 1·7m shallow and some awash rocks close in. This rock lies 1,000m SSW of Punta di Molendinu.

Pointe de Triu

A prominent pointed rocky-cliffed headland with 56m hill and coast road behind, a few rocky heads close in and a 2·7m rocky shallow 250m south of the point. It is advised to keep well clear of this point in all but calm weather.

Pointe Albellu

A point which is easy to identify due to a conspicuous tower and battery just inland standing in some trees with the coast road in front, with many dangerous rocks close in. Again keep well off.

⛵ Port de Sagone

⊕ 42°06'·7N 08°41'·5E

Sagone is a small village lying at the southeast corner of a bay at the head of the wide and deep Gulf of Sagone. A jetty and quay located on the western side of the bay offer pleasure craft a place to secure and land. Another landing is located on the eastern side of the bay and nearer the village but this quay is reserved for local fishermen. It is an attractive area with ranges of mountains rising behind a long beach with a river mouth at its western end. The area, however, is a holiday centre and in season the area is crowded with camping sites and holidaymakers and there is constant traffic on the main coast road which runs behind the area.

Approach and entry are easy as there is a conspicuous ruined tower just west of the jetty. Remember to give Pointe de Triu and Pointe Albellu a good berth if coming from the west. From the south keep outside Petra Piombata, Récif de Paliagi and Rocher de St Joseph and steer just east of north until the tower and jetty become visible.

There are no lights on the jetties so night approach is not recommended. There are swinging moorings to the north of the jetty but even if tucked away in the western corner any heavy swell from the SW can make it an uncomfortable anchorage though relatively safe.

Should a strong southwest wind be forecast and no space is available in the northwestern corner of the Baie de Sagone, it is important to leave the anchorage and work out of the Golfe de Sagone. If this is not possible some shelter can be obtained in the Baie de Liscia. Facilities are limited to everyday requirements with fuel 2 kilometres away in the village.

⚓ Baie de Sagone

This large deep sandy-bottomed bay forms an excellent anchorage in depths of 3m up to 24m. It is open to SE–S–SW but by thoughtful choice of anchorage the seas brought in by the southeast or southwest winds can be considerably reduced. The bay has low rocky-cliffed sides with a long sandy beach at its head, the coast road runs around the bay and there is a road running inland. Everyday requirements can be obtained from Sagone village, see notes above.

Pointe de St-Joseph

A sharp pointed rocky headland with an old battery on top, rocky dangers extend 300m off the point, see below.

Recif de St-Joseph and passage

A shallow area with one awash rock and one rocky islet (1·2m) with depths of 1·3m to the south. The awash rock lies 900m WSW of Pointe St-Joseph. The reef is 400m wide extending 900m SSW from the awash rock. The rocky islet lies near the centre of the reef. A 500m-wide passage lies between Pointe de St-Joseph and this reef with a least depth of 9m, take the passage in NW–SE directions equidistant between the outer awash rocks of Pointe de St-Joseph and the awash rock in the reef.

Pointe Capigliolu

A prominent sharp pointed rocky-cliffed headland with islet, rocks submerged and awash reaching 400m out from the point in a westerly direction. The Tour de Capigliolu on a hill 93m and an old tower 200m behind it are conspicuous.

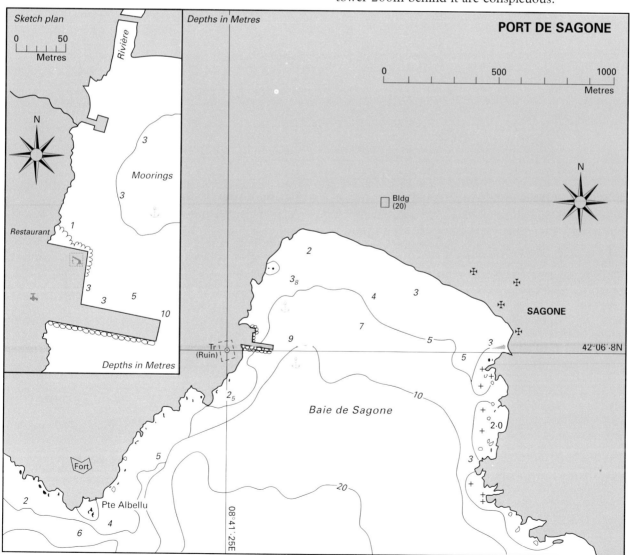

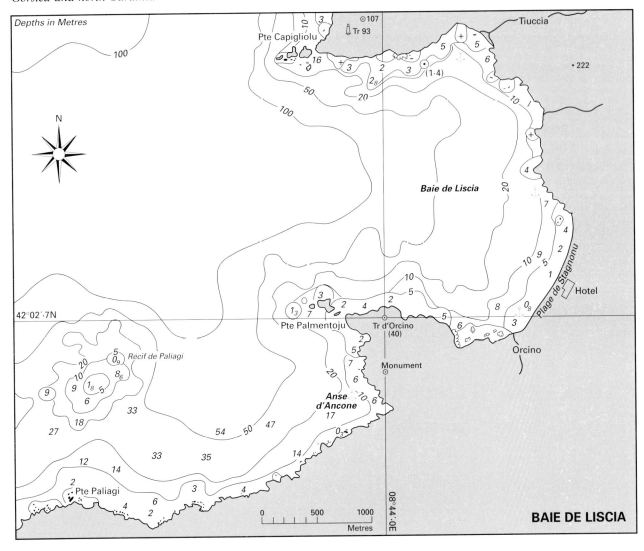

BAIE DE LISCIA

⚓ Baie de Liscia

A very wide bay with anchorage in a sub-bay to the northeast with other anchorages off a long sandy beach to south. The anchorage in the northeast corner in 5m sand and weed is close to the village of Tiuccia, where everyday requirements can be bought. There are several hotels here and a mechanic at the garage. There is a small exposed rocky islet in the approach and one awash near the shore, also near the shore are some permanent moorings. This anchorage is open to SW–W–NW. The village is famous for the Capraja Castle which belonged to the Counts of Ginarca who once ruled Corsica. This castle lies to the south of the village. The other anchorages off the sandy beach in the south of the bay are in 3m, sand, and open to SW–W–NW.

Pointe Palmentoju

A pointed headland with rocky cliffs, the conspicuous Tour d'Orcino (40m) lies near the point with a hill sloping inland to 298m. Rocky islet, rocks awash and covered, extend 500m northwestwards.

Iles de Pointe Palmentoju and passage

A short narrow passage about 50m long, 40m wide and 2·5m deep exists between the islets off the Pointe Palmentoju and the small rocks close to the point. The course to be taken is in a NE–SW direction with a good lookout and, preferably, after a reconnaissance by dinghy.

⚓ Anse d'Ancone

A small rocky-cliffed anchorage in 5m rock open to SW–W–NW in the east corner of a wide bay. Deserted.

Pointe Paliagi

A rounded headland of rocky cliffs, hills behind sloping up to 348m. Rocky islets extend 200m north with a 2m depth some 50m further on.

Recif de Paliagi

This reef is centred 1,200m to NNE of Pointe Paliagi, it has rocks covered 1m, 2m, 6m and 9m.

Pointe Parragiola and Pointe Pelusella

A high point (212m with tower on top) and small islet off the cliffs with Pointe Pelusella 800m south. This is a right-angled point with rocky cliffs, sloping up to 111m. A ruined tower stands close to the point. An awash isolated rock (0·8m deep) lies 350m northwest of Pointe Pelusella which is otherwise steep-to.

⚓ Portu Provençale

The N corner of the Baie de Lava is referred to as Portu Provençale but is only an anchorage that has many moorings laid for local fishing craft. There are good anchorages in 3m to 18m sand outside the moorings and off the sandy beach, open to SW–W–NW. There are many houses and several housing estates ashore, the village can provide everyday supplies also beach cafés, restaurants and hotels are available. There is a road to the main coast road. The south and southwest coast of the Baie de Lava is foul with many rocks including a small islet, La Figiera, 300m off the coast.

Pétra Piombata and passage

A small islet lies 700m off the coast at the southern side of the entrance to the Golfe de Lava. The islet is steep-to except for a rock 2m deep off the SE end of the islet. A 7m depth lies halfway between the island and the shore. A passage 200m wide, 100m long with a minimum depth of 10m lies 100m off the coast in E–W directions.

Cap de Feno

A very prominent point with high rocky broken cliffs and a conspicuous ruined tower standing on a 68m hill inland 200m from the point. The point has two close inshore islets on its western face and some small rocks extending 150m in a southwesterly direction, otherwise it is steep-to. In certain lights when approaching from the south the ruined tower has the appearance of a seated cat.

Écueil de Fica

A rock covered 1·6m is located 1,250m south of Cap de Feno. Unless intending to go into Anse de Fica it is recommended to go outside this rock (and La Botte) on a passage south.

⚓ Anse de Fica

Two popular anchorages the north of which is in a rocky-sided bay off a white sandy beach in 6m sand and weed open to S–SW–W. A road and a track ashore, one house. This anchorage is the best of the two and offers the best protection. The southern anchorage is in a small bay with rocky sides and a sandy beach. Anchor off the beach in 2m, sand, open to S–SW–W. Road ashore. Deserted. A rocky projection divides these two anchorages.

La Botte

This 22m-high island lies just over a mile south of Cap de Feno. With the exception of an outlier to its southwest it is steep-to.

⚓ Anse de Minaccia

This large bay has a long sandy beach with anchorages at each end. Anchor in 3m sand off the beach open to S–SW–W. Sand dunes behind the

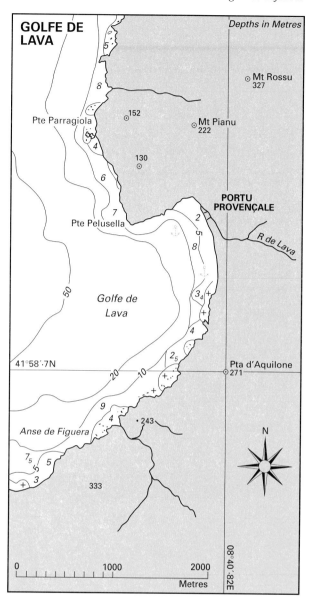

northern end of the beach. Tracks behind the beach, a few houses and a housing estate behind the southern end of the beach. Beach café. A rock covered 1·5m lies 200m off the south end of the beach.

⚓ Anse d'Alta

A small bay with a sandy beach at its head, rocky sides. Anchor off beach in 3m, sand, open to SW–W–NW. Road and housing estate behind beach.

Pointe de la Corba

A small rocky point sloping up inland to 211m. Many small rocks extend up to 200m from the coast and an isolated rock 2m deep lies 400m to WSW of the point.

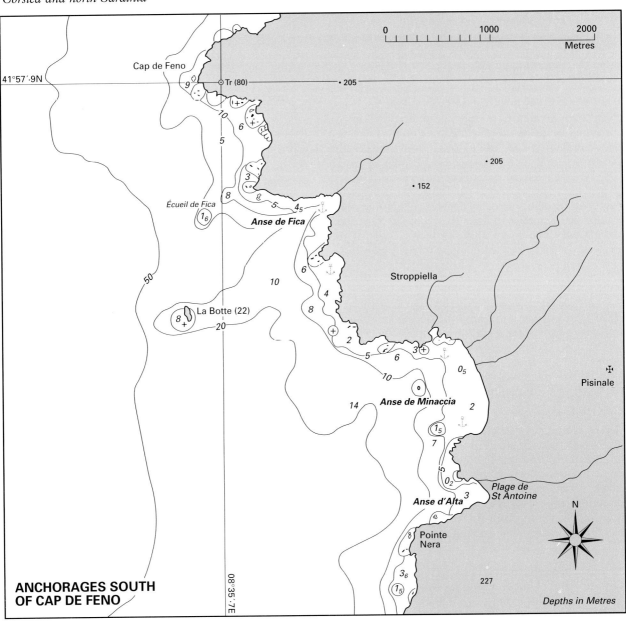

41°57'·9N

Cap de Feno

Tr (80) · 205

9

+

6 +

5

3

Écueil de Fica

8

1₆

Anse de Fica 5 4₅

· 205

· 152

6

Stroppiella

10

4

8

La Botte (22)

8 +

−20

(+)

2

5 6 3 (+)

0₅

Pisinale

10

0

Anse de Minaccia 2

14

1₅

7

5

0₂

Plage de
St Antoine

Anse d'Alta 3

Pointe
Nera

N

3₆

1₅

227

08°35'·7E

**ANCHORAGES SOUTH
OF CAP DE FENO**

0   1000   2000
Metres

Depths in Metres

Pointe de la Parata and Iles Sanguinaires

An attractive headland and islands lying in a SW – NE direction which is similar to the Raz du Sein in Brittany but without the strong tidal streams. From the northeast the high (283m) hills slope down to the Presqu'île de la Parata which consists of two distinctive parts, a low flat isthmus connected to a rounded feature with a small house and radio beacon mast on the top (86m). There is a road on the southeastern side leading to a restaurant. A second very low isthmus connects the first part to the second feature which is of a pyramid shape (58m) with a conspicuous tower on top. It is essential to identify this feature if attempting the Passe des Sanguinaires as from a distance it simply looks like 2 more islands.

Southwest of this pass lies Ile de Porri, two unnamed islets and Ile Cala d'Alga. Between these four islets it is shallow and foul with rocky heads.

The largest island, Ile de la Grande Sanguinaire, is the outer island, it has a white lighthouse, black top and white dwelling (Fl(3)15s98m24M) on the crest near the northeastern end. A signal station is located near the centre of the island and a tower stands near the southwestern end. There are rocks and shallows extending 500m southwestwards from this point. The Écueil du Tabernacle, an isolated rock 3m deep, stands 1300m to southeast of the centre of this island and it is marked by a R pillar light buoy with a square topmark (Fl(3)R.12s).

Passages des Sanguinaires

The main passage is the Passe des Sanguinaires between the Pointe de la Parata and Ile de Porri, it is 200m long, 200m wide with a minimum depth of 7m. Take the passage in E–W directions about 50m from the La Parata and 150m from Ile de Porri. For yachts drawing 2m or less the passage is 400m wide with a minimum depth of 2·8m. Currents of up to 3

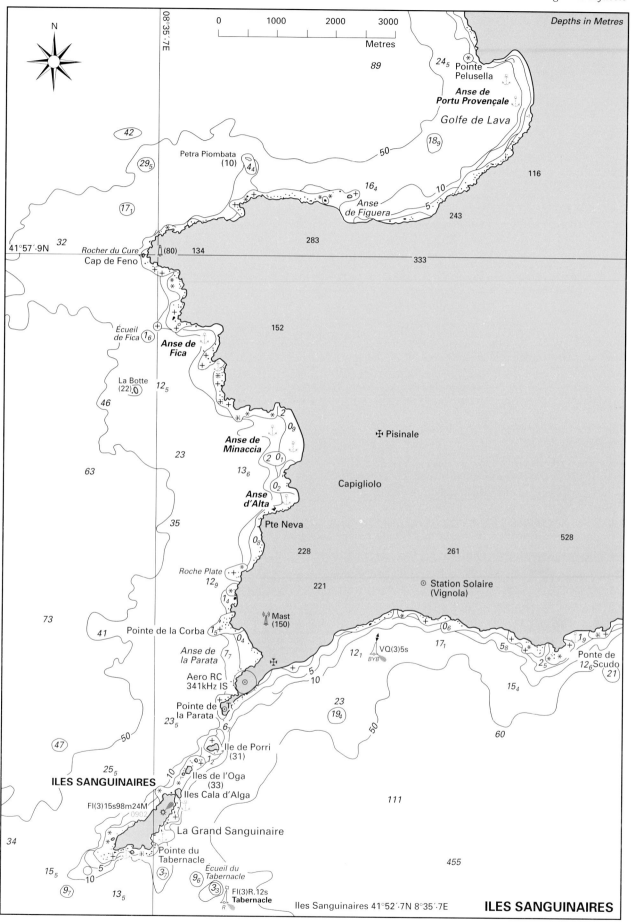

Depths in Metres

N

08°35′.7E

0   1000   2000   3000
Metres

89

24₅ Pointe
Pelusella

*Anse de
Portu Provençale*

Golfe de Lava

42

18₉

29₅

Petra Piombata
(10)

4₄

50

17₁

16₄

116

Anse
de Figuera

10

5

243

32

283

41°57′.9N

Rocher du Cure
Cap de Feno

(80)   134

333

152

*Écueil
de Fica* 1₆

**Anse de
Fica**

La Botte
(22) 0

12₅

46

2

0₉

**Anse de
Minaccia**

2 0₁

⌖ Pisinale

23

13₆

0₂

Capigliolo

63

**Anse
d'Alta**

Pte Neva

0₈

35

228

261

528

Roche Plate

12₉

221

⊙ Station Solaire
(Vignola)

1₄

73

Mast
(150)

0₆

17₁

1₉

41

Pointe de la Corba 1₅

0₄

12₁

VQ(3)5s
BYB

5₈

Ponte de
Scudo

*Anse de
la Parata*

7₇

10

2₅

12₆

21

15₄

Aero RC
341kHz IS

23

60

Pointe de
la Parata

Tr

19₄

23₅

6₇

50

47

ILES SANGUINAIRES

10

6₇

Ile de Porri
(31)

1₂

25₅

Iles de l'Oga
(33)

111

Iles Cala d'Alga

Fl(3)15s98m24M

090°

La Grand Sanguinaire

34

Pointe du
Tabernacle

3₇

455

15₅

*Écueil du
Tabernacle*

9₆

5

10

3₃

Fl(3)R.12s
Tabernacle

9₇

13₅

R

Iles Sanguinaires 41°52′.7N 8°35′.7E

ILES SANGUINAIRES

knots can be experienced in the area and these frequently set across the passage. Under conditions of heavy seas and strong winds the use of this passage is not advised, round La Grande Sanguinaire keeping over 0·5M to the southwest and pass outside the Écueil du Tabernacle light buoy.

⚓ La Grande Sanguinaire

There are three small anchorages on the SE side of this island.

1. A very small anchorage in a little bay between the Ile Cala d'Alga and the northeastern end of La Grande Sanguinaire, anchor in 3m, sand and rock, open to NE–E–SE–S.
2. A large anchorage just north of the Pointe du Tabernacle which projects in a southeasterly direction from the middle of the island. There are two 3m deep rocks and also small rocks close in along the coast. Anchor in 2m, rock, open to NE–E–SE. There is a small landing stage used by *vedettes* which unload tourists.
3. A very small anchorage just below and to the southeast of the tower on southwestern end of La Grande Sanguinaire in 4m, rock, open to E–SE–S–SW. Small stony beach.

La Botte de Canicciu

An awash rock marked by a R pole beacon with a square topmark.

Écueil de la Guardiola

A red round beacon tower with a square topmark and light (Fl.R.2·5s6m2M) erected on a small group of rocks just over 1M to SW of Ajaccio Citadelle and 500m offshore, covered by the red sector of the Citadelle light. Give it a 200m berth either side.

⚓ Anse Maestrellu

A bay open to E–SE–S–SW with a road and many houses and apartment blocks behind. Anchor off the sandy beach in 3m, sand.

Rocher Citadelle

A red round beacon tower with a square topmark and light (Fl(4)R.15s10m6M) lies 400m south of the Citadelle marking a rock and with shallows (3m) 100m to the north and (3·5m) 200m to the west. Pass to the south of this beacon.

3·5 – Ajaccio to Propriano

The wide and deep Golfe d'Ajaccio is bounded by the long chain of islands, les Iles Sanguinaires, to the north and Cap Muro, a very prominent headland, to the south. The sides of the gulf are broken and rugged and the coast at its head is low with a long sandy beach. A road follows the coast and there is an increasing number of housing estates and some camp sites, especially near the heads of the many small bays where there are beaches. South of Cap Muro there is another deep gulf, the Golfe de Valinco, again offering anchorages, although there are several unmarked off-lying dangers where care is needed. Some of the anchorages are deserted with the main centres of population near the two harbours of Porto Pollo and Propriano, although housing development is taking place around the gulf, especially at Campomoro.

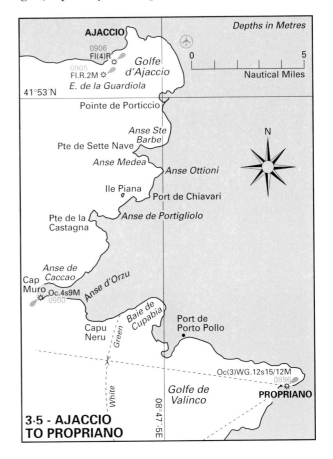

Ajaccio

General

A large commercial, fishing, naval and yachting port, which is the second largest city and port in Corsica and the capital of the island. It is an attractive city in a pleasant setting which has good facilities. There are two yacht harbours which can be approached and entered under almost any conditions and shelter found, but with strong winds from the south or southeast the swell enters the main harbour and is reflected by the Quai Napoleon into Port Tino Rossi making it very uncomfortable and occasionally dangerous. In the season both yacht harbours become very crowded. The layout is very similar to Bastia where there is a Vieux Port (Port Tino Rossi) to the south and a modern yacht harbour (Port Charles Ornano) to the north with a large ferry and commercial harbour between them. Port Tino Rossi has better facilities and is more convenient for the town but is usually the more crowded. There is naval harbour a mile to the east of the town on Pointe d'Aspretto into which entry is totally prohibited.

⚓ Port Tino Rossi

⊕1 41°55'·2N 08°44'·8E

Depth 2–7m
Number of berths 260 berths with 80 places for visitors
Maximum length 60m

Charts

Admiralty *1424*
French *6851, 6942, 7280*

Port radio

VHF Ch 19 and 9 or ☎ 04 95 21 93 28.

Lights

0906 Écueil de la Citadelle 41°54'·8N 8°44'·5E
  Fl(4)R.15s10m6M Red tower 13m
0908 La Citadelle 41°55'·0N 8°44'·5E
  Fl(2)WR.10s19m20/16M 057°-W-045°-R-057°
  White tower red top 13m,
0910 Jetée de la Citadelle Oc.R.4s13m8M White tower, red column
0911 Jetée des Capucins head Fl.RG.4s8m7/7M 110°-R-271°-G-065°-obscd- 110° White column,7m
0912 Port Charles Ornano Quai Est head
  Fl(2)R.6s5m6M White tower red top 3m
0913 Jetée de Margonajo head Fl(4)15s7m1M White post 6m

Beacons

La Campanina 41°50'·3N 8°45'E BRB beacon tower, 2 balls topmark 5M to S of harbour marking 0·3m deep rock off Pointe de Sette Nave.
La Botte de Canicciu 41°54'·3N 8°42'·4E R beacon post, square topmark 2M SW of harbour
0905 Écueil de la Guardiola R beacon tower, square topmark, Fl.R.2·5s6m2M stands on a rock 1·25M to SW of the harbour covered by the R sector of the Citadelle lighthouse.
0906 Écueil de la Citadelle R beacon tower, square topmark, 0·25M to S of the harbour Fl(4)R.15s rock 3·3m (13ft) deep.

Buoy

0957(I) Écueil de Tabernacle 41°52'·0N 8°36'·5E
  Fl(3)R.12s4m3M Red buoy, square topmark
0959·2(I) Buoy W 41°54'·5N 8°47'·6E Q(9)15s1m3M W card
0959·3(I) Buoy E 41°54'·5N 8°47'·7E Q(3)10s1m3M E card

Warnings

The Golfe d'Ajaccio has several shallow patches of foul ground extending up to 500m from the shore in places. There are some large unlit buoys in the Baie d'Ajaccio. The wash from manoeuvring commercial craft can affect yachts in the Vieux Port. Ferries, commercial vessels and naval vessels have priority over yachts in the port area and approaches.

Fire-fighting planes

Large flying boats may land in the Golfe d'Ajaccio to pick up water for fire-fighting.

Approach

By day From the north round the Iles Sanguinaires and the Tabernacle buoy to port (or take the Passe di Sanguinaires if calm) and steer along coast keeping La Botte, La Guardiola and La Citadelle beacons to port. From the south leave Cap Muro to starboard and steer a NNE course leaving Pointe de la Castagna, La Campanina and Pointe de Sette Nave well to starboard. The houses of Ajaccio will now be obvious, steer for the Citadelle.

The jetty should now be visible, steer for the end.

By night The approaches are well lit but keep more to the centre of the gulf until the jetty lights have been positively identified.

Entrance

By day Approach the head of the Jetée de la Citadelle on a northwesterly course and round it at 25m having first checked that no commercial vessels are entering or leaving. Secure to the small pontoon at the head of this jetty for berthing instructions.

By night Leave the Fl(4)R.15s and Fl(2)WR.10s to port, approach Oc.R.4s on a northwesterly course. Round it leaving it 50m to port and then secure to the small pontoon at the head of the Jetée de la Citadelle for berthing instructions

Berths

Berth where instructed – no anchoring in harbour.

Formalities

All authorities available.

Facilities

All.

⚓ Port Charles Ornano

⊕2 41°55'·80N 08°44'·8W

Depth 2–15m
Number of berths 800 with 200 for visitors
Maximum length 35m

Port radio

VHF Ch 9 or ☎ 04 95 22 31 98.

Weather forecast

Posted daily at *capitaneria.*

Lights

0913 Jetée de Margonajo Fl(4)Vi.15s7m1M White column
0912 Head of east jetty Fl(2)R.6s5m6M

Approach

As for port Tino Rossi but proceed further north keeping clear of all commercial traffic.

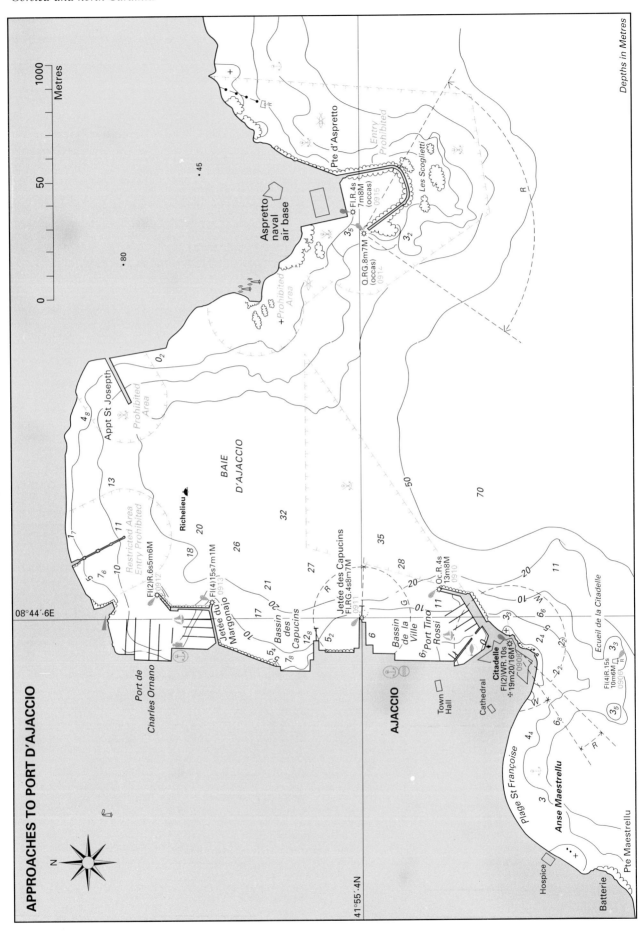

APPROACHES TO PORT D'AJACCIO

Depths in Metres

Metres

1000   50   0

N

08°44'·6E

41°55'·4N

Pte d'Aspretto

Les Scoglietti

Fl.R.4s
7m8M
(occas)
0915

Q.RG.8m7M
(occas)
0912

Aspretto naval
air base

*Prohibited
Area*

*Entry
Prohibited*

Appt St Joseph

*Prohibited
Area*

BAIE
D'AJACCIO

Richelieu

*Restricted Area
Entry Prohibited*

Fl(2)R.6s5m6M
0912

Fl(4)15s7m1M
0913

Jetée du
Margonajo

Bassin
des
Capucins

Jetée des Capucins
Fl.RG.4s8m7M
0911

Bassin
de la
Ville

Port Tino
Rossi

Oc.R.4s
13m8M
0910

Port de
Charles Ornano

AJACCIO

Town
Hall

Cathedral

Citadelle
Fl(2)WR.10s
19m20/16M
0909

Fl(4)R.15s
10m6M
0906

Ecueil de la Citadelle

Plage St Françoise

Anse Maestrellu

Hospice

Batterie

Pte Maestrellu

Bastia harbours looking SW

Vieux Port of Bastia looking SW

Macinaggio looking SW

Port di Luri looking SW

Ile de la Giraglia looking S

Centuri looking NE

St Florent looking S

Algajola looking SW

Ile and Baie de Centuri looking NE (note awash rock
200m N of Ile at lower left of photo)

...e Rousse looking SE
...wing the passage
...ween Grande Ile Rousse
... Insula dei Brucciu

...int'Ambrogio looking
...W

Ajaccio – Port Charles Ornano looking NW

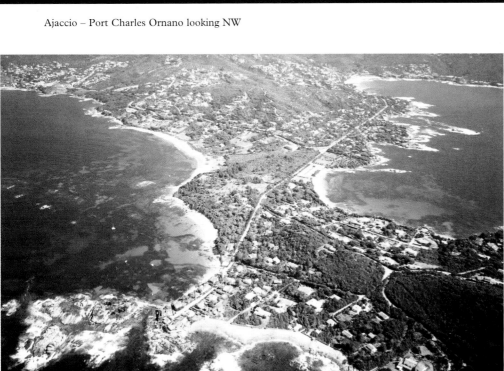

Anse Ste Barbe and Anse
Medea looking E

Port de Chiavari looking SW

neral view of Propriano looking SE

Cala di Conca looking E

Port de Pianottoli-Caldarello at the
head of Baie de Figari looking ENE –
note fish farm at the bottom of photo

Cala di Ghiuncu with Cala di u Grecu beyond looking NE and
Ile Lavezzi oratory in centre of photo

Ile Cavallo, looking just west of N, with Ile Poraggia beyond in line with Punta di u Capicciolu and Port de Cavallo in centre of photo

Port de Rondinara looking W

Bonifacio looking east

Port de Taverna looking NW

Golfe de Santa Giulia looking W

Porto Vecchio, Port de Plaisance looking SW

Port de Solenzara looking NNW

Alghero looking S

Fertilia looking N

View of Asinara looking N over the shallow Pelosa Passage,
Isola Piana at centre right with the Fornelli passage between it
and Asinara in the background

Porto Torres Porto
Commerciale (not to be
confused with Porto Industriale
to the west where pleasure craft
are not allowed) looking N

Castelsardo village and
marina looking NE

Base Nautica Porto Conte looking SW

Stintino looking ENE (note isolated rock with beacon in centre of entrance)

Isola Rossa town marina looking N

Santa Teresa di Gallura looking N with Ile Lavezzi in top right corner

View of Cannigone and south end of Golfo di Arzachena looking NE with Cala Bitta in top left corner

Porto Cervo looking NE with Cala Granu at top on extreme left

Marina dell'Orso (Poltu Quatu) looking N

Cala Bitta looking N with Capo Tre Monti at left centre

Cala Volpe looking SE with hotel complex
on left

Porto Rotondo in centre looking WSW with Golfe de Cugnana
running right to left beyond

Marina di Puntaldia
looking NW

SE corner of Golfo Marinella showing Isola
Marinella with the T pontoon of the Circolo
Nautico and the small pontoon of Yachting Club
Vela Blu to the left

La Caletta looking NE

Porto Ottiolu and Isolotto Ottiolu looking SW

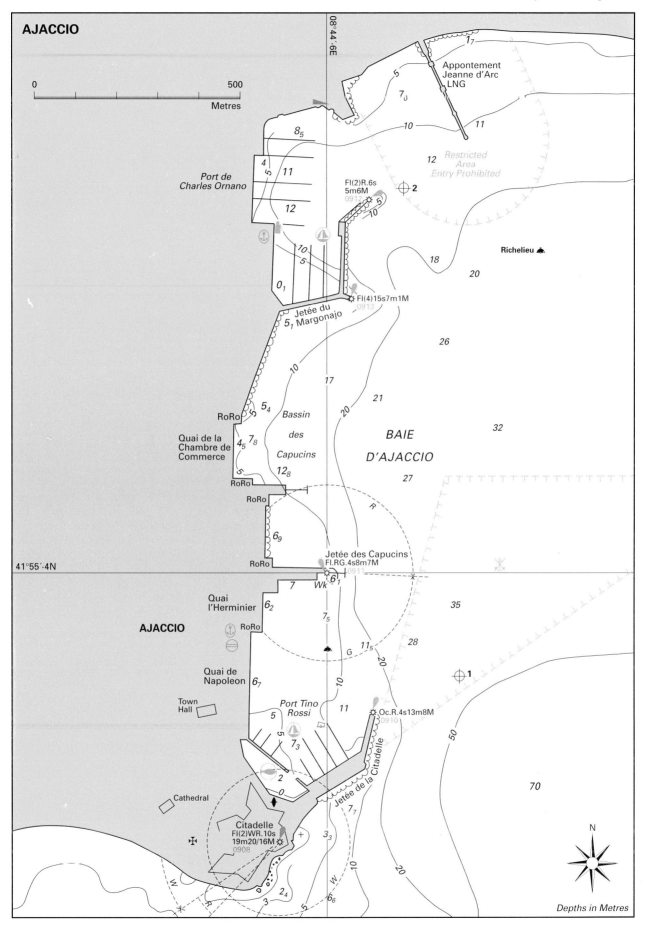

AJACCIO

0   500
Metres

Port de
Charles Ornano

8₅

4
5   11

12

Fl(2)R.6s
5m6M
0912   ⊕ 2

0₁

Jetée du
5₁ Margonajo

Fl(4)15s7m1M
0913

Appontement
Jeanne d'Arc
LNG

5

7

10

11

12   *Restricted
Area
Entry Prohibited*

18

20

Richelieu

26

21

RoRo

Quai de la
Chambre de
Commerce

5₄
7₈
4₅
5
12₈

RoRo

RoRo

6₉

RoRo

17

*Bassin
des
Capucins*

20

R

BAIE
D'AJACCIO

27

32

35

Jetée des Capucins
Fl.RG.4s8m7M
0911

7   Wk

6₁

28

Quai
l'Herminier   6₂

RoRo

7₅

Quai de
Napoleon   6₇

Town
Hall

Cathedral

*Port Tino
Rossi*

5

5

7₃

2

0

Citadelle
Fl(2)WR.10s
19m20/16M
0908

G   11₅

20

⊕ 1

11

Oc.R.4s13m8M
0910

50

70

Jetée de la Citadelle

7₇

3₃

W

0

2₄

3

5

6₆

N

41°55′·4N

AJACCIO

08°44′·6E

Depths in Metres

Entrance

By day Approach the northwest corner of the Baie d'Ajaccio and leave the head of the Jetée du Margonajo with a white tower 7m to port. Follow along the jetée est on a northerly course for 150m and then round its head at 25m entering the harbour. Secure to the first pontoon to port and report to the *capitaneria* at the root of the jetty.

By night Approach the northwest corner of the Baie d'Ajaccio leaving Fl.RG.4s 400m to port and then Fl(4)15s, 25m to port. Follow along the jetée est on a northerly course for 150m round Fl(2)R.6s at 25m entering the harbour. Secure to first pontoon to port on entering. The lights listed above are difficult to pick out against the lights of the town.

Berths

As instructed.

Formalities

All authorities available.

Facilities

All.

History

The name of this old fishing village probably originated from the Latin *adjacium* meaning a resting place and it was sited to the north of the Citadelle. In the 10th century it was destroyed by the Saracens and later reconstructed by the Genoese. The Citadelle dates from 1554 as does the Cathedral. The birth of Napoleon Bonaparte on 15th August 1769 in the Casa Bonaparte, a few hundred yards northwest of the Citadelle is the local event of importance. The fact that Pascal Paoli's partisans chased him out of his house and forced him to flee to Calvi is not so well known. They confiscated his house and used it as an arms depot.

Ajaccio, which has a pleasant temperate climate, became one of the first towns to be visited by the Victorians seeking to escape the horrors of the English winter and was developed as a resort along with Cannes, Nice and Palma de Mallorca all of which have similar architecture.

Pointe d'Aspretto

A low flat wide promontory extending south with naval air base buildings on the top where it slopes up to 50m. A spur of shallow water extends 600m south of the buildings, and around this spur there is an enclosing breakwater of a small harbour. The entrance is at the northwestern corner with depths of 3·2m to 1·5m inside. This is a naval harbour and entry is prohibited. The whole of this point including the islands Les Scuglietti, which are a mass of small islets and rocks lying to the south of this harbour, is bounded by a 200m wide band which is forbidden to all except naval personnel.

Pointe de Porticcio

A small low (36m) rocky-cliffed headland with rocky dangers extending 200m to W. Three large white buildings on the point, tree covered with houses inland.

Écueil Dorbera

An area of rocky heads awash and some 3–4m deep 500m to SSW of Pointe de Porticcio.

⚓ Pointe de Porticcio

Anchor in the small bay off a sandy beach to the southeast of this point in 5m, sand, open to SW–W–NW. Pay attention to some rocky islets close inshore, and to Écueil Dorbera 700m offshore.

⚓ Anse de Ste Barbe

Anchorage either side of a shoal area with rocky heads that jut out in a N–NE direction from the coast 400m to the east of an unnamed islet. Approach with care and anchor in 4m, sand, outside moorings, open to W–NW–N. Coast road ashore, two large slips, beach huts, houses in trees.

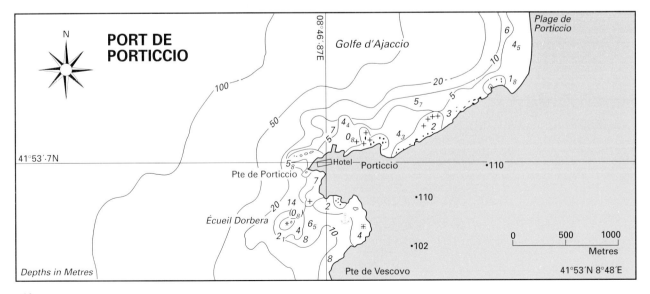

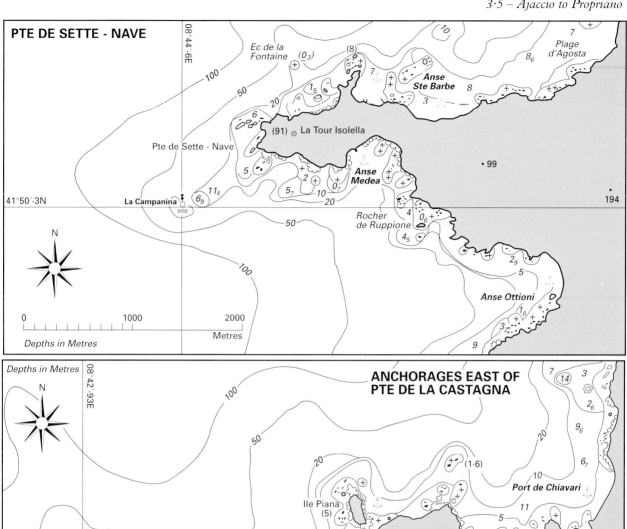

Pointe de Sette Nave

A tree-covered point with outlying rocky dangers 300m to the west and 400m to the north. The Tour de l'Isolella stands on a 66m hill behind the point and can be seen from afar there are many private houses and a coast road.

La Campanina beacon

A BRB tower with two globes topmark, located 0·5M southwest of Pointe de Sette Nave marks a rock covered 0·3m. Deep water within 100m of the beacon.

⚓ Anse Medea

An anchorage in 5m, sand and rock, in a small bay with rocky sides and a sandy beach tucked in behind Pointe de Sette Nave, keep clear of moorings. Pay attention in the approach to La Campanina beacon, to rocky shallows on the eastern side of the bay and to two small rocks in the middle of the beach. Open to S–SW.

⚓ Anse Ottioni

A small and stony beach (Plage de Ruppione) at the head of a gulf with rocky shores. Anchor off the beach in 4m, sand, open to SW–W–NW.

There are rocks at both ends of the beach. Coast road, trees and many houses and beach huts behind the beach.

Port de Chiavari

An anchorage not a port, in a wide bay open to W–NW–N. Anchor off a beach in 4m, sand. Keep to the northern half of the beach as there are rocks off the southern half. Enter the bay on a southeasterly heading as there is foul ground off the enclosing points. Main road and camps behind the beach. Small jetty, a small quay and a beach café.

⚓ Ile Piana

A beautiful little anchorage on the eastern side of the Ile Piana in 5m sand open to NW–N–NE, rocky cliff and small sandy beach ashore. An isolated rock lies 50m to the northeast of the north end of this islet. Very popular in the season and at weekends.

⚓ Anse de Portigliolo

A fine sandy bay open to W–NW–N with a camping site ashore and a road leading to a small village. Anchor in 3–5m on sand about 200m offshore due to rocks near the beach.

⚓ Pointe de la Castagna NE

A small bay behind the Pointe de la Castagna, rocky cliffs and trees ashore with some houses, a track to the road, a small sandy beach and huts on the beach.

An 0·2m shallow area inshore and rocky heads close in. Anchor in 5m, sand and rock, clear of moorings, open to NW–N–NE. Small village inland.

Pointe de la Castagna

A conspicuous promontory with a 91m hill behind the point with a conspicuous tower and an Aero RC mast on the next hill inland. Rocky dangers and shallows extend 500m to the west and southwest.

⚓ Pointe de la Castagna SE

A similar anchorage to that on the NE side of the point except yachts should anchor in 8m, rock, on the eastern side of the bay to avoid off-lying rocky dangers. This anchorage is open to S–SW–W.

⚓ Anse de Cacalu

A pleasant and useful anchorage northeast of Cap Muro which is open to NW–N–NE. Anchor in 5m, sand, in the southern corner off a small sandy and stone beach or in the northwestern corner in 7m rock. A ruined tower stands to the west of the bay. Off-lying rock at each side of the bay. Deserted.

Pointe Guardiola and passage

The northwest part of Cap Muro is called Pointe Guardiola. It has off-lying rocky dangers including the islet La Botte (the third one in the last 20 miles!) A 100m wide passage 4m deep and 200m long exists between La Botte and the point if taken in NE–SW

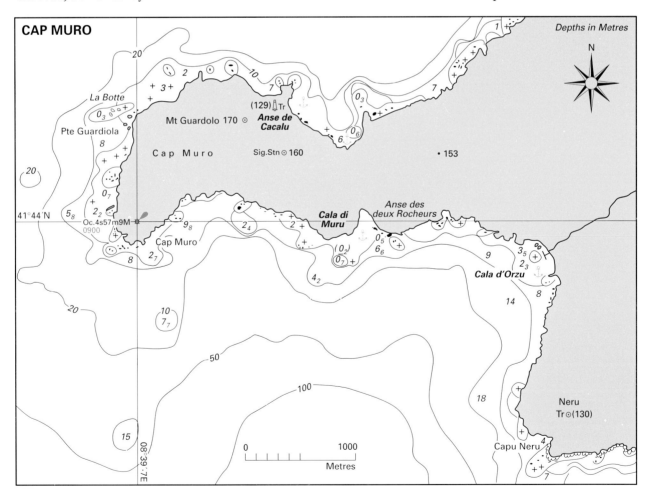

direction. However when at the northeastern end of the passage N–S directions must be taken to pass west of three isolated rocks which have only 2m depths between them and the shore.

Cap Muro

An imposing headland rising to 167m. There is a tower on the northeastern side and on the southwestern point is a lighthouse, a white square tower, black top (Oc.4s57m9M). A statue of the Madonna is carved into the cliffs on the southern point.

⚓ Cala di Muru

A small anchorage on the opposite side of the peninsula to Anse de Cacalu, with rocky-cliffed sides and a small stone and sand beach. Approach with care because there are 0·7m and 0·2m shallows 400m south-southwest of the entrance and two islets 300m to the southeast. Approach the Cala on NNW course and with a good lookout. Near the entrance there are two ball-shaped rocks. Anchor in 3m sand off the beach, open to SE–S–SW. Track along coast. Deserted.

⚓ Cala d'Orzu

A wide bay with rocky sides and a sand and stone beach. Scrub covered hills behind with signs of housing development and tracks inland. Camping

and beach cafés behind beach. Anchor in 3m sand in the northeastern side of the bay, open to S–SW–W, pay attention to two lone rocks about 100m offshore.

Capu Neru

A rounded blackish rocky-cliffed point and rocky dangers extending 300m offshore (with the fourth 'La Botte'!) Tour Neru stands on a ridge close to the

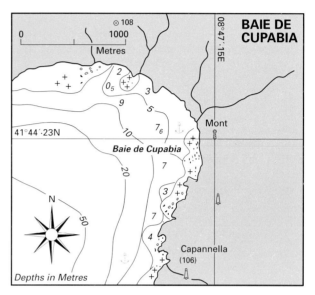

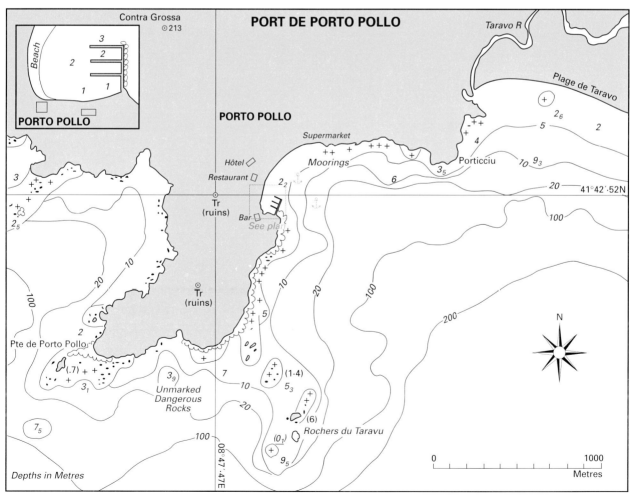

point amongst green scrub. There are tracks around the headland.

⚓ Baie de Cupabia

A large bay open to S–SW–W which has good space for anchorage. There is a long sandy beach on the northeastern side of the bay with a monument standing behind it. Anchorage is available along the beach in 3m, sand. To the south of this area an anchorage in 10m sand clear of the rocky shallows can be used. Anchorage is also possible in 17m further out. A track runs inland from the beach, some houses and a road have been built.

Pointe de Porto Pollo

Care is needed when rounding this point due to extensive off-lying rocky reefs and islets. One reef extends 500m southwest from the southwestern corner of the point and another extends 1,000m to the southeast from the southeastern corner of the point. This latter reef, known as Rochers du Taravu, has two islets (6m and 2m) near its southern extremity. If the outer islet is given berth of 200m and a course of east or west is adopted the other reef will be cleared. The point is covered with woodland and scrub. Two ruined towers stand on the crest inland but are partially hidden in the trees.

⚓ Port de Porto Pollo

⊕ 41°42'·60N 08°48'·00E

A small yacht harbour with excellent shelter from any III or IV quadrant winds. It has a 75m-long breakwater with pontoons on the inside. It is quite shallow but a 2m-draught craft can moor to the outside pontoon. Having identified Pointe di Porto Pollo with its off-lying dangers of Rochers du Taravu leave the latter well to port and then steer west of north until the jetty comes into view. If there is no room at the pontoons it is possible to anchor off the beach to the north but watch out for and keep clear of any swinging moorings. There are no facilities at the harbour but fuel and everyday needs can be obtained in the village. Propriano, which has all facilities, is only 5 miles away.

⚓ Plage de Baraci

A deep sandy beach at the head of the Golfe de Valinco, usually crowded in the summer, beach cafés and coast road behind. The mouth of Rivière Baraci lies at the northern end of the beach. Anchor in 4m, sand, off the beach, open to W–NW.

3·6 – Propriano to Bonifacio

The coast running SW from Propriano is generally low-lying with housing developments and a few quiet anchorages. South of Punta de Campomoro the coast is practically deserted until Cap de Feno is reached. Although these headlands are only 12 miles apart, the coast contains dozens of bays and inlets which make delightful isolated anchorages in settled weather. There are a number of off-lying dangerous rocks in this section, notably Les Moines, which is marked by a beacon and covered by special light sectors from two lighthouses. From Cap de Feno to Bonifacio (and beyond) is a unique feature of this coast in that it consists of high chalk cliffs.

⚓ Port de Propriano

General

A commercial, fishing and yacht harbour in attractive surroundings near the head of the deep Golfe de Valinco. The Port de Commerce is not fully enclosed and with strong winds from SW–W–NW the swell can be unpleasant. A yacht harbour, the Port de Plaisance, has been constructed to the east of Port de Commerce, and this offers good protection. Approach and entrance are easy. The small town can provide everyday requirements, it caters for thousands of tourists who pack the area in the season. The harbour also becomes very crowded.

⊕ 41°40'·80N 08°54'·00E
Depth 3m minimum
Number of berths 380 places with 200(?) for visitors
Maximum length 32m

Charts

Admiralty *1424*
French *6851, 7162*

Port radio

VHF Ch 9 or ☎ 04 95 76 10 40 (summer 0600–1200, 1400–2000; winterand 0800–1200, 1400–1800)

Weather forecast

Posted twice a day at *capitaneria*.

Lights

0896 Scogliu Longu 41°40'·8N 8°53'·9E
 Oc(3)WG.12s15m15/12M 070°-W-097°-G-137°-W-002°-obscd-070° White tower, green top 17m
0898 Jetée Nord head Iso.G.4s11m10M White post, green top7m
0899 Brise-James W head Fl(2)6s2m Red structure 1m
0899·2 Brise-James E head Fl(3)G.12s5m6M White tower, black top 3m

Warnings

To avoid the Scogliu Longu rocks, to the east of the west jetty, keep well to the north of the light tower especially at night when approaching in the white sector of the light! Remember this is mainly a commercial harbour and ferry and commercial

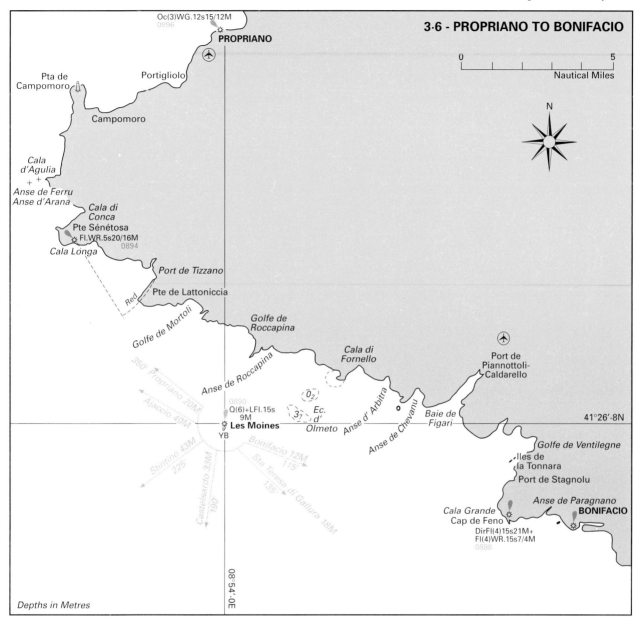

traffic have right of way. Anchoring is prohibited in the commercial port.

Approach

By day Keeping well clear of Pointe de Porto Pollo and its off-lying Rochers du Taravu (from north) or Pointe de Campomoro (from the south) steer towards the head of the Golfe de Valinco and the houses of Propriano will come into sight and it is important to identify the north jetty with its white tower so the Roches de Scogliu Longu can be avoided. Keep at least 200m north of the tower to clear all dangers.

By night From the entrance of the Gulf keep in the white sector (070° to 097°) of the north jetty light until about 1 mile from the light when a move north is made into the green sector. When the tower is about 400m away steer to leave it at least 200m to starboard.

Entrance

From north of the white tower steer about ESE and pick up the breakwater or its light and round the end carefully and enter on a course of west. Keep close to the breakwater on entering. Moor where possible and report to *capitaneria* for berthing instructions.

Berths

Stern-to on pontoons with moorings connected to pontoon by *pendillos* as instructed by *capitaneria*.

Formalities

All authorities available

Facilities

All.

History

A little fishing settlement which the Turks destroyed in 1583, 1590 and again in 1660. Most of the town

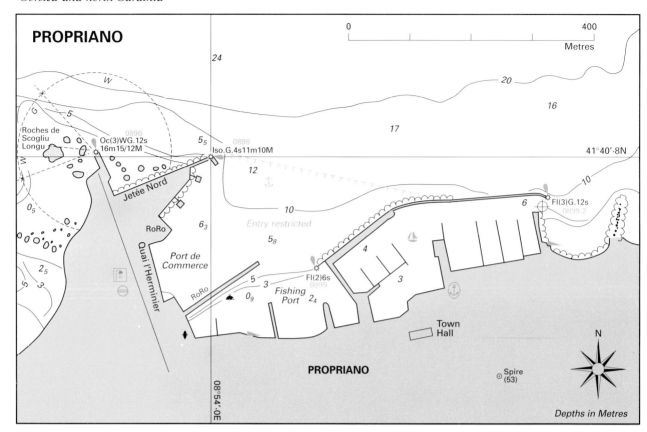

is of recent origin created when tourism came to the area.

⚓ Portigliolo

A protected anchorage a mile south of Ecueils l'Ancurella which are off the mouth of the river Rizzanesa and the small airfield that serves Propriano. Approach on a southerly heading parallel to the beach to avoid off-lying dangers to the west. Anchor in 2 to 3m off the village, open to W–NW–N.

⚓ Campomoro

A very popular anchorage in a large bay surrounded by tree and scrub-covered hills with a long sandy beach with rocks at each end and a village behind. There is a conspicuous tower on the Pointe de Campomoro which also has outlying dangers, see below. The best spot to anchor is in 6m, sand and weed, in the southwesterly corner of the bay near the 2 jetties but there are fishing boat moorings off and it may be necessary to anchor further out in 10–20m. There is a fish farm in the centre of the bay (1998) and holiday developments ashore. In common with many other areas in the islands there may be a line of small buoys off the beach to prevent yachts and RIB's approaching too close to the beach and the bathers. The bay is open to NW–N–NE.

Pointe de Campomoro

A prominent headland at the mouth of the Golfe de Valinco, with a conspicuous fort and tower just inland of the point, the hills rise to 116m behind. Rocky dangers extend to 250m in a northwesterly

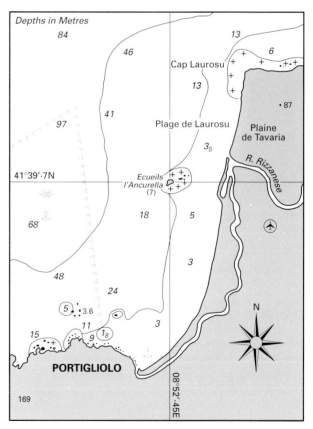

direction and 500m to the northeast, the latter partially obstructing the entrance to Campomoro bay.

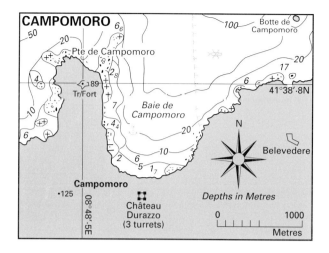

⚓ Cala d'Agulia

A remarkable anchorage 0·5M northeast of Punta d'Eccica in a narrow rocky-sided cove with a sandy beach at its head. There is room for a couple of yachts only but enter on an ESE course and moor with two anchors in 3m, sand and rock, open to W–NW. Track inland, deserted.

Punta d'Eccica

A very broken rocky point sloping down from 71m to cliffs and many off-lying rocks, exposed, awash and covered including the low rocky isle, Ile d'Eccica.

Ile d'Eccica reef and passages

A number of complicated passages exist between Ile and Punta d'Eccica which must be carefully investigated in a dinghy in calm weather before use. There is one simple and relatively safe passage which can be used by passing very close to the east side of Ile d'Eccica on a N or S course, this passage is 150m wide 400 long and 12m minimum depth. A 300m clearance is necessary from the west side of Ile d'Eccica on a N or S course when passing outside all dangers.

⚓ Anse de Ferru

A small bay tucked away behind Punta d'Eccica on

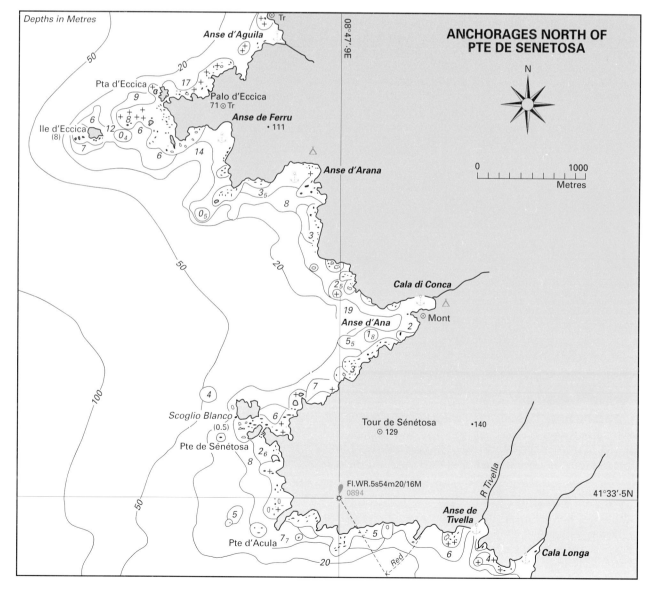

its south side with high, rocky, tree-covered hills around it. Enter on a northeasterly course to avoid rocky dangers. Anchor off head in 5m, rock and weed, paying attention to rocks close inshore, open to S–SW–W. Deserted.

⚓ Anse d'Arana

A bay surrounded on two sides by tree and scrub-covered rocky hills with a sandy beach at its head and a housing estate, the northwest side. Approach on a northeasterly course, anchor in 3m, sand, rock and weed, off the head of the bay. Open to S–SW–W.

⚓ Cala di Conca

An attractive anchorage in a narrow V-shaped cove at the mouth of a small river, it has rocky sides with coastal rocks and a sandy beach at its head. Approach on an easterly course and anchor near the bend in the channel in 4m, sand, open to SW–W–NW. Track inland. Deserted except for campers.

Pointe de Sénétosa and Pointe d'Acula

The Massif de Sénétosa has a grey tower on its peak (129m). It slopes downwards westwards to Pointe de Sénétosa and southwestwards to Pointe d'Acula. The land is scrub covered. Pointe de Sénétosa has two longish islets off its point, Scoglio Blanco (white rock) is the larger of the two and furthest to the northwest, between this islet and the point are a mass of rocky dangers. Pointe d'Acula has a long thin promontory, there is a conspicuous lighthouse consisting of a white house with two white towers (Fl.WR.5s54m20/16M). The red sector (306° to 328°) of this light covers the Les Moines (qv below) and the long banks of rocks stretching north. The point has rocky dangers extending 500m to the west. Give the whole headland a 1,000m berth when rounding these two points.

Warning

The coast from here to Cap de Feno, 18 miles to the southeast, is rocky with many off-lying dangers. There are a number of attractive anchorages but, in general, the holding is poor and there are very limited facilities, if any at all. It is only feasible to explore this section in settled and calm weather. If there are any winds forecast from the westerly direction it is recommended that you pass outside the Ile Moines and go directly to Bonifacio (or just possibly Baie de Figari).

⚓ Cala Longa

A long narrow cove with rocky sides and a small sandy beach at its head, surrounded by scrub covered rock, deserted. Anchor in 3m, sand, off the beach, open to S–SW–W.

⚓ Port de Tizzano

Not a port but an attractive and useful anchorage in a narrow estuary which has silted up near its head. There is a 40m-long jetty on the east side. There are many buildings surrounding its rocky shores and a

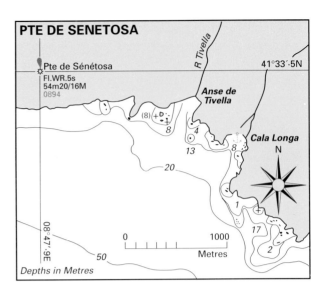

road to the main coast road. The houses and old fort can be seen from afar. Enter on a northerly course and leave the breakwater to port, anchor in 2m sand off the quay, open to S–SW. There is a small village with restaurant, café and a mobile food shop but little else in the way of facilities.

Pointe Latoniccia

A large promontory with hills reaching 146m a short distance inland. It has rocky dangers close inshore. On the south-facing point there are three patches of rocky heads which extend 100m.

La Botte de Tizzano and passage

La Botte de Tizzano (13m) lies 300m offshore and has rocky dangers to the north. A passage 100m wide, 200m long with a minimum depth of 3m to be taken E or W halfway between the Corsican shore and the *botte* detailed above. Use with care and with a good lookout.

⚓ Cala di Brija

A small bay on the eastern side of the Massif de Latoniccia. It is surrounded by scrub-covered rocky hills. Approach on a northerly course, enter and anchor in 3m, sand, off the rock and stone beach, open to E–SE–S–SW. Tracks ashore but otherwise deserted.

⚓ Golfe de Murtoli

A large bay with anchorages off the beaches to the northwest and southeast. The sides are very broken rocky cliffs and there is one long sandy beach and one short sandy beach. A very small village of Zivia with a few houses and a road inland in the northwest corner. Summer camp sites. Anchor in 3m, sand, off the beaches, open to SE–S–SW–W.

Pointe de Murtoli

A point with a hill 48m high inland rising to 89m, it has a broken rocky-cliffed coastline with rocky dangers projecting 200m towards SW.

⚓ Golfe de Roccapina

A large open bay at the foot of a wide valley of the

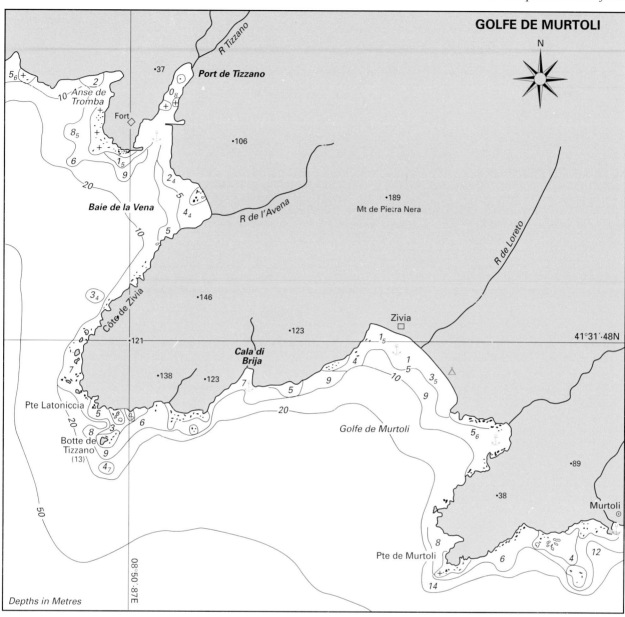

GOLFE DE MURTOLI

Depths in Metres

Rivière l'Ortolo. There is a group of rocks 1M east of Pointe de Murtoli and the coast in the western part of this bay has rocky dangers close in. The eastern half consists of a long sandy beach, anchorage is available off this beach in 3m, sand, open to SE–S–SW–W. There is a beautiful one- or two-yacht anchorage by the village of Murtoli behind a small rocky projection for use by very experienced navigators. There is a track to the main coast road from here.

Pointe de Roccapina

A high (134m) narrow promontory with a forked point and rocky dangers extending 200m to the southwest. The crest of the hill behind the point has the appearance of a lion from some directions and in certain lights. There is also a tower on the crest.

⚓ Anse de Roccapina

A popular anchorage in a square-shaped bay. The sides of which are of rocky scrub-covered hills. There are many rocks exposed, awash and covered near the eastern side of the entrance and three more isolated islets further up the bay. The recommended entrance is to keep very close to the western side of the bay, inside of all rocky shallows and anchor in the north corner as shown on the sketch plan. The head of the bay consists of a sandy beach, anchor in 3m, sand, open to SE–S–SW off this beach. There is a track to the main road, holiday buildings and camp sites ashore.

Les Moines (islets, reefs and passage)

A very dangerous area of islets, exposed, awash and covered rocks lying between 1·5M and 3M to the south-southwest of Pointe de Roccapina. It lies half way and on the direct line between Pointe de Sénétosa and Cap de Feno. The Grand Moine (6m) lies near the centre of the group. There are many exposed rocks at the northern end and Les Moines

69

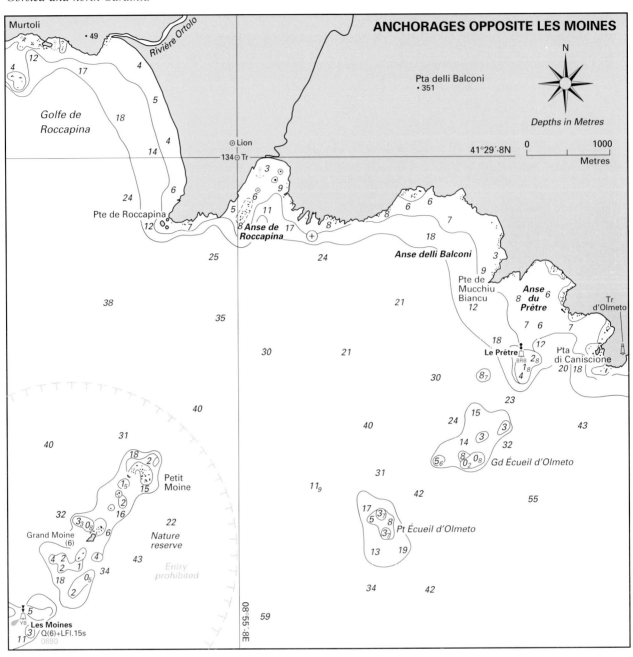

ANCHORAGES OPPOSITE LES MOINES

beacon tower S cardinal, black tower, yellow top (Q(6)+LFl.15s26m9M) marks the southern end.

Punta di Caniscione

A low rounded rocky point with the conspicuous Tour d'Olmeto on its southeastern side. Rocky dangers on the western side extend up to 150m and on its southwestern side up to 250m.

Écueils d'Olmeto and Le Prêtre and passages

Three shallow areas lying in a line approximately south-southwest of the Punta di Caniscione. Le Prêtre lies 800m from this point with shallows of 1·7m and 1·8m and an awash rock. This rock was marked by a BRB beacon tower but it has been partially destroyed and has not been replaced. Further out from Le Prêtre beacon lies the Grand Écueil d'Olmeto which has depths of 0·2m and

0·8m with shallows of 3m and 5m on the landward side of them. 1·25M still further out the Petit Écueil d'Olmeto has shallows of 3·7m.

The passage between Le Prêtre and the Corsican shore is 600m wide and should be taken in SSE–NNW directions to avoid dangers extending 250m from the Punta di Caniscione. Keep about equidistant from the ruined beacon and this point.

The passage between Le Prêtre and the Grand Écueil d'Olmeto is about 900m wide and should be taken in NW–SE directions equidistant between the ruined beacon and the broken water over the 0·2m and 0·8m shallows at the south end of the Grand Écueil d'Olmeto.

The passage between the Grand and Petit Écueil d'Olmeto is 1·25M wide and should be taken in NW–SE directions. Except in heavy seas the Petit

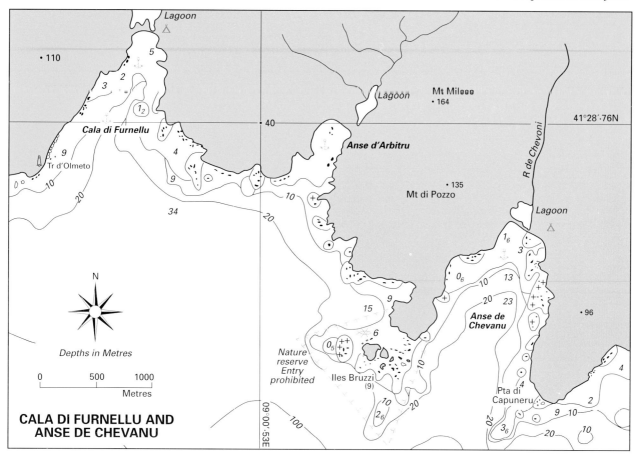

CALA DI FURNELLU AND
ANSE DE CHEVANU

Depths in Metres

Écueil d'Olmeto can be ignored by yachts drawing less than 3m.

⚓ Cala di Furnellu

A large pleasant V-shaped bay with rocky low hills, tree and scrub covered. The Tour d'Olmeto on Punta di Caniscione on the western side of the entrance is conspicuous. There is a 1·2m deep rock near the centre of the bay halfway in. The eastern shore has rocky outliers extending 50m. Anchor in 3m, sand and weed, off a sandy beach at the head of the bay, open to SE–S–SW. Summer camp sites, track to main road, otherwise deserted.

⚓ Anse d'Arbitru

A small bay with a low rocky coastline and a large sandy beach at its head but with some rocks extending 150m out from the centre of the beach. Anchor in 3m, sand and rock, but the holding is not good, open to S–SW. There is a large red house on the western side of the bay and some smaller apartment blocks and houses behind the beach. Tracks leading inland, usually deserted. Behind the beach is a lake and marshes fed by the Rivière Agninaccio.

Iles Bruzzi

A group of one large and eight small rocky islets with many rocky heads and shallows covering a dog-leg shape 1,000m NW–SE and 1,000m N–S. Located 200m off the unnamed headland that lies between the anchorages at Anse d'Abitru and Anse

de Chevanu, as detailed above and below. Yachts should keep at least 1,000m from the headland and preferably 1,500m in bad weather.

⚓ Anse de Chevanu

A large bay with low rocky sides and a big sandy beach at its head. There are many off-lying rocks close inshore on the eastern side of the bay and another group extends 150m from the centre of the beach. Two isolated rocks lie 300m to the south and southwest of Punta di Capuneru. The Iles Bruzzi (see above) obstruct direct entrance to this anchorage from SW–W–NW. Enter on a northerly course and anchor in 3m, sand and weed, (poor holding) off the beach, open to SE–S–SW. Summer camp site and track inland, otherwise deserted.

Punta di Capuneru

A rocky headland with two islets and many rocky heads extending 300m to south and southwest.

⚓ Baie di Figari

This is a 2-mile long inlet relatively deserted at its outer end with many rocky patches and shallows on the approach. In strong south to southwest winds the entrance would be dangerous. Take a position midway between Punta di Capuneru and Punta de Ventilegne and steer north towards a conspicuous tower, Tour de Calderello, bringing the tower into line with the church tower in Calderellu on a transit of 008°. As Rocher St Jean comes abeam to port,

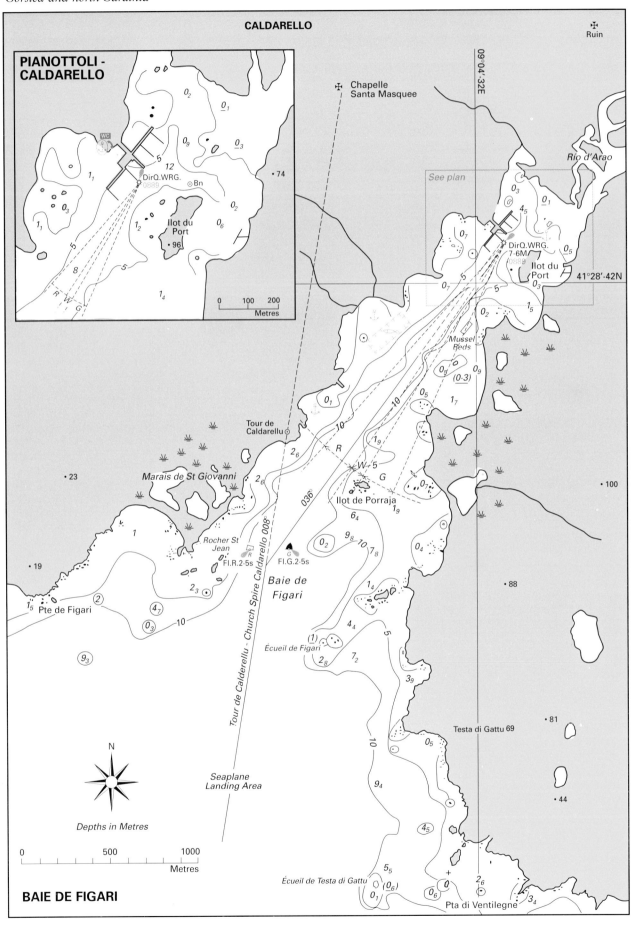

CALDARELLO

⌖ Ruin

PIANOTTOLI - CALDARELLO

0₂

0₁

WC

0₉

0₃

12
DirQ.WRG. ⊙ Bn
0889

1₁

• 74

0₂

0₃

1₁

1₂

Ilot du Port
• 96

0₆

5

8

5

R W G

1₄

0   100   200
Metres

Chapelle
Santa Masquee

09°04′·32E

Rio d'Arao

See plan

0₃

0₁

4₅

0₇

DirQ.WRG.
7·6M
0889

0₅

Ilot du
Port

41°28′·42N

0₇

5

0₃

1₅

0₂

Mussel
Beds

0₅

0₉

(0·3)

0₁

10

0₅

1₇

Tour de
Caldarellu ⌀

2₆

R

W 5

G

Marais de St Giovanni

• 23

2₆

036

1₉

Ilot de Porraja

1₉

0₇

• 100

6₄

1

Rocher St
Jean
Fl.R.2·5s   R

G
Fl.G.2·5s

0₂

9₈ 10 7₈

0₄

• 88

Tour de Calderellu - Church Spire Calderello 008

Baie de
Figari

1₄

• 19

2₃

1₅   Pte de Figari

②

4₇

4₄

5

0₃   10

Écueil de Figari

(1)

2₈

7₂

3₉

9₃

N

Testa di Gattu 69

• 81

Seaplane
Landing Area

10

0₅

9₄

• 44

Depths in Metres

4₅

0   500   1000
Metres

5₅

Écueil de Testa di Gattu

(0₆)

0₆

2₆

3₄

BAIE DE FIGARI

0₁

0₁

Pta di Ventilegne

two small light buoys should be seen. Pass between them and steer 036° which takes you up the main channel. The sides are steep-to and 8m can be carried up to the yacht harbour. One can anchor to the NE of the Tour or farther up the channel behind the Ilot du Port. There are several fish farms and mussel beds in the area and these must be given a wide berth.

⚓ Port de Pianottoli-Caldarello

⊕ 41°28'·42N 09°04'·32E

This is a relatively new yacht harbour on the east side of the inlet opposite the Ilot du Port. Approach is as for the Baie di Figari above and simply proceed up the main channel until the pontoons become visible. There is a light on the outer jetty DirQ.WRG.7·6M (sectors 026°-G-035°-W-037·5°-R-046°). The white sector illuminates the main channel and, at night, you should steer up this passing between the two light buoys, Fl.R.2·5s and Fl.G.2·5s at the lower part of the inlet. Communication is on VHF Ch 9 or ☎ 04 95 71 83 57 and there are 200 places (120 for visitors) with maximum length of 40m. Depths are 1·5–5m at the pontoons. There are reasonable facilities here (electricity and water on pontoons, showers, WCs, gash bins etc.) but no fuel, and supplies may have to be obtained at the village 2km away out of season.

Punta di Ventilegne

An inconspicuous headland with foul ground extending 700m from the shore in a southwesterly direction, to the Écueil de Testa di u Gattu, an unmarked awash rock, and 500m in a southerly direction!

⚓ Anse de Pesciucane

A smallish V-shaped bay with a lagoon behind it. Both rocky shores have some close inshore rocks. Anchor in 5m, sand and weed, off head of bay, open to S–SW. Deserted. Main road 0·75M inland.

⚓ Golfe de Ventilegne

A large gulf which has several anchorages around its head for use with care due to shallows and several areas foul with rocky heads. The bay is open to SW–W. The coast road runs behind this gulf.

⚓ Iles de la Tonnara

A group of three rocky islets extending up to 600m from the coast with outlying rocky dangers. A small anchorage lies between the northeasternmost island which is the largest, and the coast where there are several ruined houses and a sandy beach. Approach this anchorage from the Golfe de Ventilegne on a southerly course with care. Anchor in 3m, rock and sand, open to NW–N. Road to main coast road, usually deserted.

⚓ Port de Stagnolu

A bay with rocky coast and sandy beach at its head. There is a small islet in the entrance of the bay. This is not a port but a deserted anchorage. Pass north or south of this islet and anchor off the beach in 3m, sand, open to SW–W–NW. Track to main road.

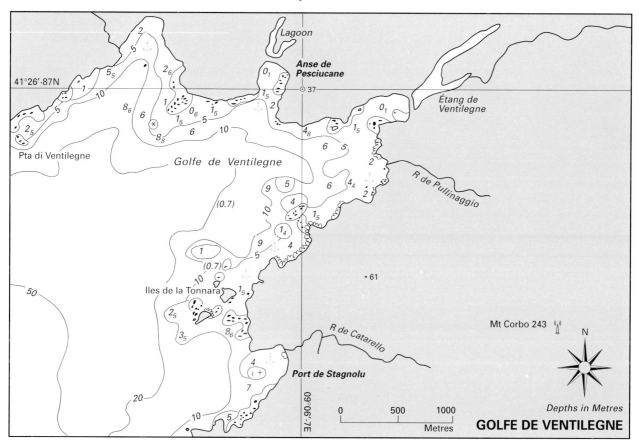

GOLFE DE VENTILEGNE

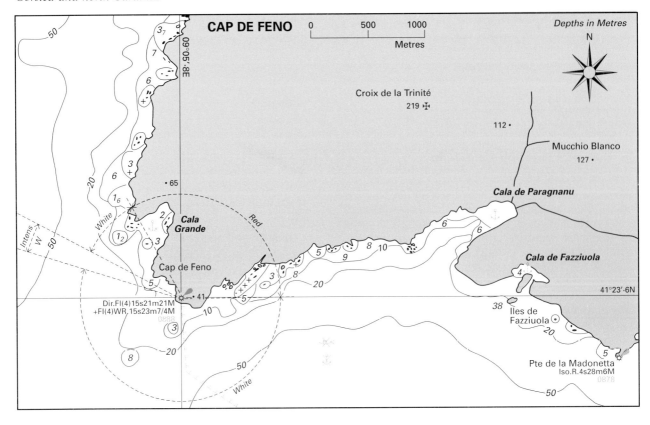

⚓ Cala Grande

In spite of its name this fantastic anchorage is very small and situated on the west side of Cap de Feno in a rocky-sided bay. The eastern side of the bay has some close-in rocky heads and there is an exposed rock in the centre of the bay. Enter on a NNE course close to the west side of the bay with a good lookout forward. Anchor in 3m, rock and sand, short of the head of the bay where there is a sand and rocky beach. Open to S–SW. It may be necessary to take a line ashore. Footpath, deserted.

Cap de Feno

A broken rocky promontory sloping up to 114m inland with irregular cliffs. Two small rocky dangers exist 200m to the west of the lighthouse and a 3m shallow patch 200m to the south. The lighthouse is a white square squat tower with a black top marked 'Feno' (DirFl(4)15s21m21M). This intense white sector covers the Les Moines beacon tower (109·4°–111·4°). The white sector of the upper light in the same tower (Fl(4)WR.15s23m7/4M) covers the safe approach to Cap de Feno (270°-150°).

⚓ Cala de Paraganu

A long thin bay, high broken hills with two towers to the west, light grey cliffs to the east and a white sandy beach at the head of the bay. It is popular with summer visitors and tourist boats. A patch of rocky heads extends 100m on the west side of the entrance. Anchor off the beach in 3m, rock and sand, open to S–SW. Road to main road.

⚓ Iles and Anse de Fazziolu

A fantastic small creek and bay with two islets almost blocking the entrance leaving two entrances/exits, the western entrance being the wider and deeper of the two. The sides are of layered whitish-grey cliffs and there is a small beach at the head of the bay. There is a Glénans Centre here. Yachts should use the west entrance and smaller boats can use the east entrance. Anchor to the north of the islet in 2·5m, sand, open to S–SW. There is a path to Bonifacio and in summer there are many visitors who come by land or by tourist boats.

3·7 – Bonifacio to Porto Vecchio

(including les Bouches de Bonifacio)

The section of white cliffs from Cap de Feno to Cap Pertusato is quite unique and only includes the port of Bonifacio and 2 anchorages. The channels between Corsica and Sardinia, Les Bouches de Bonifacio with its two Corsican islands, Lavezzi and Cavallo, are included in this section. The Corsican islands are lower, very rocky and have many off-lying dangers, while the Sardinian islands, to the south, are higher and are described in detail in Section 4.3 (page 105). From Cap Pertusato to Punta di a Chiappa, on the south side of the Golfe de Porto Vecchio, the coast is interspersed with large gulfs and bays. The hills have a more rounded

tree-covered appearance in contrast to the markedly jagged mountains of the W and SW coasts. The Iles Cerbicale and some isolated rocks and shallows lie offshore and are marked by two buoys. The main road runs well inland along this section of coast and there are camp sites, holiday centres and sailing schools at the head of many bays and few of the anchorages remain deserted.

⚓ Port de Bonifacio

General

This commercial, fishing and yachting harbour, which is the only harbour on the south coast of Corsica, almost defies description. It is certainly the most spectacular and attractive natural harbour in Corsica and probably in the Mediterranean. The narrow, deep, fjord-like inlet with high almost vertical sides of white rock crowned by a medieval walled town and Citadelle is certainly unique. The approach and entrance are easy and almost complete shelter is available once inside. The facilities for yachtsmen are good but unfortunately the harbour becomes very crowded in the season. There are two *bureaux de port*, the *club nautique* (a private affair) and the Port de Plaisance (the municipality).

⊕ 41°23'·1N 09°08'·9E

Depth 1–6m
Number of berths 400 berths with 220 for visitors
Maximum length 55m

Charts

Admiralty *1213*, *1424*
French *7024*, *7096*

Port radio

VHF Ch 9 or ☎ 04 95 73 10 07.

Weather forecast

Posted twice-daily at *club nautique*.

Lights

0878 Pointe de la Madonetta 41°23'·1N 9°08'·8E
    Iso.R.4s28m6M Red square tower, grey corners
    12m
0882 Pointe Cacavento Fl.G.4s6m5M White pyramid,
    dark green top
0886 Pointe de l'Arinella Oc(2)R.6s9m3M Red tower
    on grey base 035°-R-059°.

Warnings

Large commercial craft use this harbour and yachts must keep out of the way.

Restricted area

A nature reserve lies along the coast from Cap de Feno to Ile St Antoine and extends 1M seawards. Fishing, subaqua diving and anchoring is forbidden in this area.

Approach

Although the actual entrance is difficult to make out from a distance the two conspicuous headlands of

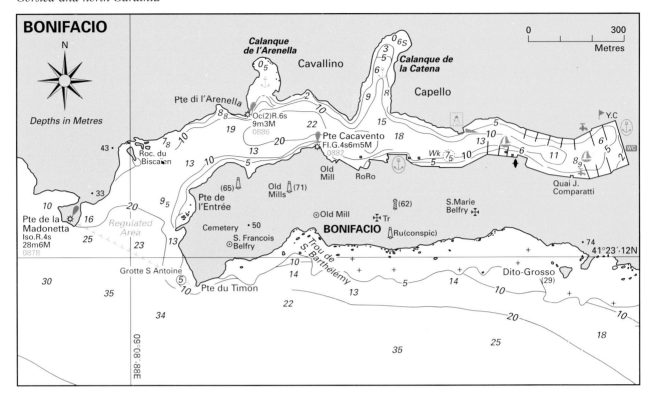

Cap de Feno and Cap Pertusato should be easily seen, by day or by night, and a course set towards the distinctive Pointe de la Madonetta light. The town and Citadelle can be seen high up and well to the east of the entrance.

Entrance

By day Enter on a northeasterly course leaving the steep-to white-cliffed Pointe de la Madonetta with a red square lighthouse tower on its top 100m to port and the similar steep-to white-cliffed Pointe du Timon, which has a large cave, 100m to starboard. Follow the inlet around to starboard in mid-channel. It is advised that one should be under engine because of (a) the vicious downdraughts that exist in the entrance in certain winds and (b) the possible need to avoid commercial traffic which have right of way in the harbour.

By night Approach Pointe de la Madonetta light (Iso.R.4s) on a northeasterly course and then alter towards Pointe de l'Aranella light (Oc(2)R.6s). When about 50m short of the light proceed on an easterly course up the inlet leaving Pointe Cacavento light (Fl.G.4s) to starboard.

Berths

Yachts berth near the head of the harbour. The northern section is administered by the *centre nautique* and has the usual facilities. The southern section is controlled by the municipality. In the northern section yachts secure stern-to the quay or pontoons with bows-to small buoys. In the southern section yachts secure stern-to the quay or pontoon with moorings from the bow. Pontoons have fingers for berthing. The use of anchors is forbidden.

Anchorages

There are two secluded anchorages in the harbour both with poor holding. The Calanque de la Catena with a mud bottom of 15m sloping to 0·5m and the much shallower Calanque de l'Arenella 10m rapidly sloping to 0·5m. This anchorage is not so sheltered as the Calanque de la Catena.

Formalities

All authorities available.

Facilities

All.

History

This superb natural harbour must have been used by local fishermen since time immemorial but the real foundation of the town dates from AD 828 when Bonifacio, Marquis de Toscane, arrived here on his return from an expedition against the Saracens. In 1195 during celebrations after a marriage ceremony, a force of Genoese seized and occupied the town driving out all of the inhabitants. They have held the town virtually ever since and even today many of the inhabitants still speak a Genoese dialect. In 1420 Alfonso of Aragon arrived with a strong force at the request of the local Corsican lords who had succeeded elsewhere in driving the Genoese off the island but their attacks on Bonifacio failed. The population of the town was decimated in 1528 by the plague and in 1554 a combined French and Turkish force captured the town but it was returned to Genoa by a treaty a short time afterwards.

In 1963 the French Foreign Legion took over the barracks in the Citadelle and in subsequent years the development of the tourist industry has slowly taken place.

Cap Pertusato

A major headland of whitish-grey rock 86m high with an off-lying islet, St Antoine, which has a chapel on its top. The outer rock of this cape is shaped like a French Marine's cap. There is foul ground west of the cape extending 100m. The lighthouse stands 400m to the east of the cape and is housed in a white square tower with black top and corners (Fl(2)10s100m25M). A conspicuous signal station stands 800m northwest of the cape. Contact by flag, light or VHF Ch 10 or 16 and (☎ 94 73 00 32), permanent watch.

Ile St Antoine and passage

This islet is 150m long, 80m wide and 30m high of layered whitish-grey rock. There is a 30m wide passage between this islet and the cape about 1·5m minimum depth, it is most spectacular. Take in NE–SW direction when the sea is calm and with great care. Boats with tall masts cannot get through due to over-hanging rocks.

Le Prêtre beacon

A pole beacon painted black, red and black 6m high with 2 spheres topmark, is located on a 4·6m shoal 500m southwest of Punta de Sperono.

Punta de Sperono

A low headland which can easily be recognised because the rear mark (a wall) of the transit for the Passage de la Piantarella stands on the point.

⚓ Anse Piantarella (plan on page 79)

A small shallow cove with white sandy beach and small river at its head. Caution is necessary when approaching due to shallows between Ile Piana and the Corsican coast, depths can also change during storms, deep water is usually near the Corsican coast. Anchor in 2·5m sand near the mouth of the cove, open to NE–E–SE–S. Track ashore, popular with summer visitors.

⚓ Cala Longa (plan on page 79)

A small bay on the high rocky coast that stands out towards Pointe Cappiciolo. Anchor in 2·5m sand off the centre of the bay, open to E–SE–S. A few houses ashore and a road inland. A group of rocks extend 150m from the shore from the southwest corner of the bay.

Note

In the following sections the compiler has been surprised at the plethora of names applied to any particular place. Differences occur (naturally?) not only between similar charts of different countries but also between different issues of charts by the same country. For this volume the compiler has used the names given in the 2000 editions of French and Italian pilots which, for the most part, agree with one another and use the original dialect names of older charts.

Les Bouches de Bonifacio

General

The 3·5M passage between the Corsican and Sardinian islands is considered as a separate section because of the numerous off-lying dangers and the adverse weather that is sometimes encountered here. Experienced navigators, especially those used to a similar type of coast such as is found in North Brittany and around the Channel Islands should experience no difficulty. The less experienced should take extra care and should avoid the area in poor weather conditions. The passages between the Italian islands off Sardinia are described in Section 4 that follows. The large scale French chart *7024* or the Italian charts *2142* or *3350* are advised for those exploring this most attractive and challenging area.

The passages

Although technically there are six passages between the islands on the north or Corsican side of the *bouches* only three are advised in view of the normal weather and current patterns that occur locally. The three recommended are as follows:

1. Grande Passe des Bouches which is the main deep-water commercial route running between Sardinia and the Écueil de Lavezzi. 3M wide, 3M long, 19m deep.
2. The pass between the Écueil de Lavezzi and Iles Lavezzi, a deep-water route useful for yachts. 1M wide, 1M long, 5m deep.
3. The Passage de la Piantarella, a daytime only passage for small craft, between Ile Ratino and Ile Piana in reasonable weather. 300m wide, 2M long, 3·5m deep.

Important note

Both Ile Lavezzi and Isola Razzoli light sectors and characteristics have been recently (early 2000) been radically altered and this has made the use of the pass between Iles Lavezzi and the Écueil de Lavezzi by night a more difficult affair, especially after strong winds when unknown surface currents can be flowing. Newcomers to the area are not recommended to use this pass at night.

Currents

During and after a NW–W gale, east-going currents of up to 3 knots can be experienced. Strong winds from NE–E create weaker west-going currents. In winter this west-going current is semi-permanent.

Lights

0876 Cap Pertusato 41°22'·0N 9°11'·2E
  Fl(2)10s100m25M 239°-vis-113° White square tower with black top and corners 21m
0938 Capo Testa 41°14'·6N 9°08'·7E Fl(3)12s67m17M 017°-vis-256° White tower on 2 storied house 23m
0872 Lavezzi (Capu di u Beccu) 41°20'·1N 9°15'·6E Oc(2)WR.6s27m17/14M 243°-W-351°-R-243°- partially obscd-138°-obscd-218° Square tower, red band, on white house 12m
0874 Écueil de Lavezzi 41°19'·0N 9°15'·3E Fl(2)6s18m9M Black tower, red band 2 balls(vert) topmark

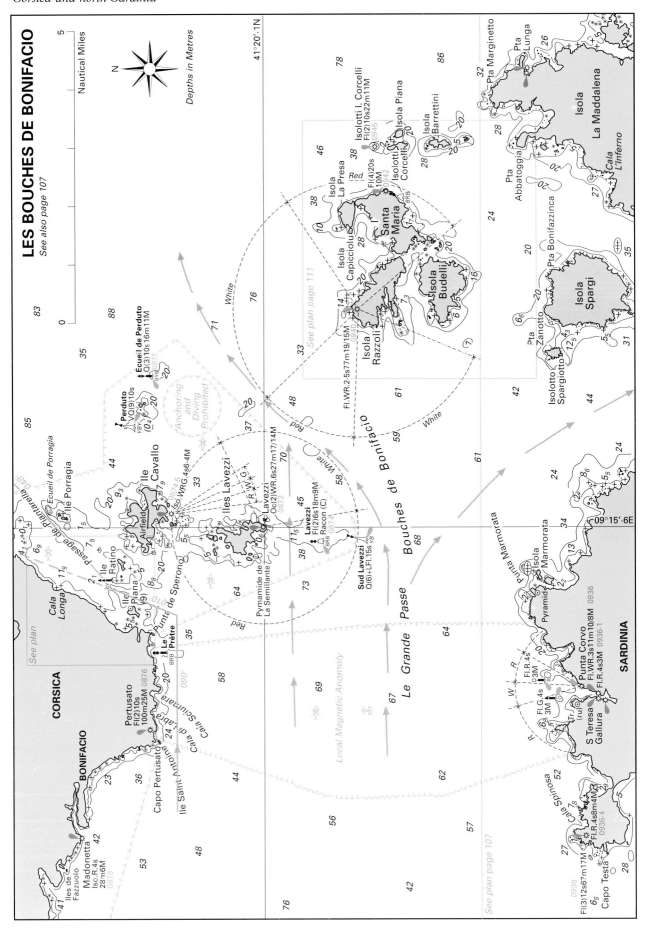

LES BOUCHES DE BONIFACIO

See also page 107

Nautical Miles

Depths in Metres

41°20′·1N

0875 Écueil de Perduto 41°22'·0N 9°19'·0E
  Q(3)10s16m11M E card beacon tower BYB 28m
0940 Isola Razzoli 41°18'·4N 9°20'·4E
  Fl.WR.2·5s77m19/15M 022°-W-092°-R-137°-W-
  237°-R-320° Stone tower 12m

Buoys
0925·2(I) Sud Lavezzi 41°18'·6N 9°15'·3E
  Q(6)+LFl.15s7m4M S card YB
0926·2(I) Perduto 41°22'·4N 9°17'·9E VQ(9)10s4m6M
  W card YBY

Beacons
Pyramide de la Sémillante – Pyramid tower on rock
  SW of Iles Lavezzi commemorating the sinking of
  the frigate *La Sémillante* in 1854
La Prêtre BRB post with 2 balls topmark marking a 4m
  rocky patch 0·3M SW of Punta de Sperono
Tignosa di Ratino N card post BY, 0·25M NW of Ile
  Ratino
Passage de La Piantarella leading marks
  Front, a white wall on Ile Piana
  Rear, a white wall on Punta de Sperono bearing
  228·5°

1. La Grande Passe des Bouches

A 3M wide deep-water passage for commercial
shipping and the easiest and safest route by day and
the recommended passage at night. There is a local
magnetic anomaly 2M to the south of Cap Pertusato
with a maximum deflection of 3°.

Approach by day

From the west Approach the pass on an easterly
heading approximately 2M north of the Sardinian
coast and at least 1M to the south of the Écueil de
Lavezzi, marked by a beacon tower, with a topmark
of 2 spheres. Leave the Sud Lavezzi S cardinal buoy
well to port and when this buoy has been passed
round onto a northeasterly course and pass between
Iles Lavezzi and Isola Razzoli and then leave the
Écueil de Perduto marked by a E cardinal light buoy
1M to port.

From the east The directions given above are taken in
reverse order but it is essential to make a positive
identification of Iles Lavezzi and Isola Razzoli before
entering the area.

Approach by night

From a position some 2M north of Capo Testa,
approach Isola Razzoli (Fl.WR.2·5s) on a course
between 080° and 085° in its white sector, leaving
Sud Lavezzi S cardinal buoy (Q(6)+LFl.15s) well to
port. When Iles Lavezzi light (Oc(2) WR.6s)
changes from red to white (351°) alter course to
045°. When Écueil de Perduto E cardinal buoy
(Q(3)10s) is abeam the passage has been completed.

From the east Enter the pass on a southwesterly
course with the Capo Testa light (Fl(3)12s) on 235°
showing halfway between Isola Razzoli
(Fl.WR.2·5s) and Iles Lavezzi (Oc(2)WR.6s); both
in their white sectors leaving Écueil de Perduto
(Q(3)10s) over 2M to starboard. When Iles Lavezzi
(Oc(2)WR.6s) changes from white to red (351°)
change to a course of west leaving Sud Lavezzi
(Q(6)+LFl.15s) to starboard which ends the
passage.

2. Iles Lavezzi – Écueil de Lavezzi pass

This pass is very suitable for yachts though in bad
weather it will be rougher than the Grande Passe
due to the shallower water. The pass is 1M wide
minimum depth 5m.

Approach by day

From the west enter the pass on an easterly course
halfway between the Iles Lavezzi and the Écueil de
Lavezzi beacon tower, BRB, topmark of 2 spheres.
When the lighthouse on Lavezzi bears NW change
course to northeast and leave the Écueil de Perduto
East cardinal buoy 1M to port.

From the east the reverse course holds good provided
positive identification of Iles Lavezzi has first been
made.

Approach by night

From a position some 1·5M south of Cap Pertusato
enter the pass by approaching the light on Isola
Razzoli (Fl.WR.2·5s), in the red sector, on a course
of 106°. When the red sector of the Iles Lavezzi light
(Oc(2)WR.6s) turns white (351°) alter to a course
of 080° and remain in the white sector of this light
passing 1M southeast of Écueil de Perduto E
cardinal buoy (Q(3)10s).

From the east Approach Écueil de Lavezzi (Fl(2)6s)
on a WSW course until the light on Isola Razzoli
(Fl.WR.2·5s) bears 106° (in its red sector!), turn
onto a course of 286° and keep the stern bearing of
Isola Razzoli on 106°.

3. Passage de la Piantarella

This is the usual inshore passage for yachts by day
and in normal weather. It cannot be used at night or
in bad weather.

From the west Steer towards the south point of Ile
Cavallo on a course of 090° passing some 0·25M off
the coast of Corsica and outside Le Prêtre beacon,
BRB with two balls topmark. When the high land of
Sant'Amanza peninsula to the north is in line with
the Tignosa di Ratino, alter to a course of 010° and
pass equidistant between these islets and Ile Piana.
When the white wall (front) leading mark on Ile
Piana bears 225° and nearly abeam of the Tignosa
to starboard, alter to a course of 048° leaving
Tignosa di Ratino beacon, N cardinal BY 150m to
starboard. The rear leading mark, also a white wall,
on Punta de Sperono will soon appear. Keep these
in line astern. When Ile Porraggia is abeam you can
make a little to NW of the leading line which passes
very close to this group of rocks and islands.

From the north Navigate to a position where the Ile
Porraggia group of islands lie 300m to the southeast
and proceed on a course of 228°. The two white wall
leading marks will be seen and should be brought
into line and followed. This course passes some
150m to N of the Tignosa di Ratino beacon N
cardinal BY. When this beacon is 200m to the east
turn onto a course of 190° passing equidistant
between Ile Piana and the off-lying rocks of Ile
Ratino. When the lighthouse on Cap Pertusato
appears course may be altered towards the west.

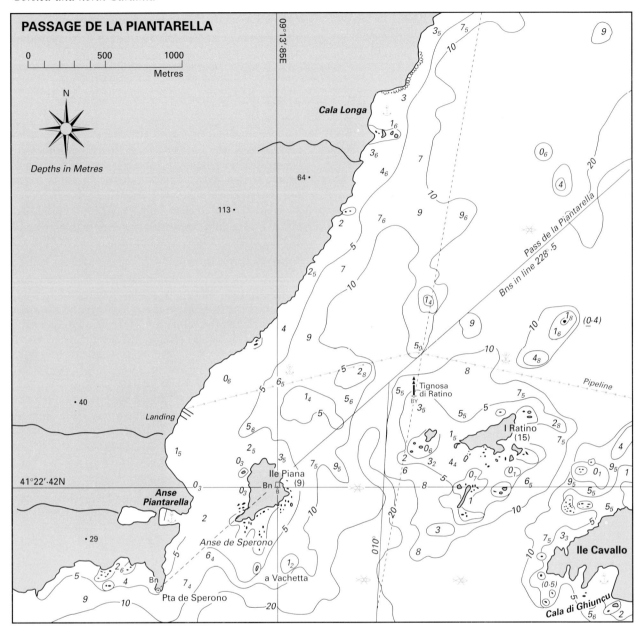

PASSAGE DE LA PIANTARELLA

Iles Lavezzi

(41°20'·5N 09°15'·5E)

General

A delightful, almost bare, group of rocky islands which offers three beautiful anchorages with crystal clear water over a white sandy bottom. The islands are deserted though in the season tourists are brought over by motor boat from Corsica in their hundreds and many yachts use the anchorages. The approach and entrance require some care due to off-lying rocks and shallows. The various anchorages offer good protection from wind and sea though it may be necessary to change anchorage if the wind direction should alter.

Currents

An E–going current of up to 2 to 3 knots may be experienced during and after a west to northwest gale. Weaker west-going currents may be encountered after strong winds from northeast or east especially during winter months when there is a west-going current of a semi-permanent nature.

Lights

0872 Lavezzi (Capu di u Beccu) 41°20'·1N 9°15'·6E
Oc(2)WR.6s27m17/14M 243°-W-351°-R-243°
138°-partially obscd-218° Square tower, red band, on white house 12m

0874 Écueil de Lavezzi 41°19'·0N 9°15'·3E
Fl(2)6s18m9M Black tower, red band 2 balls (vert) topmark

Buoys

0925·2(I) Sud Lavezzi 41°18'·6N 9°15'·3E
Q(6)+LFl.15s7m4M S card YB

Beacons

Pyramide de la Sémillante – Pyramid tower on rock SW of Iles Lavezzi

Warning

In bad weather especially from the northwest the

0

500

Metres

13

13

13

12

12

4

7₅

0₂

6₅

11

0₅

9₈

2₆

10

3₆

3

4₅

6₆

1₅

0₅

11

13

4₆

10

15

4₅

FI(2)R.6s

R

14

2₅

9₆

+

18

23

9₆

9₂

5₆

1₆

31

2

6₆

2₅

+

0₅

+

8₅

2

2₇

2₂

1₄

0₁

20

26

Cala della Chiesa

1₃

6₆

5₆

16

20

10

LAVEZZI

• 37

1₆

1₆

1₆

2

(0·2)

1₃

Cala Lazarina

21

7₇

△
Pyramide de la Semillante

9

9₇

10

20

37

3₃

12

+

+

1₆

1₇

2₅

9₂

1

Cala di Ghiuncu

4₆

1₆

0₆

9₇

5

6₇

0₆

2₇

Cala di u Grecu

22
Obscured

Partially

⊞
Oratory

Lavezzi
Oc(2)WR.6s
17–14M
0872

2₅

3₅

White

8₆

7₆

Red

26

20

41°20′·1N

21

Capu di Beccu

8₆

⊞

2₈

16

31

18

24

N

10

28 Red

7₅

18

White

09°15′·6E

Depths in Metres

ILES LAVEZZI

seas and winds can be considerably increased by the funnel effect between the high hills of Corsica and Sardinia.

Restrictions

A large part of the area around these islands is a nature reserve and all forms of sport which destroy animals, fish, birds and vegetation etc. are forbidden.

Approach by day

From the west round the high white cliffs of Cap Pertusato with its conspicuous lighthouse and signal station and set an ESE course towards the SW point of Iles Lavezzi which has a pyramid-shaped tower La Semillante on the point which will be seen in the closer approach.

From the wide and deep Golfe de Sant'Amanza round the prominent Punta di Capicciolu steer a SSE course. Leave the small group of rocks Ile Poraggia 0·5M to starboard and pass between Ile Cavallo and Ile Perduto leaving a W cardinal light buoy, YBY VQ(9)10s, just to east. Then steer a SSW course towards the lighthouse on the southern tip of the Iles Lavezzi which should be rounded at 400m.

Approach by night

Though there are numerous navigational lights for a night approach to the area a close approach to this island would be hazardous due to the number of off-lying rocks and shallows and is not recommended.

Entrances to the 3 anchorages

1. *Cala Lazarina* Take up a position where the memorial pyramid La Semillante is some 300m to the northwest and proceed on a NNE course leaving a series of small above-water rocks 75m to port. There is an anchorage about 220m NNW of the large islet to starboard in 5–8m but the venturesome can work their way, with care, deeper into the bay. A bow lookout is advised. This anchorage is open to the south.
2. *Cala di u Ghiuncu* From a position where the Lavezzi lighthouse bears northeast 300m make a northerly course leaving the shore 50m to starboard to the head of the *cala* where the anchorage lies. Anchor in 2m of sand at the head of the *cala* with the white-walled cemetery bearing northeast and some 25m from the beach. Anchorage is open to S–SW and take care when anchoring as cables run ashore here.
3. *Cala di u Grecu* Approach the north half of the island on a westerly course and in the close approach identify the small white building and wall around the cemetery. Approach it on a SSW course leaving a small isolated rock 30m to port. Proceed with care and a bow lookout to the anchorage at the head of the *cala*. Anchor in 2m on sand 30m from the beach. Anchorage open to NE.

Moorings

There are some private moorings in these *cala*s which could be used if not required by their owners. Some are used by the ferry boats.

Formalities

Customs officers may make snap inspections of yachts.

Facilities

None.

Ile Cavallo

(41°22'·0N 09°16'·0E)

General

A rocky island with a certain amount of low scrub and small trees which has been developed as a high-class holiday area by an Italian consortium. It has four possible anchorages which need some care in the approach and entrance. Shelter from winds from all directions is possible. Facilities ashore are very limited and the house owners do not like visitors. An airfield has been built for small private planes. A small private harbour and hotel complex has been built to the south of Cala di Palma.

Approach

By day The island is best approached from the southwest or northeast directions as these minimise the off-lying dangers. However close approach to all the anchorages described below needs care and a lookout forward. It is not recommended to approach Cavallo at night except from the southeast where lights are available to enter Port de Cavallo, but note entry is only permitted between 0600 and 2200 from June to September!

Anchorages

1. *Cala di Palma* Entrance to this anchorage requires considerable care for the first visit and slow speed with a bow lookout is essential. Enter from a position where the island is contained between north and west on a northwesterly heading. An alternative approach may be made on a westerly course from a position 100m to south of the southeastern extremity of the island then keeping close to the north shore. Open from E–S. Sand beach, several small landing pontoons and a slip. Anchor off mouth of southern sub-bay in 4m, sand.
2. *Cala di Zeri* Enter on a southwesterly course towards the western corner of the *cala*. The centre and eastern side is rock filled. Open to NE. A large and a small beach at head of *cala* with a small pontoon (2m) between them. Anchor 100m from the head of the *cala* close to the northwest shore in 3m, sand.
3. *Cala di u Grecu* Enter on a southerly course leaving an outlying rock 75m to port and a shallow (1·5m) to starboard. Open to N. Keep in mid-*cala*, landing slip at head of *cala*. Anchor 100m from head of *cala* in 2m, sand, and keep

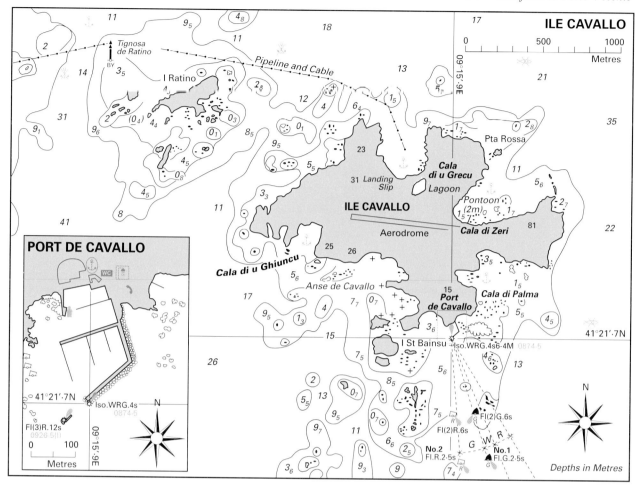

clear of pipeline and cable – see plan. There is a restaurant ashore which is famous for its prices!

4. ***Cala di u Ghiuncu*** Enter on a northeasterly course. Open S–SW. Several small sandy beaches. Anchor in 3m, sand.

⚓ Port de Cavallo

General

A relatively new, privately-owned yacht harbour built as part of a holiday complex on the south end of Cavallo. Visiting yachtsmen are not encouraged to make use of the facilities ashore here.

41°21'·8N 09°16'·0E
Depth 2–5m
Number of berths 230 berths with 37 for visitors
Maximum length 30m

Port radio

It is obligatory to call *capitaneria* on VHF Ch 9 or ☎ 95 70 10 09 before entering.

Lights

0874·5 Jetty head 41°21'·7N 9°15'·9E
Iso.WRG.4s7m6/4/4M 328°-G-337°-W-344°-R-353° White tower
0926·4(I) in same structure Fl(3)G.12s5m2M
0926·5(I) on left of entrance Fl(3)R.12s4m2M

Buoys

800m south of above lights there are **Boa 1** Fl.G.2·5s2M (stbd) and **Boa 2** Fl.R.2·5s2M (port)

250m south there are **Boa 3** Fl(2)G.6s2M (stbd) and **Boa 4** Fl(2)R.6s2M (port)

Warnings

Many rocks and shallow patches exist outside of the approach channel.

Approach

Pick up the outside pair of buoys and steer a course of 340° towards the jetty head. Note that although there are lights entrance is only allowed between 0600 and 2200 (June to September). On reaching the jetty turn to starboard and take up the berth that has already been allocated.

Formalities

Report to *capitaneria* when berthed.

Facilities

All in season – basic out of season.

Returning to the Corsican coast

Punta di u Capicciolu

A prominent point with high cliffs sloping up to a hill (105m). Just under a mile southwest of the point stands the Tour Sant'Amanza (127m). There are a few close inshore rocks to the south of the point otherwise it is steep-to.

⚓ Golfe de Sant'Amanza

A large deep gulf with yellow-white cliffs which offers excellent protection but is open to NE–E; it is very easy to enter and the channel is in the centre of the gulf with rocks extending from both shores. Attention must be paid to the many oyster beds which occupy an area 2,500m by 500m to the southwest of Punta di u Capicciolu. The best and most sheltered anchorage lies in the southern corner near the village of Gurgazo where there is a landing and where provisions may be obtained, there is also a road here. An alternative anchorage is at the head of the gulf, both anchorages are in 3m, sand and weed. Sailing clubs, houses, hotels and summer camps occupy much of the shore along the beach which has caught a lot of flotsam. The very beautiful Cala di Stentinu should be visited by dinghy while

craft with less than 1·3m draught can anchor inside. Another anchorage lies just south of Capu Biancu.

⚓ Anse de Balistra

An anchorage which is in the northwest corner of a bay, in front of a sandy beach behind which is a lagoon. Anchor in 3m, sand and weed, but the anchorage is subject to more swell than further up the gulf as it is open to NE–E–SE. Main road 1M inland.

Punta di Rondinara

A large round headland of reddish rock with a narrow isthmus connecting it to the Corsican shore. The top is scrub covered, there is a small islet on the point and an isolated rock 200m to S the southeast, the point has many close-in rocky dangers on its north side.

⚓ Golfe de Rondinara

An excellent anchorage in an almost landlocked sandy bay, there is an 0·8m shallow patch in the middle of the bay (occasionally buoyed). A white sandy beach lines the sides of the bay. Anchor in 3m, sand, to suit wind direction. The bay is open to NE–E–SE. The Club Nautique de Glenans has a base here. There is a track inland to the main road.

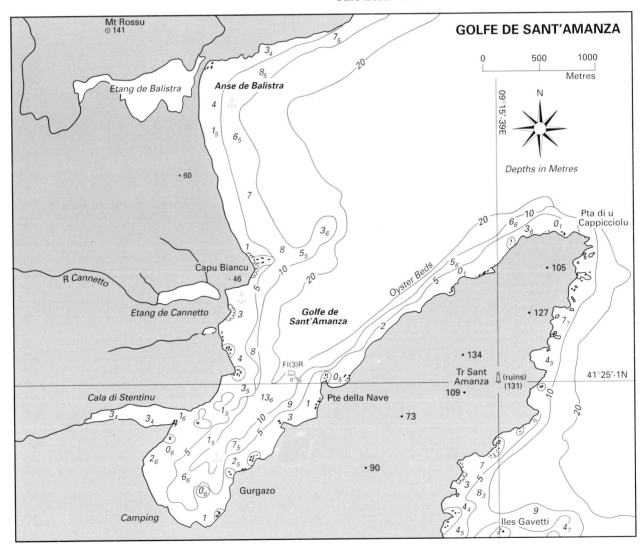

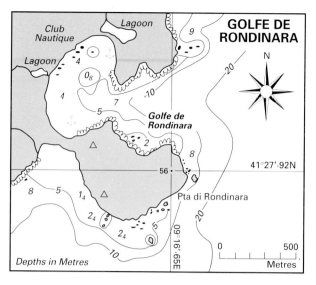

GOLFE DE RONDINARA

Pointe de Sponsaglia

A small hooked headland of whitish rocky cliffs with a conspicuous ruined tower on its summit. A small islet lies 50m east and an isolated rock lies 90m to the south of this point, otherwise steep-to, a track runs inland to the coast road.

⚓ Golfe de Porto Novo

A large deep bay with two areas for anchoring. Entrance is easy but note a 0·8m rocky shallow patch 150m north of the point on the south side of the gulf. Anchor in 3m, sand off the sandy beach at the western end of the bay, open to N–NE–E. Sand dunes and a lagoon lie behind the beach, track inland. The Bocca d'Alesia is a sub-bay on the southern side of Porto Novo with rocky sides and close inshore rocky dangers, it is shallow on the western side. Enter with care, anchor off sandy beach in 3m, sand, shell and weed, open to N–NE–E. Deserted.

⚓ Golfe de Santa Giulia

A large semi-landlocked bay surrounded by low scrub-covered hills. A white sandy beach runs around the shore with a river mouth in the southern corner. It is a beautiful setting but is always overcrowded in the season. There are a number of shallows and several groups of rocky islets

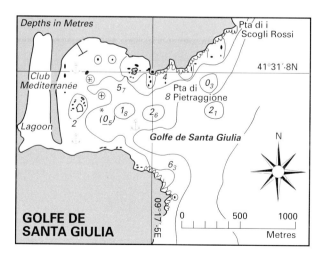

GOLFE DE SANTA GIULIA

surrounded by covered rocks. Enter with care using a bow lookout and continuous sounding. Anchor on north or south side of the bay in 3m, sand, open to NE–E–SE. There is a large Club Mediterranée base on the N side of the bay, also a jetty which is used by numerous ferries in high season. A road runs inland to the main road.

Ile du Toro

A 40m-high rock lying 4·5M off the coast surrounded by three rocks, islets and some awash and covered rocks. 0·5M to the east of the Ile du Toro lies a 2·6m shallow, the Haut-fond du Toro, which has a S cardinal light buoy, YB Q(6)+LFl.15s, on its south side.

⚓ Plage de Palombaggia

A long shallow bay with a popular sandy beach. The points at each end of the beach have off-lying rocks extending 200m. There are also a few rocks extending 250m from the centre of the bay. Anchor off beach at either end of the bay in 3m, sand, open to NE–E–SE–S–SW. Some houses ashore, also a road.

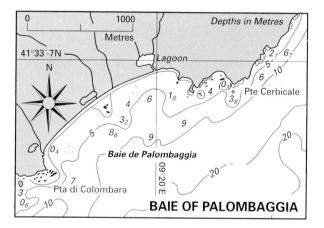

BAIE OF PALOMBAGGIA

Pointe Cerbicale

A headland which is not conspicuous unless coasting close in. It slopes up to a 145m hill which is scrub covered. There is a good view from here of the coast and islands. The coast is free from obstructions with the exception of a rocky projection to the southwest.

Iles Cerbicales

Four of these islands lie in a 2M long NE–SW line about 1M southeast of Pointe Cerbicale. The fifth island lies 0·5M further to the east. At the northeast end Ile Forana (34m) is sloping with one peak, Ile Maestro Maria (7m) is flat and has good beaches. Ile Piana is the largest with 34m and 31m peaks, Ile Pietricaggiosa (10m) at the south end. Rocher de la Vacca (21m) which is 0·5M to the east is high and pointed. The Danger de la Vacca with 4·0 and 4·5m shallows lies 1·5M to the east of Ile Piana and is marked by an E cardinal light buoy, BYB Q(3)10s. Passages are available between all the islands with

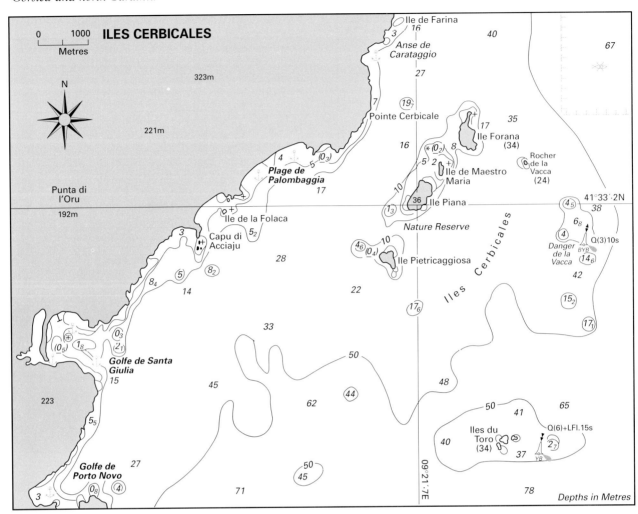

minimum depth of 9m except for the passage north of Ile Piana where there is a 1·4m submerged rock. There are several shallow patches and an isolated rock on the western side of the islands, which are best seen from the chart. The islands are a nature reserve and landing without permission is forbidden between 1 April and 31 August.

Rocher de la Vacca is sometimes used as a target for naval firing practise. Should this occur close the Corsican coast and keep within a 0·25M of it.

⚓ Anse de Carataggio

A small sandy bay with white sandy beach and rocky sides. Anchor in 3m sand and weed near the centre of the bay, open to NE–E–SE–S. Track to road inland, deserted.

Punta di a Chiappa

A major headland on the south side of the mouth of the Golfe de Porto Vecchio, steep whitish-grey rocky cliffs, scrub-covered top 44m high. A conspicuous lighthouse on the summit with white square tower, red lantern on white building (Fl(3+1)15s65m23M), also a red and white banded radio mast. A signal station stands 250m to the west of the light. The point is steep-to except for some rocky dangers which extend 100m to the south of the point.

Roches de Chiappino (and Tourelle)

300m to the north of Punta di a Chiappa lies this group of rocks which was marked with a BRB beacon tower, Tourelle Chiappino, until it was destroyed in 1989. It has not been rebuilt since and now only the old base is just visible in calm weather. The passage inshore of the beacon has a minimum depth of 11m but is not recommended in anything but calm weather.

3·8 – Porto Vecchio to Bastia

The sixty-five mile section of coast northwards from Porto Vecchio to Bastia covers the larger part of the east coast of Corsica and is in general quite different from the rest of the island's coasts.

The high ranges of hills and mountains draw further and further back from the coast as progress is made north and even the foothills cease near Solenzara where a flat sandy plain commences and continues as far as Bastia. From Campoloro northwards, the foothills are again in evidence but stand back from the coast.

As would be expected on a flat sandy coast good sheltered anchorages are not to be found.

From Porto Vecchio to Solenzara some 14M to the north there are six anchorages which are described, these are in various bays where the foothills come down to the coast. The remaining 41M has only the artificial harbour of Campoloro where yachts can seek shelter.

The coast is not deserted and there are many holiday houses. Inland, vast areas of fruit, cereal and vines are under cultivation. A main road parallels the coast at a varying distance usually about 2M. Between Porto Vecchio and the lighthouse at Alistru local magnetic deviations of the order of up to 5° may be encountered.

Porto Vecchio

General

A modern yacht harbour and a commercial harbour at the head of a large and beautiful gulf, easy to enter in most weather conditions and offering complete shelter in the harbour. Adequate facilities for yachtsmen and everyday requirements can be obtained from an attractive walled town close by. There are several very attractive anchorages around the gulf and many places including a river to explore. Yachts are not to enter the commercial harbour unless they are longer than 40m (the maximum size in the Port de Plaisance). This is a very popular harbour and during the season it becomes very overcrowded.

⚓ Port de Plaisance

⊕1 41°36'·40N 09°22'·50E (at gulf entrance)
⊕2 41°35'·50N 09°17'·00E (at entrance of Port de Plaisance)
Depth 1·3 to 3·5m in basin, 3·5m in entrance channel
Number of berths 540 berths with 150 for visitors
Maximum length 40m

Charts

Admiralty *1425, 1992*
French *6911, 6929*

Port radio

VHF Ch 9 or ☎ 04 95 70 17 93.

Weather forecast

Posted daily at *capitaneria*.

Lights

0866 Punta di a Chiappa 41°35'·7N 9°22'·0E
   Fl(3+1)15s65m23M 198°-vis-027° White square tower, red lantern, 21m
0866·4 Tourella Pecorella 41°36'·7N 9°22'·3E
   Fl(3)G.12s6M White tower green top 14m
0867 Punta San Ciprianu 41°37'·0N 9°21'·4E
   Fl.WG.4s26m11/8M 220°-W-281°-G-299°-W-072°-G-084°-obscd-220° White square tower black lantern 13m
0869 Punta di Pozzoli 41°36'·6N 9°17'·5E
   Oc(2)WRG.6s10m15-13M 258·7°-G-271·7°-W-275·2°-R-288·2°-obscd-258·7° White tower, black top 5m
0870 Commercial port 41°35'·2N 9°17'·5E
   Iso.WRG.4s9m11-9M 208·5°-G-223·5°-W-225·5°-R-240·5°-obscd-208·5° White framework tower, red top 12m
0870·6 Digue Est head Fl(2)R.6s5m6M 212°-vis-302° White tower, red top 4m
0870·8 Digue NE head Fl(2)G.4s4m5M 200°-vis-290° White tower, green top 2m
Beacons
0866·4 Tourella Pecorella 41°36'·7N 9°22'·3E (see above)

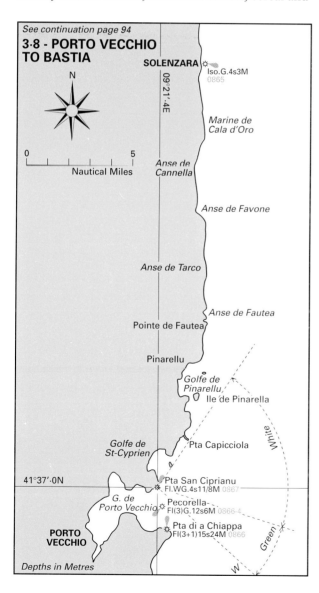

See continuation page 94

3·8 - PORTO VECCHIO TO BASTIA

N

0 — 5
Nautical Miles

SOLENZARA ☆
Iso.G.4s3M
0865

09°21'·4E

Marine de Cala d'Oro

Anse de Cannella

Anse de Favone

Anse de Tarco

Anse de Fautea

Pointe de Fautea

Pinarellu

Golfe de Pinarellu
Ile de Pinarella

Golfe de St-Cyprien
Pta Capicciola

White

41°37'·0N
Pta San Ciprianu
Fl.WG.4s11/8M 0867

G. de Porto Vecchio
Pecorella ☆
Fl(3)G.12s6M 0866·4

Pta di a Chiappa
Fl(3+1)15s24M 0866

PORTO VECCHIO

Green

W

Depths in Metres

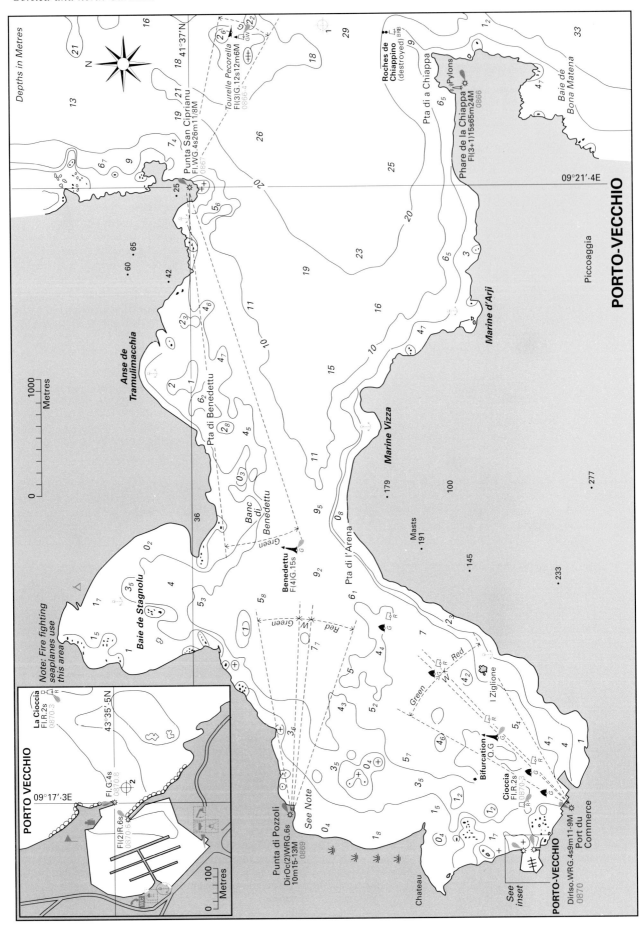

Depths in Metres

1000 Metres 0

N

16

21

13

6₇ 9

7₄ 19 21

7₄

18 41°37'N

Punta San Ciprianu
Fl.WG.4s26m11/8M
0867

Tourelle Pecorella
Fl(3)G.12s12m6M
0866.4
GW 2₂

2₆

2₂

1

29

18

26

20

25

23

19

25

20

6₅ 3

Roches de
Chiappino
(destroyed)

9

Pylons

Pta di a Chiappa

6₅

Phare de la Chiappa
Fl(3+1)15s65m24M
0866

1₂

33

Baie de
Bona Matena

4₇

4₇

09°21'·4E

PORTO-VECCHIO

Piccoaggia

25

•60 •65

•42

4₆

2₃

4₇

11

10

*Anse de
Tramulimacchia*

Pta di Benedettu

6₂

2₈

4₅

0₃

Banc
di
Benedettu

Marine d'Arji

10

16

4₇

15

11

9₅

0₈

Pta di l'Arena

6₁

Marine Vizza

•179

100

•277

Green

Benedettu
Fl(4)G.15s

9₂

5₈

Green
W
Red

1

7₇

5

4₄

5₂

4₃

2₃

7

G R

I Ziglione

G R
W
Red
4₂

Green

5₄

4₇ 4

1

1₂

Bifurcation
Q.G.

4₆

G G

G G

5₇

3₅

5₃

36

0₂

3₅

1₇

4

Baie de Stagnolu

1₅

1

*Note: Fire fighting
seaplanes use
this area*

3₆

See Note

3₅

0₄

0₄

1₈

3₅

1₅

Chateau

Punta di Pozzoli
DirOcl(2)WRG.6s
10m15-13M
0869

Masts
•191

•145

•233

Ciocca
Fl.R.2s
0870·2

CR

1₇

0₄

See
inset

PORTO-VECCHIO
DirIso.WRG.4s9m11-9M
0870

Port du
Commerce

Tourella Chiappino – destroyed 1989 – base still
   visible
0870·3 Écueil de la Cioccia 41°35'·4N 9°17'·5E
   Fl.R.2s3m2M red tower 5m
Buoys
0923·2(I) Haut-fond de Toro 41°30'·4N 9°23'·6E
   Q(6)+LFl.15s4m7M S card, YB
0871·5 Danger de la Vacca 41°32'·7N 9°24'·0E
   Q(3)W10s4m6M E card, BYB
0921·4(I) Benedettu 41°36'·6N 9°19'·1E
   Fl(4)G.15s4m4M G pillar buoy, triangular top off
   Punta di l'Arena where leading lines change
0922·2(I) Bifurcation 41°35'·6N 9°17'·9E Q.G.3m4M
   Green buoy, cone point upward top marking the
   stbd turn into the channel to the marina
Four G buoys, with cone topmarks and green reflecting
   strips, mark the stbd side of the main entrance
   channel
Four R buoys, with cylindrical topmarks and red
   reflecting strips, mark the port side of the channel

Warning

The shallow sandy area north of Pointe de l'Arena is
slowly extending. Do not attempt to cut this corner.
For a first visit follow the marked channels carefully,
do not attempt to follow local yachts which are
making use of large areas of deep water with
unmarked dangers.

Fire-fighting planes

Large flying boats may land in the Golfe de Porto
Vecchio to load water to fight fires.

Restricted areas

A nature reserve is established 2·5M to the east of
Punta di a Chiappa which is 3M long in a
north–south direction and 1M wide in an east–west
direction. Fishing, subaqua diving and anchoring in
the area is forbidden.

   The whole of the area around the Iles Cerbicales
including the outlying islets and shallows are also a
nature reserve and the same restrictions apply
between 1 April and 31 August and include landing
on any island or islet.

Approach

By day Take up a position near ⊕1 between the
Tourelle Pecorella, W tower, G top, and Roches de
Chiappino and set a westerly course down the
centre of the outer part of the Golfe de Porto
Vecchio to a point halfway between Punta di
l'Arena, a rounded rocky tree-covered promontory,
and Punta di Benedettu, a lower tree-covered
headland to the north. In this area Benedettu, G
pillar light buoy with up-pointed cone topmark
(Fl(4)G.15s) will be found. Now set a southwest
course between a series of G buoys with up-pointed
cones and R buoys with cylinder topmarks towards
a group of large metal sheds painted white at the
RoRo terminal. When the small conical tree-covered
Ilot Ziglione (13m) is abeam, a small G light buoy
(Q.G) will be seen ahead. Round this buoy to a
course of 254° leaving it to starboard. 0·75M ahead
will be seen a small red beacon tower, Fl.R.2s,
Écueil de la Cioccia. Leave this tower close to port

and the two light towers at the yacht harbour
entrance will be seen ahead.

By night Enter the outer part of the Golfe de Porto
Vecchio and make for a point near its centre. Course
should be set to avoid the dangers around the
beacon towers of Chiappino off Punta di a Chiappa
and Pecorella (Fl(3)G.12s) off the Punta San
Cipriano (Fl.WG.4s). The directional light Pozzoli
(DirOc(2)WRG.6s) will then be seen. Navigate into
the white sector and follow it on a 273° course until
the commercial harbour light (DirIso.WRG.4s) is
seen. When in the white sector of this light turn to
225° and follow it. After 1·25M a small buoy (Q.G)
must be rounded onto 254° course leaving it to
starboard. The course is now towards a Fl.R which
is left to port then towards a Fl(2)R.6s and Fl.G.4s
at the entrance to the yacht harbour.

Entrance

By day Approach the entrance on 254° from Écueil
de la Cioccia R beacon tower and round the head of
Digue Nord-Est at 15m to avoid shallows onto a
northwest course entering between the two digue
heads.

By night Approach Fl.G.4s on 254° and when close
divert to round it at 15m leaving Fl(2)R.6s to port
onto a northwest course.

Berths

Secure to head of Digue Nord-Est close to the
fuelling berth and report to the *bureau de port* on the
west side of the harbour for the allocation of a berth.
Then secure stern-to quay or pontoon with mooring
chain from the bow. This chain is attached to a line
which is connected to the pontoon or quay.

Formalities

All authorities available.

Facilities

All.

History

This ancient Genoese walled town with its small
fishing harbour below was probably built on the site
of a prehistoric settlement, because the area has
been in occupation since 3000 BC and the town is
located on the best natural defensive site. Porto
Vecchio means 'old port' in Italian.

   The town never expanded greatly due to the
unhealthy marshy salines at the mouth of the
Stabiacco river where malarial mosquitoes used to
breed.

   The Golfe de Porto Vecchio has been praised
since Roman times, Diodorus Siculus called it a
most beautiful port and even Boswell said that it
may vie with the most distinguished harbours in
Europe. In recent times due to the extermination of
the mosquito and to the tourist trade the area is
expanding and becoming more prosperous.

Anchorages in the Gulf

There are numerous anchorages around the Gulf,
details of some are given below.

Marine d'Arji A small sandy bay open to N–NE–N with an anchorage 200m off the beach in 3m, sand. A few houses, a large salt pan and the road behind the beach. There is an uncompleted harbour for dinghies and small fishing boats on the west side of the bay.

Marine Vizza A deserted anchorage 150m off the small beach in 3m, sand, open to the NW–N–NE but otherwise well protected.

Ilot Ziglione Anchorage between the island and the coast in 3m, sand, well protected but open to N. There are some private moorings in the area, a landing stage and houses on the shore. Sound carefully.

Baie de Stagnolu Anchor in 3m, sand, off the east side of the bay, well protected but strong winds from SW send in short waves. There is a Touring Club de France base here and summer camps.

Anse de Tramulimacchia A shallow bay open to SE–S–SW. Anchor 100m off the beach at the north side of the bay in 3m, sand. Due to shallows, approach this anchorage on a NW course sounding carefully.

Bay to W of Punta San Ciprianu A very small bay open to S–SW. Anchor near the moorings sounding carefully at the head of the bay. Houses around the bay. Many rocks in the southeast corner.

Roches de Pecorella and beacon

Near the centre of the mouth of the Golfe de Porto Vecchio lies a shallow area 500m long by 200m wide with awash and covered rocks 2·0 to 2·6m deep. A tower, Tourelle de Pecorella, stands near the middle of the dangers, it is a masonry beacon G over W. There are four wrecks on the west and north sides of the beacon.

⚓ Baie de San Ciprianu

A superb sandy bay which is being spoilt by developments around the shores. Enter on a

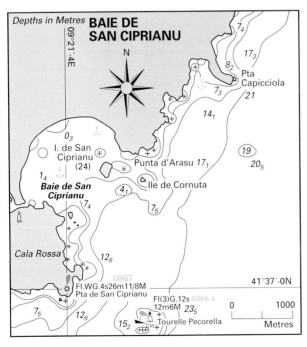

northwesterly course and anchor off the beach NNW of the island. Take care to avoid an isolated rock 200m NNW of the island.

Punta d'Arasu

A rounded headland at the north side of the entrance to the Golfe de Porto Vecchio. Two islets of red rock, Ile de Cornuta (11m) 500m south of the point and Ile de San CipriAnu (23m) 400m southwest. These islands have foul ground extending 150m north. A passage 4m minimum depth equidistant exists between the islands and the point but care is needed to avoid a lone awash rock in the passage lying north of Ile de San CipriAnu.

⚓ Punta Capicciola W

A pleasant deserted anchorage behind the Punta Capicciola, rocky cliff sides to high scrub-covered hills. Small sandy bay with rocks at northeast end at head of bay, anchor in 3m, sand and weed, off this beach, open to E–SE–S.

Punta Capicciola

A 46m hill which slopes to the coast where a reddish tongue of rock 30m high projects 500m. One small rock stands close to the point.

Ile de Pinarellu

A very conspicuous and prominent rocky-cliffed island 500m by 400m and 51m high, lying off the southern point of the Golfe de Pinarellu. A small detached islet on its north side and a group of rocks extending 100m south from its south side. A conspicuous square tower stands on the scrub-covered top.

⚓ Golfe de Pinarellu

A large gulf with a white sandy beach 1·5M long at its head. Ilot Roscana, a bare reddish rocky islet 20m high is located near the centre of the entrance to the gulf, at certain angles and light this island looks like a face with long hair. Rocky dangers extend 100m to east and west of this islet. The whole of the northwestern side of the bay has rocky dangers which extend up to 500m from the shore but with a good lookout these rocks can be seen in the clear waters making careful navigation in the area possible. Anchor in 3–5m, sand with some weed, off the sandy beach, open to NE–E–SE–S. Near the centre of the head of the bay are large red apartment blocks and many houses, there are more to the north side of the bay. There is a launching slip to the south of the red apartment buildings. There is a mechanic at Lecci 3M inland.

⚓ Pointe de Fautéa SW

A small anchorage just behind the Pointe de Fautea on the western side with a sandy beach at its head. Anchor off the beach in 2·50m on sand and weed, open to E–SE–S.

Ile et Pointe de Fautéa

A small roundish rocky scrub-covered promontory sloping uphill to 79m with a conspicuous round

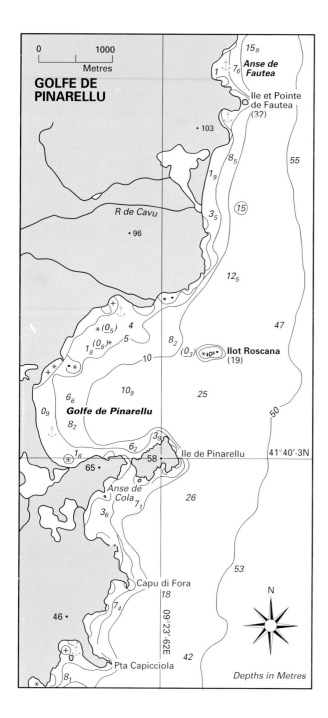

GOLFE DE PINARELLU

Depths in Metres

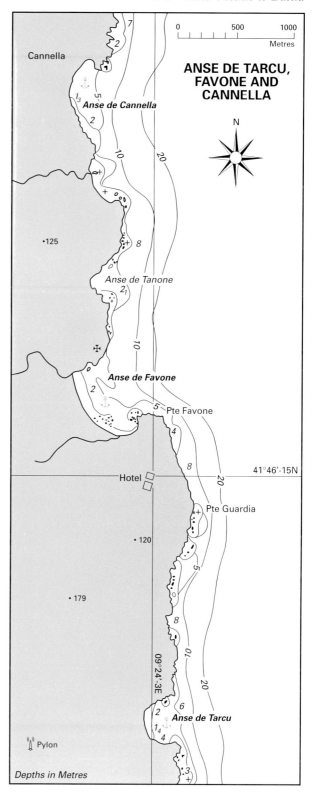

ANSE DE TARCU, FAVONE AND CANNELLA

Depths in Metres

tower on its point. The coast road runs behind this feature. Off the point and almost joined to it is a small pyramid-shaped islet the Ile de Fautea 32m high.

⚓ Anse de Fautéa

An open bay between rocky cliffs with a white sandy beach at its head behind which runs the coast road, a conspicuous road bridge with three round tunnels lies at the northern end of the beach, a housing estate is on the west side of the bay. Anchor off the beach in 3m, sand, open to NE–E–SE.

⚓ Anse de Tarcu

A small bay with sandy beach at its head and landing slip protected by a small breakwater. The coast road runs behind the beach where there is a large apartment block and a group of houses at each end of the beach, a housing estate is up the river valley further inland. There is a high road bridge over the river at the southern end of the beach which has three arches. Anchor off the beach in 3m, sand, open to NE–E–SE. The PTT and TV towers 1M inland to the south are conspicuous.

⚓ Anse de Favone

A bay with a 800m long sand beach at its head and the coast road running behind it. There are many houses scattered around the area. Beach restaurants/cafés, an hotel and some shops. Anchor in the southern part of bay in 3m, sand, off the beach, open to N–NE–E.

⚓ Anse de Cannella

A small bay with stony beach and reddish cliffs and coast road running behind, two houses and beach café. Anchor in 3m, sand in the north corner, open to NE–E–SE.

⚓ Marine de Cala d'Oru

A very small bay with a white stony beach and coast road behind. There is a house on the southern side of the bay and a housing development behind. The bridge over a river is conspicuous. Anchor in 3m, sand and weed. Open to NE–E–SE.

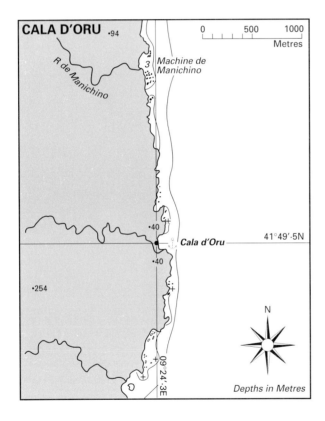

⚓ Port de Solenzara

General

A superb little yacht harbour situated just south of the Solenzara river mouth close to the pleasant village of Solenzara. The village and surroundings (and the harbour) tend to become very crowded in season.

⊕ 41°51'·3N 09°24'·2E

Depth 2–4m
Number of berths 450 berths with 150 for visitors
Maximum length 30m

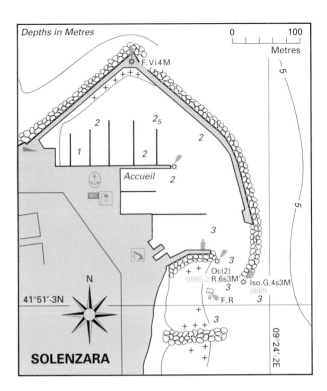

Charts

Admiralty *1999*
French *6855*

Port radio

VHF Ch 0 or ☎ 04 95 57 46 42.

Weather forecast

Posted twice-daily at *capitaneria*.

Lights

0865 Jetée Est head 41°51'·4N 9°24'·3E Iso.G.4s3M
0865·2 Quai d'Armement Oc(2)R.6s3M
Quai Nord head F.Vi.4M at entrance to river
To the north
0917(I) Oléoduc 41°55'·2N 9°25'·6E Q(3)10s4m6M E card BYB buoy marking the inshore fuelling berth

Warnings

It is recommended that craft proceeding north from Solenzara should keep at least 1M from the coast to avoid military areas, bombing ranges and shallow sandy patches. Certainly off Foce de Tavignano the depths are much less than those given on even modern charts.

Note Access to the harbour is only permitted between 0700 and 2100 in summer and 0800–1800 in winter.

Approach

By day From the south and the wide and deep Golfe de Porto Vecchio, the coast has two large gulfs, those of San Ciprianu and Pinarellu, and a number of smaller bays. The conspicuous tower on the Ile and Pointe de Fautea and the wide Anse de Favone which has some houses around the bay can be recognised. In the closer approach the large blocks of flats located just inland of the harbour will be seen.

The coast from Campoloro, some 31 miles to the north, has few easily identifiable features. The lighthouse Alistru on a hill inland is one. A very tall water tower some 2M inland from the mouth of the Tavignano river and the airfield at Solenzara with its off lying buoys may also be recognised. In the closer approach the houses and blocks of flats at Solenzara will be seen. Keep at least 500m from the coast near the airfield, it is foul with rocks inshore.

By night The lights of the harbour are not bright and a night approach is not permitted (see warnings above).

Entrance

Approach the east jetty head on a westerly course and follow it round 20m off to a NNE course and enter the harbour. Keep close to the starboard side of the entrance channel as there is a shallow patch half way between the two eastern breakwaters which may be marked with a buoy. The entrance is dangerous in strong SE winds and should be avoided if at all possible.

Berths

Secure to the pontoon 'I' near the *capitaneria* in the south basin and await berthing instructions or obtain them from the bureau.

Formalities

Just the bureau staff; customs and other authorities are in Porto Vecchio.

Facilities

All.

Aérodrome de Solenzara

A military airfield located 4M to the north of Solenzara. A forbidden area runs for 2M to the north of the river and extends 500m from the coast. This area is shallow and has many dangerous covered rocks, give it a wide berth. There is a line of trees between the runways and the coast and only a radio beacon tower, the control tower, some hangars and a water tower can be seen from the sea.

Offshore fuel terminal Solenzara

This terminal is located 700m from the shore near the centre of the runways. There may be a number of buoys inshore but on the seaward side is a E cardinal light buoy, Oléoduc, Q(3)10s6M. Keep well clear and to seaward of this area.

Foce di u Fium Orbu (Calzarello)

This river mouth has a conspicuous white house with a tower, Tour de Calzarello just to the south. 0·5M further south is a conspicuous wreck – it is forbidden to approach within 200m of this wreck. Just over 1M to the north of the mouth of the river a 0·5m submerged rock lies 200m from the shore.

Foce de Tavignano Fleuve

Dark green trees mark the south side of the entrance and a group of huts the north. It is a large river with a complex sand bar across its mouth. Shallows extend well offshore and there is an extensive area of

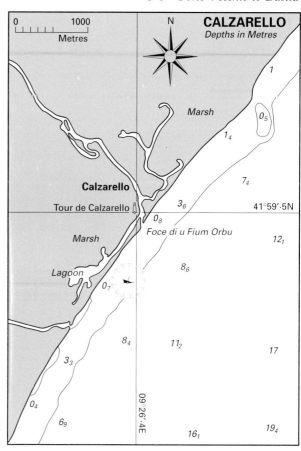

3 by 9 miles off the coast to the north where bombing practice takes place. See plan on page 94.

Phare d'Alistru

An important light situated 0·75M inland on a hillock, it has a grey 8-sided tower black lantern and red house and is surrounded by dark green trees and other houses (42°15'·6N 9°32'·5E Fl(2)10s 93m22M).

⚓ Port de Taverna

General

This modern yacht harbour has been built on the coast some distance from any town or village. Approach and entrance are easy but would become difficult and dangerous with heavy swell and strong winds from NE or E. The immediate area around the harbour is flat and rather dull but the hinterland is attractive with mountains, old villages and forests.

42°20'·50N 09°32'·5E
Depth 1–3·5m
Number of berths 460 with 100 for visitors
Maximum length 25m

Charts

Admiralty *1999*
French *6823, 6713*

Port radio

VHF Ch 9 (24 hrs) or ☎ 04 95 38 07 61 (0600–2100 summer 0800–1800 otherwise).

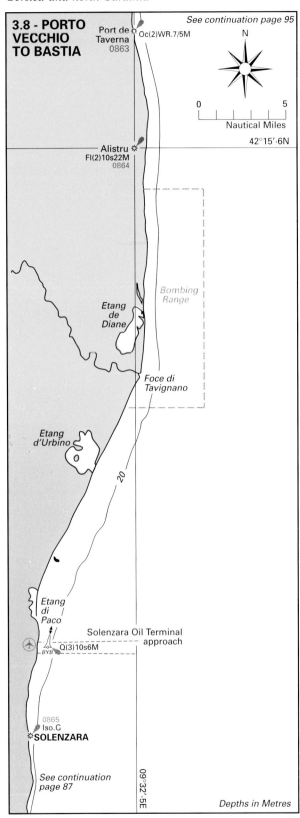

3.8 - PORTO VECCHIO TO BASTIA

Port de Taverna ☼ Oc(2)WR.7/5M
0863

See continuation page 95

N

0   5
Nautical Miles

42°15'·6N

Alistru ☼
Fl(2)10s22M
0864

Bombing Range

Etang de Diane

Foce di Tavignano

Etang d'Urbino

20

Etang di Paco

Solenzara Oil Terminal approach
Q(3)10s6M
BYB

0865
Iso.G
☼SOLENZARA

See continuation page 87

09°32'·5E

Depths in Metres

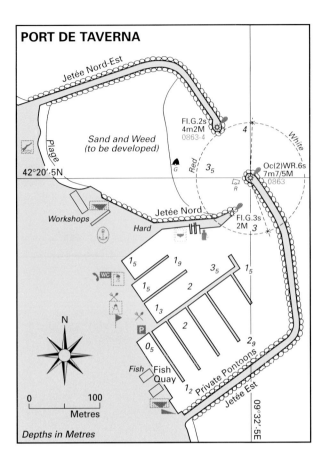

PORT DE TAVERNA

Jetée Nord-Est

Sand and Weed (to be developed)

Fl.G.2s 4m2M
0863·4

4   White

42°20'·5N

Plage

G   Red   3₅

Oc(2)WR.6s 7m7/5M
0863
R

Workshops

Jetée Nord

Hard

Fl.G.3s 2M   3

1₅   1₉   3₅   1₅

WC   1₅   2

1₃   2   2₉

N

P   0₅   2

Fish Fish Quay   1₂   Private Pontoons   Jetée Est

0   100
Metres

09°32'·5E

Depths in Metres

0863·4 Jetée Nord-est head Fl.G.2s4m2M

Warnings

Due to silting the depths may not be as shown on the charts, especially in the avant port. The entrance can be dangerous in strong NE or E winds. No anchoring is allowed in the harbour.

Approach

By day From the south the lighthouse on a small hill inland at Alistru and the town of Cervione on a mountain spur are conspicuous some 5 miles from Taverna. The harbour itself is not conspicuous and will not be seen until close-in, but the workshop is conspicuous as are the masts of the yachts already there.

From the north there is a large white domed building (Aero RC Poretta) with some other buildings 6 miles to the north of Taverna. The harbour itself is difficult to see from a distance but the workshop and masts are conspicuous.

By night The light at Alistru Fl(2)10s93m22M is a guide but the east jetty light should be positively identified before approaching the coast to closely.

Entrance

Approach the head of the east jetty and leave it 20m to port coming round to a course of south leaving the north mole to starboard.

Berths

Secure to the reception berth immediately ahead on entry and report to the bureau for berthing

Weather forecast

Posted twice a day on *capitaneria*.

Lights

0863 Jetée Est head 42°20'·5N 9°32'·5E
Oc(2)WR.6s7m7/5M 184°-W-342°-R-184° White column, red top 5m

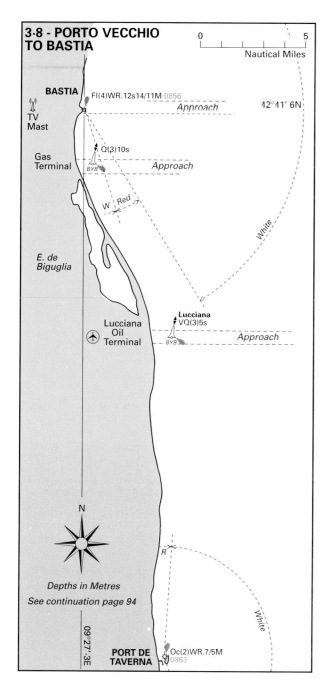

3·8 - PORTO VECCHIO TO BASTIA

0 — 5 Nautical Miles

BASTIA
TV Mast
Fl(4)WR.12s14/11M 0856
Approach
42°41′ 6N
Gas Terminal
Q(3)10s
BYB
Approach
W Red
White
E. de Biguglia
Lucciana VQ(3)5s
BYB
Approach
Lucciana Oil Terminal
N
Depths in Metres
See continuation page 94
09°27′·3E
PORT DE TAVERNA
Oc(2)WR.7/5M 0863
R
White

Lucciana Offshore Fuel Terminal – Aérodrome de Bastia-Poretta

A number of buoys moored off the coast and an E cardinal light buoy, Q(3)5s is moored further offshore. Keep well to seaward of this area.

Offshore Fuel Terminal – Bastia

A fuel terminal lies 500m offshore and 2M south of Bastia. There are a number of buoys close inshore and an E cardinal light buoy, BYB, Q(3)10s, is moored on the seaward side. Note that underwater cables come ashore 600m north of this terminal where there are four yellow beacons. Anchoring is prohibited in the area.

⚓ Anse de Porto Vecchio

An anchorage in a small bay with a popular beach of sand and stone. Behind the beach are roads and the buildings of Bastia, anchor in 2·5m sand and mud, open to NE–S–SE–S. A deeper open anchorage is 400m southeast in 20m, sand and mud. For facilities see Port de Bastia (page 19).

instructions. Berth as instructed with stern to the pontoon with mooring chain forward secured to pontoon by a light chain/rope.

Formalities

All authorities available.

Facilities

All.

Résidence des Iles, Dome and Aero RC beacon

A group of apartment blocks and very distinctive and conspicuous dome with an Aero RC Beacon No. 1069 Bastia. BP (·—···/·——·) 369kHz located here. In summer a T-shaped floating pontoon is installed in front of the buildings.

4. North Sardinia

General description

Sardinia is the second largest island in the Mediterranean after Sicily. It is 260km long and 135km wide with an area of 24,093sq km. It has a coastline of 1,850km (which is almost exactly 1,000 nautical miles) long. It lies 110 miles from the Italian mainland, 7 miles from Corsica, 120 miles from Africa and 200 from the Balearic Islands. It is a mountainous island with the main range running down the east coast with the highest peak, Punta La Marmora, reaching 1,834m (6,000ft). There is another range in the southwest corner, around the mining area of Iglesias, with the high point of 1,236m (4,050ft) of Monte Linas. It has a population of around one and a half million but as it is quite barren for much of its area, the population is concentrated around the main towns. The mountains are covered with small bushes – *macchia* in Italian or *maquis* in French – which give out a scent in the spring which once experienced is never forgotten and is unmistakably the perfume of the islands.

History

As can be imagined the early history of Sardinia is closely linked to that of Corsica. Around 2000 BC groups of settlers arrived and possibly developed into the Nuraghi Civilisation who built large stone block domed towers, called *nuraghe* similar to the towers on Corsica and the *talayots* of the Balearics. They also buried their dead in caves and tombs called 'tombs of the giants'. Then the Phoenicians occupied various parts of the island – remains can still be seen on the islands of San Pietro and Sant'Antioco off the southwest corner. The Romans arrived in 236 BC and Sardinia was a Roman province with various civil, Greek and Etruscan wars until final capitulation about 46 BC when Caesar made Cagliari a Municipality. Roman domination now lasted for 400 years with much building going on. Cagliari, Nora and Tharros were large Roman towns with temples, spas, hot and cold water systems etc. Over the centuries there has been a rise in sea level and areas of Tharros and Nora can be seen on calm days under the sea.

From about AD 500 to 1000 the island was ravaged by the Vandals, Ostrogoths, Byzantines and finally the Saracens. In 1077 the Pope assigned Sardinia (along with Corsica) to the Pisans which was disputed by the Genovese. Then another Pope gave it to the Aragons who finally put in a king around AD 1430 and Spain ruled it for some years – still with local unrest from the natives.

In 1708 Cagliari surrendered to a British fleet under Admiral Lake and Sardinia was ceded to Austria and the Dukes of Savoy and it has remained Italian ever since, the language was changed from Spanish to Tuscan in 1764 for example. However Sardinia remained a largely forgotten part of Italy. It is interesting to note that Nelson wanted to take the island for England (rather than Malta) and used many of its anchorages on its northeast coast during the blockade of the French in the early eighteen hundreds.

During the 20 years of Fascist Government great works were completed on the island, draining of swamps, new roads, assistance with mining. It was important as an airfield during the Second World War and several towns were severely damaged by bombs of both sides. The island was granted political autonomy in 1948.

Data and warnings

From Asinara Island on the northwestern corner to Punta Coda Cavallo on the east coast there are numerous islands and each of these is bordered by even more numerous rocks and shoals. Some of these are marked with posts or buoys but the majority are not. It is not recommended to sail close inshore at night, if you must sail at night and miss the glorious scenery keep well offshore and keep a prudent eye out for isolated rocks and islands.

Bonifacio Straits are well known for their strong west (and east) winds. Winds, mainly the *maestrale*, can be quite strong, force 6 or 7 even in summer, and blow for several days at a time.

Prohibited areas

1. Navigation, anchoring, fishing and landing are prohibited in the areas surrounding Isola Asinara (41°N, 8°16'E) except for vessels in difficulties. (It used to be a penal colony but is now a nature reserve with the same prohibitions about landing etc. as before). Navigation is permitted through the Fornelli passage in daylight, as is landing on Isola Piana.
2. It is prohibited to navigate or berth at the Italian Naval Base east of Cala Gavetta on La Maddalena.
3. It is prohibited to enter the NATO Naval Base on the NE corner of Santo Stefano Island.

4. The whole of the NE part of Tavolara Island is a military area and anchoring is prohibited.

As well as these the Italians are establishing nature reserves on some of the small islands and more interesting coastal areas, like around the Maddalena archipelago for example. No anchoring, fishing or diving is allowed but it is very difficult to enforce these rules. UK yachtsmen should note any local areas and abide by the 'request' to maintain the reserve.

Major lights

The original idea behind the light ranges in these waters was to ensure one could always see a light when cruising along the coast. In areas like La Maddalena there is a plethora of lights which can confuse the unwary (especially with the flashing neon signs of new developments and the general street and car lights that abound). In other, more remote, areas there are hardly any lights to be seen at all. It is interesting to note that the ranges quoted in the list below are from up-to-date documents and they have not changed for many years. It is also a known fact that the intensities of virtually all lights have been markedly reduced over the past 10-year period. It is the compiler's experience that these ranges are only achieved in excellent visibility and then with binoculars trained on the bearing. At times only half these ranges are achieved so be advised not to panic when a light does not show up – keep going and it will hopefully appear in adequate time.

1124 Capo Caccia 40°33'·6N 8°09'·8E Fl.5s186m24M White tower on 3-storied building 24m

1130 Punta dello Scorno (Asinara) 41°07'·1N 8°19'·1E Fl(4)20s80m16M White tower on 3-storied building 35m

1138 Porto Torres 40°50'·1N 8°23'·8E LFl(2)10s45m16M White tower on 2-storied building 20m

0938 Capo Testa 41°14'·6N 9°08'·7E Fl(3)12s67m17M 017°-vis-256° White tower on 2-storied building 23m

0940 Isola Razzoli 41°18'·4N 9°20'·4E Fl.WR.2·5s77m19/15M 022°-W-092°-R-137°-W-237°-R-320° Stone tower 12m

0942 Isola S Maria 41°17'·9N 9°23'·1E Fl(4)20s17m10M 173°-vis-016° White 2-storied building 12m

0950 Punta Sardegna 41°12'·45N 9°21'·8E Fl.5s35m11M White 2-storied building 13m

0992 Capo d'Orso 41°10'·6N 9°25'·4E Fl.3s12m 10M White tower 10m

0998 Isolotti Monaci 41°12'·9N 9°31'·0E Fl.WR.5s24m11/8M 246°-R-268°-W-317°-R-357°-W-246° White tower

1002 Capo Ferro 41°09'·3N 9°31'·4E Fl(3)15s52m24M White tower on 2-storied building 18m

1014 Isola della Bocca (Olbia) 40°55'·2N 9°34'·0E LFl.5s24m 15M 180°vis-264° White tower on 2-storied building, 22m

1028 Punta Timone (Tavolara) 40°55'·6N 9°44'·0E LFl(2)10s72m15M White octagonal tower 7m

1030 Capo Comino 40°31'·7N 9°49'·7E Fl.5s26m15M White tower on building 7m

4·1 – Alghero to Porto Torres

From the safety of Alghero's superb harbour the coast runs west to Capo Caccia and then the coast, going north to Asinara Island, has high cliffs with virtually no harbours and certainly no safe refuges from the prevailing westerlies. From Asinara east to Capo Testa, south of Bonifacio, the land is mainly low-lying and again there are only few natural harbours but both Stintino and Castelsardo have excellent shelter in almost any weather.

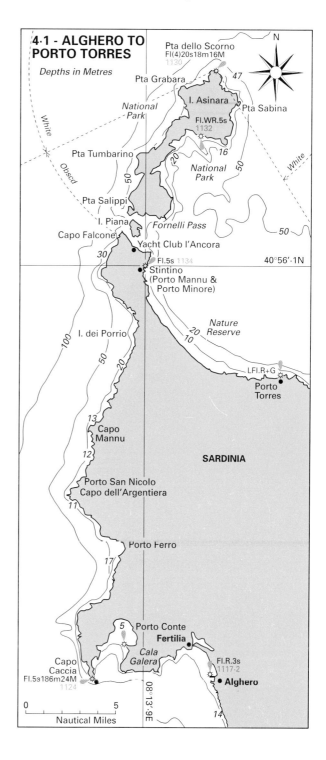

⚓ Alghero

General

Alghero was a delightful old walled Catalan city with Spanish (and Gothic) style buildings and street names set amid groves of olive, eucalyptus and parasol pine trees but is now becoming more and more a tourist resort with hotels taking the place of the trees. However it is well worth a visit and the harbour authorities are making great efforts to attract the charter fleets down from Corsica by putting in a lot more pontoons in the harbour during the summer season.

40°33'·8N 08°18'·5E

Depth 0·5–3·5m
Number of berths In excess of 1000

Charts

Admiralty *1985, 1202*
Italian *48, 292, 911/05*

Port communications

VHF Ch 16 or 11 from 0700–1900. ☎ 98 68 11 079.

Lights

1124 Capo Caccia 40°33'·6N 8°09'·8E Fl.5s186m24M
    White tower on 3 storied building 24m

1122 Isolotto della Maddalena 40°34'·3N 8°18'·9E
    Fl.R.5s10m4M White tower, red bands 6m
1117 Molo Sud head 40°33'·9N 8°18'·4E
    Fl.G.3s10m8M Green column 6m
1117·2 Molo Sottoflutto head Fl.R.3s10m8M Red
    column 6m
1119·2 Secca delle Murge Fl.G.4s6m5M Green pylon
    4m
1119 Molo Nord head 2F.R(vert)7m3M Red post 6m
1118 Banchina Sanità 2F.G(vert)7m3M Green post
    6m
1117·3 Molo Sottoflutto spur head 2F.R(vert)6m2M
    Red post 5m
1119·4 New basin left hand entrance F.R.5m4M Red
    post 4m
1119·5 Molo Furesi (right hand ent) F.G.5m5M
    Green post 4m

Warnings

Secca delle Murge is the only danger in the harbour and has a green pylon on it with a Fl.G.4s5M light.

Approach

Both day and night approaches are straightforward as all major construction work has now been completed but pontoons are still being installed in various parts of the harbour.

By day The suburbs of large hotels and villas to the south of Alghero and the Isolotto della Maddalena

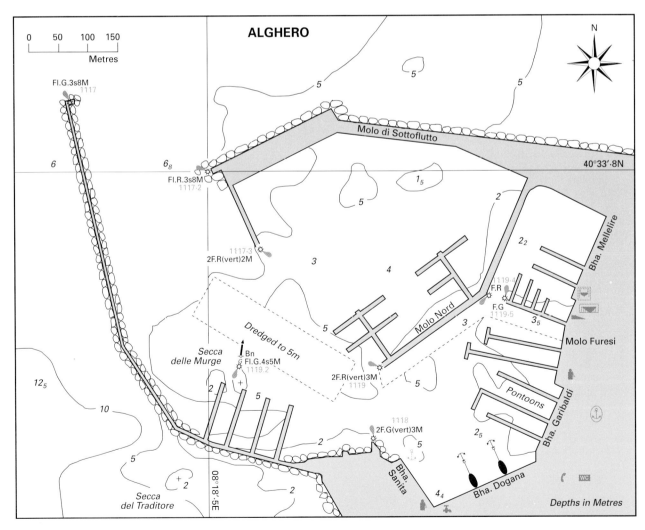

to the north are conspicuous as the harbour entrance is approached. There are no particular dangers and when the southern breakwater is identified make for the outer end.

By night Use the light on Isolotto delle Maddalena to approach on a northeasterly heading until the light on the southern breakwater is picked up.

Entrance

This is quite simple but note the course to enter between the breakwaters is a southerly one.

Berths

There are now six or seven mooring areas for pleasure craft with over 1,000 berths and it is probably sensible to call the *capitaneria* before entering to enquire where there are places rather than do a tour of the harbour searching for a berth.

Formalities

All authorities available.

Facilities

All.

⚓ Fertilia

40°35'·6N 08°17'·4E

This small harbour lies at the very north of the Alghero bay on the exit canal from the Stagno di Calich. The village, to the left of the harbour, has a conspicuous steeple and there is a large off-white low building to the right of the harbour. The harbour consists of a long breakwater running east-west, which is rounded on the port hand to enter on a westerly course. The quay to the east is reserved for the private company moorings but space may be available there for visiting yachts (no VHF but ☎ 079 93 00 88). Pleasure craft can also moor to the pontoons on the western side or to the inside of the southern mole in depths of 0·5 to 3m. The moles are lit with F.R and F.G lights. There are about 150 berths (90 on the east side) but few facilities. The village close by can supply food and fuel, however.

⚓ Cala Galera

On the west side of the Alghero Bay is Capo Galera. About half a mile north of the point is another small headland with Tour Galera on it. In strong westerlies good shelter can be found in the bay just to the north of the tower where you can anchor quite close to the shore, in 5m, in sand and weed. Do not go too far north as rocks protrude from the headland at the north end of the little bay.

⚓ Base Nautica Porto Conte

40°35'·7N 08°12'·8E

Just to the east of Capo Caccia lies the large bay of Porto Conte with a headland half way up on the eastern shore with Tour Nuova on it. It is lit Fl.3s10M and about half a mile to the east of the point lies the yacht harbour. This is a private marina

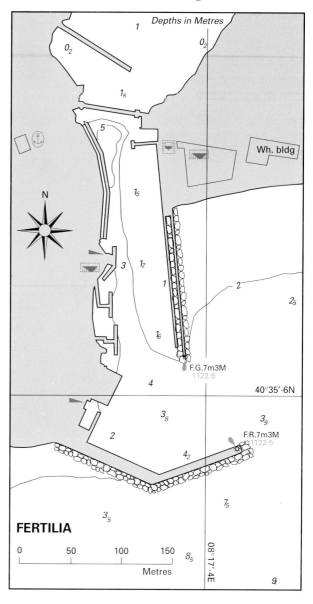

FERTILIA

with a long concrete jetty with pontoons attached. The ends of the jetty are lit with F.G and F.R and the harbour is approached along a dredged channel (to 4m). The depth at the pontoons is 0·5 to 4m and VHF Ch 9 (or ☎ 079 94 20 13) contacts the authorities. Care must be exercised on the approach as it is very shallow outside of the dredged channel. This is a very sheltered harbour with only very strong *maestrale* setting up a chop in the mooring area. All normal facilities are available here.

⚓ Cala Tramariglio

On the western side of the bay, opposite Tour Nuova, there is a small bay with a private jetty which can be used for mooring by small yachts in depths of 0·2 to 2m. You can also anchor off in 3 to 4m in sand and weed.

⚓ Cala del Bollo

In this bay just south of Tramariglio there is a large

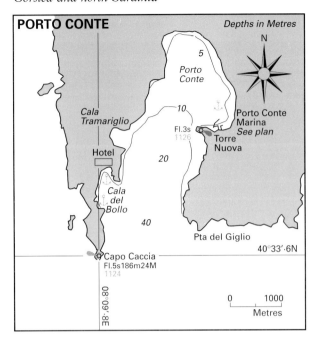

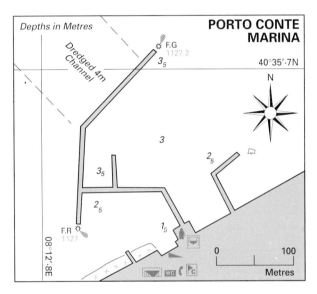

hotel complex at the north end where you can anchor off in 3 to 6m in sand and weed. From the south end of this *cala* it is an easy walk to the famous Grotto di Nettuno (Neptune's Cave) down the 760-odd steps of the L'Escala del Cabirol.

Capo Caccia

Capo Caccia is a very conspicuous headland with its 150m-high chalk cliffs dropping straight into the sea. There are no off-lying dangers and the 2 small islets of Piana and Foradada just north of the point can be passed inside in settled weather without any concern. There is a lighthouse on the point (Fl.5s186m24M) and numbers of caves of which the Grotto di Nettuno is the most famous.

From Capo Caccia to Capo Falcone there are 23 miles of high rocky cliffs with virtually no beaches. The prevailing westerly winds drive big seas against this forbidding coastline with very confused

reflections and it is well to seek calmer waters further north or south. However in calm weather there are two possible anchorages.

⚓ Porto Ferro

Some 8 miles north of Capo Caccia is a small bay with a beach with Tour Negra at the north end and Tour Rossa at the south. Anchor off in 4 to 6m in sand with excellent holding. Note that it is totally exposed to the prevailing winds and you should not stay overnight unless convinced of a stable weather pattern.

⚓ Porto San Nicolo

Five miles north, round Capo Argentiera, there is a small anchorage with a 20m jetty with depths of 4m along it. You can moor here free of charge or anchor in the middle of the bay in 10–12m. Again this must only be contemplated in settled weather.

Capo Falcone

This is another impressive headland with 100m high cliffs on the west side but sloping more gently down on the east side. There is a conspicuous tower on a high point (189m) one mile south of the point.

Fornelli passage

North of Capo Falcone lies Isola Asinara, a 9 mile long fairly hilly island which was, until recently, an Italian penal colony. It is now a large nature reserve and, note, it is still totally prohibited to land or anchor near the island. There is a shallow passage, the Fornelli Passage, between the island and Capo Falcone which saves about 25 miles of sailing around Asinara. The Pelosa Passage between Isola Piana and Capo Falcone should not be used. It has a minimum depth of less than 2m and if there is any swell, which there usually is, the depth is correspondingly less.

By day To use the Fornelli passage from the south or west identify the conspicuous tower 1 mile south of Capo Falcone itself at the top of a hill of 183m high and take up a position about half a mile NNW of the cape. Steam towards the north end of Isola Piana or the tower on its north shore until the leading marks are identified. These are on the south shore of Asinara and are white masonry towers with a black line. The leading line is 072° and should be kept until just past a small islet (Is Bocca) to port when two further masonry beacons will be seen on the port beam/quarter. When these come into line alter course to 121° and steam out keeping them in line. The shallow 3m patch is just off the Isolotto Bocca. For the passage west simply reverse the above i.e. steer 301° until the eastern leading markers come into line astern and then alter course to 252°.

By night Some two years ago 2 sectored lights were placed at the front marker of each leading line which enables craft to proceed through the passage at night (previously it was a daylight only passage (but see warning note below)). These lights are:

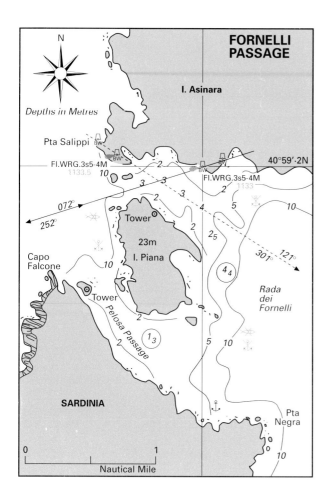

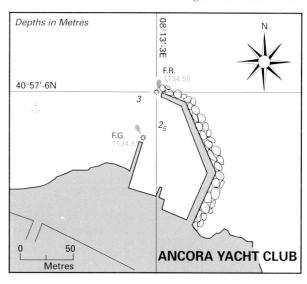

1133 Ldg line 072° Fl.WRG.3s6m6-4M 065·2°-G-
068·2°-W-076·2°-R-079·2°

1133·5 Ldg line 301° Fl.WRG.3s6m5-4M 293·3°-G-
297°-W-305°-R-308·7°

Thus it is merely a matter of steaming to a position
where one is in the white sector of one light and
following the course towards the light, keeping in
the white sector until one steams into the white
sector of the other light and altering course as
appropriate.

Warning note After strong winds have been
blowing in one direction for some days there may be
up to a 2-knot surface current flowing through the
passage so it is advised to use this passage in settled
weather only, especially at night.

⚓ Yacht Club l'Ancora

40°57'·6N 08°13'·3E

This is a private club lying just west of Punta Negra
but visitors are welcome. It consists of a 110m
breakwater running northwards from the shore.
There are some pontoons inside but these are in
depths of less than 1m and visitors moor up (stern-
to) to the outer end of the jetty in 2·8m. Anchor
outside in 3 to 5m in sand (and excellent holding)
off the beach if the harbour is full. There are lights
(F.G and F.R) on the jetty ends. Sgr. Salah Bornaz
on ☎ 079 52 70 85 is the local contact.

Punta Negra

This is a low headland which has shallow reefs off to
the north and the south of the point. It should be
given at least a 400–500m berth to ensure clearance
of these reefs. There are holiday homes built
apparently randomly all over this headland.

Stintino

⊕ 40°56'·20N 08°13'·80E

This is a small town set on a peninsula that separates
two yacht harbours. It lies just over a mile south of
Punta Negra and is protected by a long breakwater
running south. There is a rock southwest of the
breakwater end with a white beacon with a black
stripe to seaward (Fl.5s3M) which can be passed on
either hand but do not go between the beacon and
the shore! Some yachts might prefer to anchor in the
north of the harbour in 3 to 7m in sand and rock
with good holding and this is possible but there is an
idea to put pontoons in the area. This harbour is
well sheltered from all the prevailing winds.

⚓ Porto Mannu

40°56'·6N 08°13'·50E

This is the northern harbour and has been dredged
to 2·5m. There are a lot of finger pontoons and quay
walls for mooring but much of it is allocated to local
yacht clubs and charter firms. Visitors should moor
to the southern quay if possible where there is the
fuelling point. VHF Ch 16, 9, 14, gets Porto Torres
capitaneria but Ch 73 or ☎ 079 52 35 19 should get
the local Stintino *circolo* (responsible for the north
side of the harbour) while the south side is run by
the company Nautilus ☎ 079 52 37 21. Out of
season ☎ 079 52 30 92 for berthing instructions.
Italian pilots say that there are persons available to
assist with mooring but do not say how to attract
their attention.

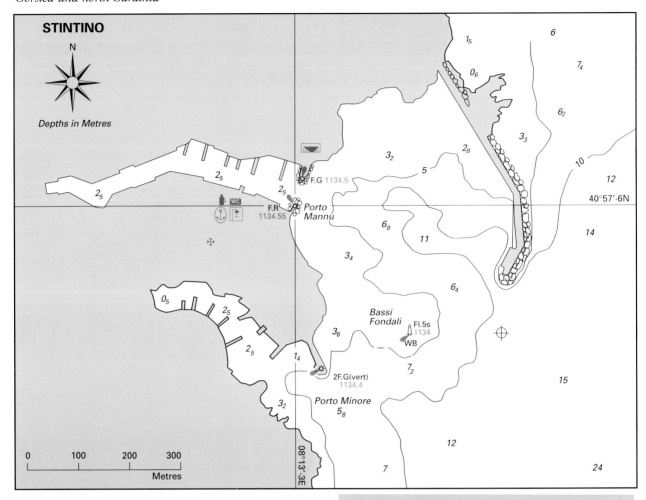

STINTINO

N

Depths in Metres

0   100   200   300
Metres

08°13'·3E

⚓ Porto Minore

40°56'·19N 08°13'·48E

This harbour is to the south of the town and has several jetties and pontoons but again most are allocated to various societies. On entering keep fairly close to the end of the small mole as there is a reef of rocks on the south shore opposite the mole end. There is a light on this inner mole F.G(vert)3M and visitors should moor to No.8 pontoon (if there's room).

4·2 – Porto Torres to Santa Teresa di Gallura

From the low lying land around Porto Torres the land slowly rises as one moves NE but there is really only one harbour, Castelsardo, in this section of coast which offers protection from the prevailing (generally strong) NW winds. After that only a small anchorage in the lee of Isola Rossa affords any type of shelter until one reaches Santa Teresa.

Porto Torres

General

Porto Torres is the main commercial port for Sassari and the north of Sardinia. It lies on a flat plain and the tall chimneys and oil storage tanks to the west of the harbour are the first things seen. There is also a large electricity generating plant to the west of the oil terminal with a pipeline into the sea terminated in a yellow tower with a Fl.Y.3s3M light. The western harbour is for commercial traffic only and pleasure craft are prohibited from entering. In an unfortunate choice of names the harbour for pleasure craft is called Porto Commerciale and lies to the east of the industrial harbour. This is the only harbour described below.

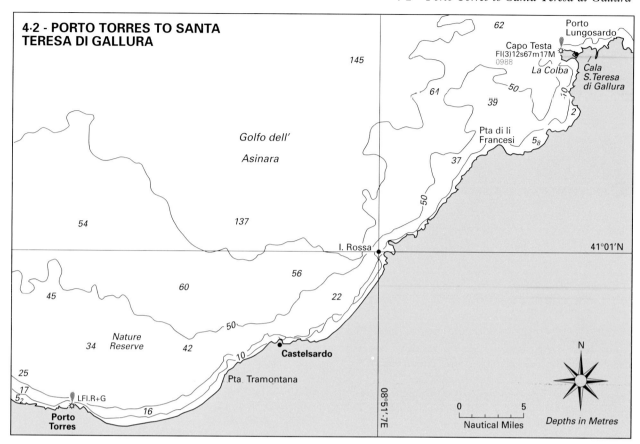

4·2 - PORTO TORRES TO SANTA TERESA DI GALLURA

⚓ Porto Commerciale

⊕ 40°50'·80N 08°24'·20E

Depth 2·5–4·3m in Darsena Interna
0·5–3·3m in Darsena Nuova
Number of berths About 70 in Darsena Nuova
(under the local commune)
150 in Darsena Interna (under private company
Cormorano)

Charts

Admiralty *1985, 1204, 1202*
Italian *49, 289, 286*

Port communications

VHF Ch 16, 9, 12, 14 or ☎ 079 50 22 58 for *capitano*.
VHF Ch 74 or ☎ 079 51 22 90 for Cormarano Marina
(in Darsena Interna).

Lights

1138 Main light 40°50'·1N 8°23'·8E LFl(2)10s45m10M
White tower on 2 storied building SW of town 20m
1139 Molo di Ponente head 40°50'·9N 8°24'·0E
LFl.G.6s11m8M Green column on hut 9m
1140 Molo di Levante head LFl.R6s11m8M Red
column on hut
1141 Pontile del Faro head 2F.RG(vert)7/6m3M Red
and green striped pole 5m
1142 Commercial Quay head 2F.G(vert)6/5m2M
Green column 4m
1144 Darsena Interna left hand entrance F.R.5m3M
red pole 3m
1144·2 Darsena Interna right hand entrance
F.G.5m3M green pole 3m
Pontoons may have 2F.RG(vert) at ends

Warnings

Keep well clear of the commercial and ferry traffic in
the Avamporto.

Approach

By day There are no problems in the approach but
do not enter the western harbour by mistake. The
houses of Porto Torres behind the harbour are a
good indication that you are entering the Porto
Commerciale.

By night The lights of the western harbour are quite
different from the eastern and the flares of the oil
refinery chimneys stand out well. Make for the
western mole end light and enter between the mole
ends.

Entrance

Enter on a SW course, round the eastern mole and
make for the Darsena entrances.

Berth

Normal alongside/stern-to moorings are provided.

Formalities

All authorities available.

Facilities

All.

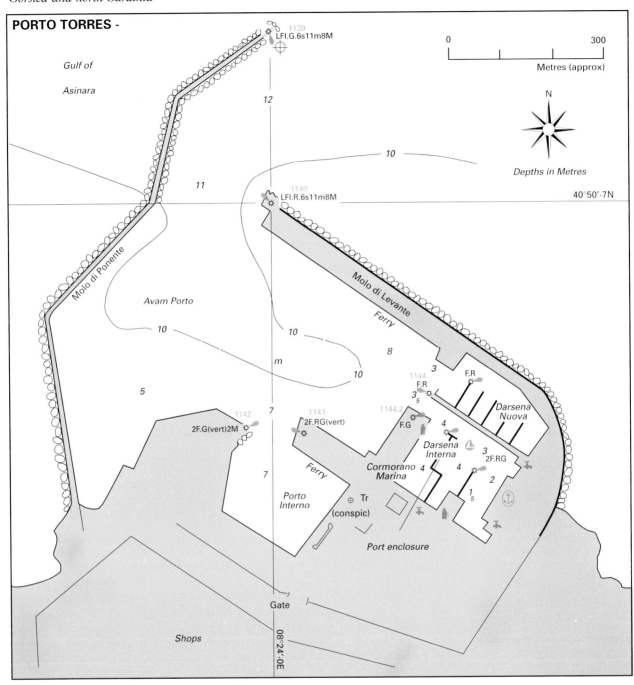

PORTO TORRES -

Gulf of

Asinara

1139
LFl.G.6s11m8M

0   300

Metres (approx)

12

10

N

Depths in Metres

1140
LFl.R.6s11m8M

40°50'·7N

11

Molo di Ponente

Molo di Levante

Ferry

Avam Porto

10

10

8

3

F.R

1144
F.R

Darsena
Nuova

10

10

m

5

3
5

1142
2F.G(vert)2M

7

1141
2F.RG(vert)

1144.2

F.G

4

3
2F.RG

*Darsena
Interna*

*Cormorano
Marina*

4

4

5

3

2

7

Ferry

*Porto
Interno*

Tr
(conspic)

Port enclosure

1
5

Gate

08°24'·0E

Shops

08°24'·0E

⚓ Castelsardo

40°54'·8N 08°42'·2E

About 15 miles east of Porto Torres is Castelsardo, an attractive village set on a hilly promontory with a conspicuous belfry and castle. Closer in the high harbour breakwater wall and Torre Frigiano can be identified west of the town. The western mole is built over the small islet of Frigiano and the Molo Curvilinio joining it to the mainland has had a high wall built to reduce the effect of the maestrale in the harbour. Although the entrance is well lit with

1145·2 Molo Sopraflutto head 40°54'·9N 8°42'·1E
Fl.G.3s8m4M Green pole 5m
1145 Scogliera Sottoflutto head Fl.R.3s8m4M Red
pole 5m

1145·4 Scogliera Isola Frigiano F.G.8m1M
090°-obscd-180° Green pole 5m

it is advisable to enter in daylight initially as there is quite a tricky chicane at the entrance. Enquiries for berths should be addressed to the Commune ☎ 079 07031 or the local Maritime Office ☎ 079 470916.

A very large development has taken place over the past few years and there is now a modern marina at the SE end of the harbour with 200 berths. Most of the shoreside support is now available and work is going on to refurbish the old pontoons at the NW end which will allow a total of 500 berths to become available. The reef and beacon south of Isola Frigiano has been removed and water depths at the pontoons are now 2 to 4·5m. This is a superb yacht

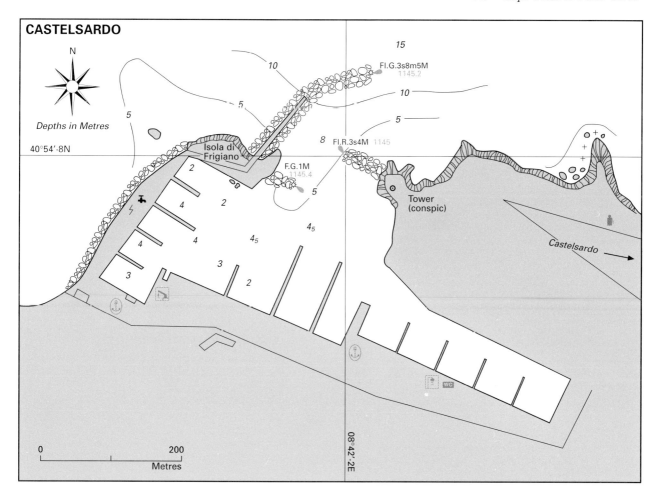

harbour now, totally sheltered from all wind directions and is well worth a visit.

⚓ Isola Rossa

Some 10 miles along the coast there is a conspicuous island 27m high of distinctly reddish rock. In reasonable west or northwest winds excellent shelter can be found behind this island but be careful of a 2m shallow patch 50m off the western coast of the island. On the shore southeast of the island is a tourist complex, named Isola Rossa, on a low promontory with a conspicuous round tower. Two breakwaters enclose a brand-new marina which has four pontoons but it is understood that the depths at the pontoons are only about 1m. It used to be totally private and moored the owners' *gommones* but some berths may be available for visitors in the future.

⚓ Portobello di Gallura

A further 10 miles along the coast there is another totally private development which has constructed a small port, again for the owners' *gommones*. It is very small and visitors are not really welcome because there really is no room, it is shallow (1m) and there are no shoreside facilities at all.

4·3 – Capo Testa to Porto Cervo
(including La Maddalena archipelago)

From Capo Testa to Porto Cervo, the coast is indented with many small harbours and even more bays with superb beaches. There are many islands with off-lying rocks which can make navigation tricky but with up-to-date large-scale charts and GPS even the most cautious navigator should enjoy sailing in this wonderful cruising ground.

The next part of the coast forms the south side of the Bonifacio Strait. It is bordered by numerous islands which are in turn bordered by even more numerous rocks, shoals and reefs. The Strait is used by large numbers of merchant vessels and ferries as well as pleasure craft and a good lookout and giving way in ample time is vital. It has a well-deserved reputation as a rough area especially with a strong *maestrale* (west wind) or *levante* (east wind) and yachtsmen cruising in the area for the first time should exercise caution. However, it is a superb cruising ground with many attractive anchorages and safe harbours. It should not be missed.

The winds in summer blow mainly from the IV quadrant sometimes getting up to force 5 or 6, while around the islands there are frequently southwest or

CAPO TESTA ANCHORAGES

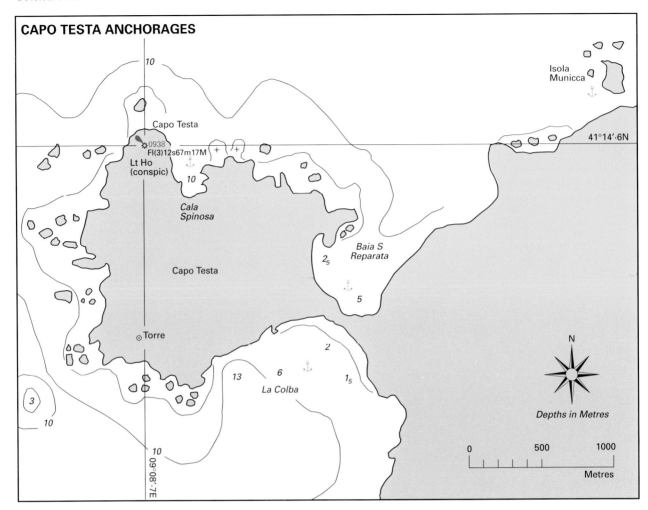

10

Isola
Municca

Capo Testa
☼ 0938
Fl(3)12s67m17M
Lt Ho
(conspic)

10

41°14'·6N

*Cala
Spinosa*

*Baia S
Reparata*

Capo Testa

2_5

5

◌ Torre

2

13   *6*

1_5

La Colba

3

N

Depths in Metres

10

09°08'·7E

10

0	500	1000

Metres

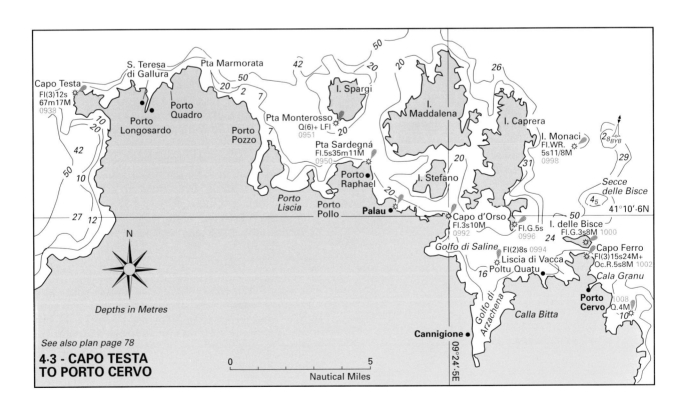

Pta Marmorata

50

42

20

26

Capo Testa
Fl(3)12s
67m17M
0938

S. Teresa
di Gallura

50

20   *2*   *7*

I. Spargi

Porto
Quadro

I.
Maddalena

I. Caprera

Porto
Longosardo

Porto
Pozzo

Pta Monterosso
Q(6)+ LFl
0951

20

10
20

7

I. Monaci
Fl.WR.
5s11/8M
0998

2_{8BYB}

42

Pta Sardegná
Fl.5s35m11M
0950

☼

29

50
10

Porto
Raphael

I. Stefano

20

31

*Secce
delle Bisce*

4_5

41°10'·6N

27   *12*

*Porto
Liscia*

Porto
Pollo

Palau ●

20

Capo d'Orso
Fl.3s10M
0992

50

I. delle Bisce
Fl.G.3s8M 1000

N

Fl.G.5s
0996

24

Capo Ferro
Fl(3)15s24M+
Oc.R.5s8M 1002

Golfo di Saline   Fl(2)8s 0994

☼ Liscia di Vacca
Poltu Quatu

Cala Granu

Depths in Metres

16

**Porto
Cervo**
Q.4M
10

1008

*Golfo di
Arzachena*

Calla Bitta

See also plan page 78

**4·3 - CAPO TESTA
TO PORTO CERVO**

Cannigione ●

09°24'·5E

0					5

Nautical Miles

southeast winds. In spring the winds are northwest or northeast while in autumn the winds are mainly from northwest and southeast. As stated previously the currents follow the prevailing wind but are diverted by the islands and headlands. The currents are quite variable in strength and direction but since most navigation in the vicinity of the Strait is by eyeball the currents can, in general, be ignored.

Capo Testa

Approaching Sardinia from either the west (Bonifacio or Asinara) or the northeast (Passage de la Piantarella) this rugged promontory is easily recognisable. The lighthouse, a low white square tower on a two-storied building (67m high) is conspicuous. The cape is fringed with rocks, some above water and yachts must exercise caution close to the cape. There are 3 anchorages round the cape:

⚓ *Baia La Colba* – on the south side of the isthmus. Anchor in 5m on sand

⚓ *Cala Spinosa* – east of the lighthouse. Anchor in 10m on sand.

⚓ *Baia S Reparata* – north of isthmus. Anchor in 4-6m on sand.

There is also a small bay, sheltered from the east only, at the south end of the small Isola Minicca off

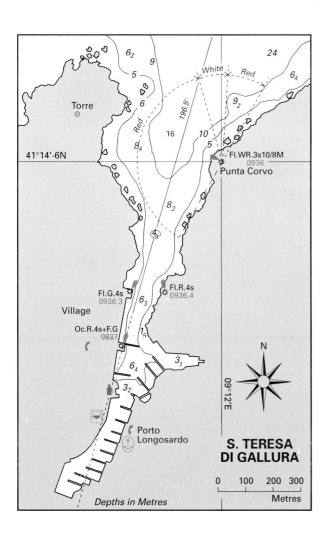

a point 2 miles east of the light on Capo Testa. It is surrounded by rocks but does offer reasonable holding for a lunch stop for example.

Santa Teresa di Gallura

General

Santa Teresa di Gallura is quite a large village on the west side of a ¾ mile long fiord-type harbour in which there is a brand-new yacht harbour (summer 1998), Porto Longosardo. It is a very well sheltered harbour but there is some swell effect during and after strong northerlies.

⚓ Porto Longosardo

41°14'·6N 09°12'E
Depth at entrance 20m, in harbour 2m
Number of berths 300

Charts

Admiralty *1189*
Italian *325, 326*

Port communications

VHF Ch 16, 9. ☎ 0789 75 46 02.

Lights

0936 Punta Corvo 41°14'·6N 9°12'·0E
Fl.WR.3s11m10/8M 030°-R-164°-W-184°-R-210° White hut
0936·3 Entrance light (W) Fl.G.4s8m4M Green pole 6m
0936·4 Entrance light (E) Fl.R.4s8m4M Red pole 6m
0937 Ldg Lts 196·5° *Front* Oc.R.4.s12m3M 181·5°-vis-211·5° White and green pole 10m
0937·1 Rear *(1280m away)* Fl.R.4s45m7M 151·5°-vis-241·5° White and green pole 5m
1020·2(I) Marina entrance light F.G.6m3M on same pole as 0937

Warnings

As with most commercial ports of the islands commercial craft and ferries have right of way in restricted channels and port entrances and must not be obstructed. Anchoring is not permitted in the harbour itself.

Approach

Capo Testa, 2 miles to the west of the entrance, is conspicuous on an approach.

By day Two buoys marking shallow patches (3 and 5m) some half a mile north of the entrance should be seen although they are quite small and difficult to see if any sea is running. A conspicuous 42m high tower (Tour Longosardo) on the western entrance and the village behind it is the clearer indication of position. Go between the buoys and steer a course to keep in the middle of the channel (remember the need to keep clear of ferries!) of 196·5°. The west side is clearer of rocks than the east side. On approach to the quays steer to enter the harbour.

By night The 2 buoys are not lit but Punto Corvo

light, on the east side of the entrance, has a white sector that covers the passage between the shoals. Steer towards Punto Corvo light until the leading lights are in line and steer 196·5° until the quay is reached.

Entrance

The entrance itself is quite narrow (75m) but is clear from obstructions.

Berths

On entering go slightly to starboard into a large new yacht harbour and contact should be made by VHF on approaching the harbour to receive berthing instructions. If this fails try ☎ 0789 75 46 02 and there should be assistants on the pontoons to guide you to your berth.

Formalities

All authorities available.

Facilities

All.

⚓ Porto Quadro

A bay adjacent to the east of S. Teresa entrance with a large hotel complex on the shore. Care should be taken of the rocks at the entrance but inside anchor in the middle of the bay in 3–5m. This bay is totally untenable in *maestrale* conditions.

⚓ Marmorata Bay

Lies about half a mile south of Marmorata Point which has a couple of daymarks, one on the point and another higher up. Anchor just south of the Marmorata islands in 5m with excellent shelter except for northeast to southeast winds. There is a large Club Mediterranean complex above the beach.

⚓ Porto Pozzo

This is not really a port but a long (1·5M) inlet with the large Isola di Coluccia (which is not really an island as it is attached to Sardinia at its southern end) forming the east shore. Coming from the north the beacon at the north end of the Paganetto Rocks stands out clearly and should be left to starboard. Keep to the middle of the inlet and anchor at the head in 3 to 5m in reasonable holding. There are 2 small bays on the east side of the inlet that you can also anchor off in 3–5m.

⚓ Conca Verde

There is a small wooden landing pier with some floating pontoons attached on the west side of the above inlet about 0·7M from the entrance. Depths alongside vary from 5m at the extreme end to 1·5m near the land. This is a private harbour owned by a yacht club but visitors are welcome and there are some simple facilities – fuel! You can also anchor off in 5+m.

⚓ Porto Liscia

Coming from the north keep Punte delle Vacche at least 2 cables clear to avoid the rocks and watch out

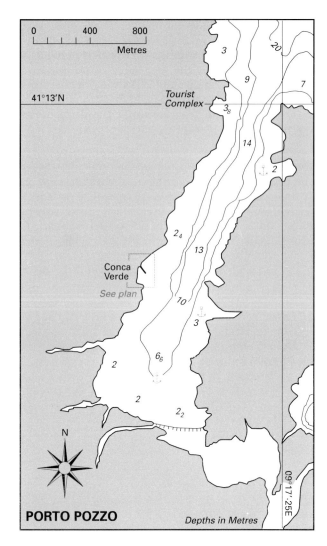

PORTO POZZO *Depths in Metres*

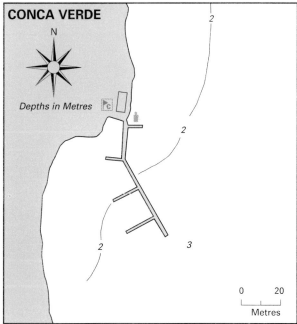

CONCA VERDE *Depths in Metres*

for the iron pole on the Secca di Macchiamata, again leaving it to starboard. Anchor at the west end of the large bay in 3 to 5m on a good holding sandy

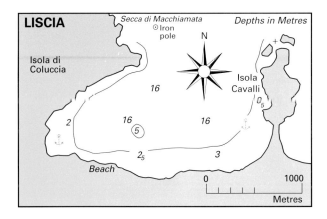

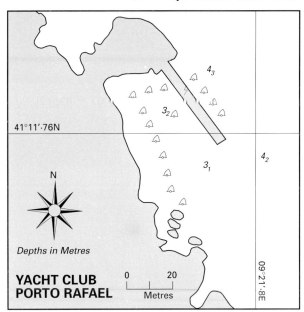

bottom. The anchorage is exposed to winds from the first quadrant but sheltered from all the rest. In calm weather there is a delightful anchorage on the east side of the bay, under Isola Cavallo. There are beaches all round the bay.

⚓ **Porto Pollo (or Puddu)**

Another small inlet, very sheltered from all winds. Keep well clear of Punta Cavalli with its large rock 1·5 cables off and keep to the centre of the bay when entering to avoid extensive rocks on both shores. Anchor SE of the island in 8 to 10m – it shelves very quickly to 1m so exercise caution. Rocks extend all round the island for at least 100m. There are no facilities but, again, there are lovely beaches around the bay with a hotel complex and camp sites mainly at the eastern end of the bay.

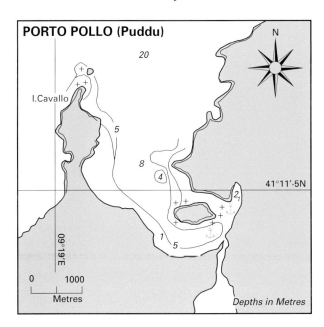

⚓ **Yacht Club Porto Rafael**

41°11'·76N 09°21'·8E

Just under 1M south of Punta Sardinia there is a small private harbour with a quay with stern-to moorings outside and small dinghies etc. inside. All of the moorings are usually occupied but one or two may be available if their owners are away cruising.

Note It may be of interest to note that you are sailing in waters that Nelson often used. He used to anchor his fleet here in the early 1800s when blockading the French fleet in Toulon. The Italian and English charts still bear the names of Cala Inglese (where the YC Porto Rafael is located), Baia di Nelson (about half a mile south of the YC moorings)) and the whole gulf is called Rada de Mezzo Schifo. *Schifo* can be translated as 'skiff' so it might be called 'Bay of Half a Skiff' but *schifo* also means disgusting or loathesome and it probably takes that meaning as the holding in the area is known to be suspect and with the anchors of Nelson's time many a ship will have dragged its anchor hereabouts.

⚓ **Palau**

General

At one time a small farming village, Palau is now a modern town which serves as an 'R and R' town for Americans stationed at the NATO base on Santa Stefano Island and as the mainland ferry port for La Maddalena.

41°10'·9 N 09°23'·2E
Depth 2–4m in harbour.
Number of berths 500
Maximum length 14m

Charts

Admiralty *1213, 1212*
Italian *42, 324, 282*

Port communications

VHF Ch 9. ☎ 0789 70 94 19.

Lights

0988 Punta Palau 41°11'·2N 9°22'·9E
Fl(2)G.10s15m4M White tower, green band 10m
0990 Outer Mole head 41°10'·9N 9°23'·2E
2F.GR(vert)6/5m3M Red and green striped post
0990·6 Shelter Mole head F.G.6m3M Green post 5m
0990·4 Breakwater head F.R.6m3M Red post 5m

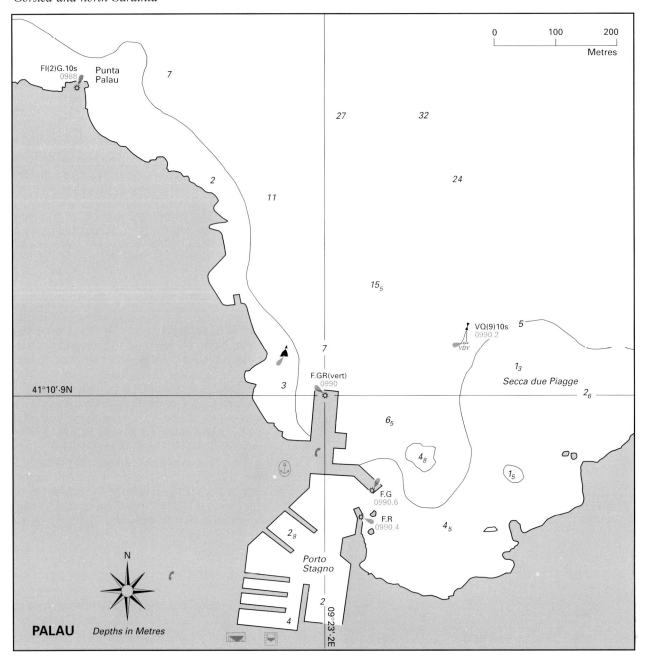

0990·2 Secca due Piagge 41°10'·9N 9°23'·3E
VQ(9)10s5m5M W card buoy YBY (250m at 065°
from outer mole head)

Warnings
There is an extensive reef of rocks, Secca due
Piagge, extending over 2 cables from the eastern
shore marked with a W cardinal buoy. There are
many ferries using the outer mole and all
commercial traffic has right of way so keep fairly
close to this buoy on a southerly course to give the
ferries as much room as possible.

Approach
By day A straightforward approach with the town
easily identified. Ferries are constantly running
between Palau and the islands and are useful for
locating the harbour. The W cardinal buoy is also
obvious as one gets close to the mole.

By night Use the light on Palau Point and the mole
head fixed lights to approach.

Entrance
The entrance is simple but keep closer to the
northern arm as there are rocks projecting northeast
from the southern arm.

Berths
There are floating pontoons and it is possible to go
alongside the quay at the south end of the harbour.
It is always crowded in the harbour.

Formalities
All authorities available.

Facilities
All.

La Maddalena archipelago

Bocche di Bonifacio passages

This group of islands lies to the northeast of Sardinia island and form the southern edge of the Bouches (or Bocche) di Bonifacio. The 3 main passages through the Bocche on the Corsican side are described on page 77. There are 2 further passages, one main one for those vessels going south which simply keeps fairly close to the Sardinian coast leaving all the islands of the Maddalena group to port. The narrowest sections (0·5 miles wide) are between Punta Sardinia and Isola La Maddalena, Isola Santo Stefano and Punta Nera (near Palau) and Capo d'Orso and Punta Fico on Caprera. From Capo d'Orso a course of 120° should be steered for 2 miles which will take you between the south point of Caprera (Punta Rossa buoy) and the isolated Secca di Tre Monti marked with a BRB buoy with two spherical topmarks (Fl(2)8s5M). When abeam of this buoy either a course of east should be steered to pass through the Passo di Bisce (in settled weather only) or a course of 065° should be steered to take you north of Isola delle Bisce and its off-lying

dangers. All isolated rock dangers are well marked in this channel and there is at least 15m depth throughout its length. The second, less important, passage is from a point north of Santa Teresa, take a course just south of east and go between the islands of Budelli and Spargi (keeping closer to Budelli). When abeam of Budelli steer just north of east and go through the Passo di Barrettinelli between the north point of Isola La Maddalena and a group of rocks to the northwest.

The islands are composed of red granite and for the most part are bare of vegetation except for the usual Mediterranean *macchia*. The islands are surrounded by above- and below-water rocks and caution must be exercised when navigating around them. There are seven principal islands, 3 in the northern group Razzoli, Santa Maria and Budelli and 4 in the southern group, La Maddalena, Caprera, Spargi and Santo Stefano.

The Northern Group

This group has few inhabitants and little in the way of vegetation or water.

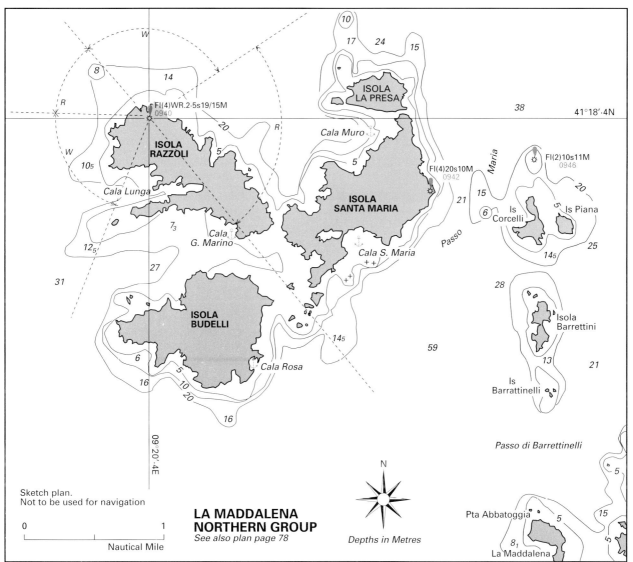

Sketch plan.
Not to be used for navigation

0 ————————————— 1
Nautical Mile

**LA MADDALENA
NORTHERN GROUP**
See also plan page 78

Depths in Metres

Isola Razzoli

The northwesternmost of the group, it is low (65m) with a distinctive square black and white striped lighthouse on its northwest point, Fl.WR.2·5s19/15M, with red sectors over the Lavezzi rocks (092°–137°) and Santa Maria (237°–320°). There are 2 anchorages.

⚓ Cala Lunga

Care is needed to avoid the rocks on both sides of the entrance. Anchor in 3 to 4m on sand. It is open to the west but otherwise is well sheltered.

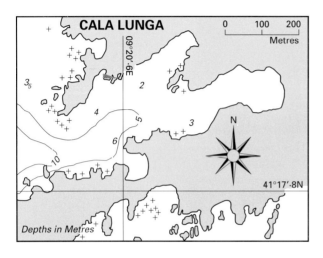

⚓ Cala Giorgio Marino

This is on the south side of the island but effectively sheltered by all the islands. Anchor in 3 to 5m on a sandy bottom – again open to the west.

Isola Santa Maria

Lies to the east of Razzoli from which it is separated by Passo degli Asinelli which is impassable for keel yachts. To the north of the island lies Isola La Presa and off the east coast a number of small islets. The passage between these latter islets and Santa Maria is clear except for a 6·5m shoal. There is a distinctive lighthouse on the east coast Fl(4)20s10M and a light on the northernmost islet to the east from a white stone tower on Isola Barrettinelli di Fuori Fl(2)R.10s7M. There are 2 bays on the island providing reasonable shelter.

⚓ Cala Muro

Near the north tip, south of the Isola La Presa. There is a rocky reef in the middle of the bay and rocks around the shores. Anchor in 6 to 10m on the south side of the bay. Open to the west.

⚓ Cala Santa Maria

On the southeast side of the island and care must be taken of 2 reefs south of the entrance. There is a nondescript port-hand buoy off the northernmost reef which should be left to port on entering. Take up a position east of the buoy and, leaving it to port, steer about 300° until 4 to 6m is reached (keep in

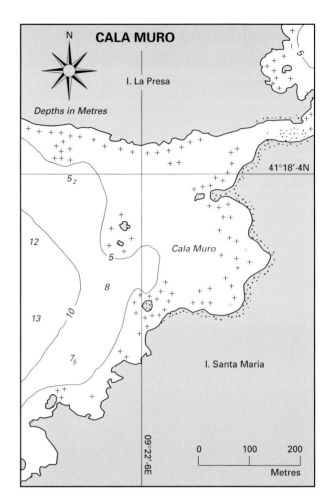

the clear sandy patch which is obvious from the buoy inwards). Good sandy bottom with splendid beach which is flooded with tourists in season. Open to the south.

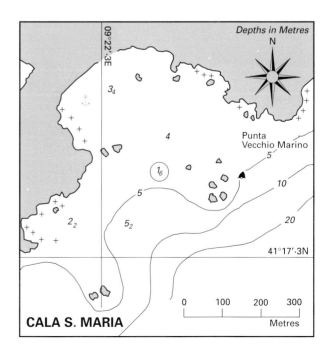

Budelli

Lies to the south of Razzoli and southwest of Santa Maria. It is separated from the latter by the Passo Secca di Morto (Deadman's Rock) which has a minimum depth of 1·2m and is not recommended. There's really only one decent anchorage.

⚓ Spiaggia Rossa (Cala Rossa)

This is a small cove on the southeast shore with reasonable shelter from all but easterly winds. The cove took its name from the red colour of the sand which came from the dead coral that grew around the islands in profusion long ago. Not only has the coral succumbed to mans' harvesting (for jewellery) and pollution but all the visitors to the beach over the centuries have taken a small sample home with them and today the beach is a normal beach colour. It is, however, a delightful spot if you can visit it on a quiet day.

The Southern Group

These 4 islands are larger and greener than the northern group. There are numerous anchorages and the sea is crystal clear turquoise and aquamarine over a rock and sand bottom.

Isola Spargi

The westernmost of this group is a rocky isle with a high point of 153m. Some 3·5 cables off its southern tip lies the Secca Corsara (3m depth) which is marked by a S cardinal light buoy (Q(6)+LFl.15s5M). A small islct, Spargiotto, lies 6 cables off the NW corner. There are 3 anchorages.

⚓ Cala d'Alga

Lies on the west side of the southern tip. Anchor in 3 to 5m on sand and rock. Open to the W and S but has a nice beach.

⚓ Cala Corsara

Lies on the east side of the southern tip. Again anchor in 3 to 5m on sand and rock.

⚓ Cala Ferrigno

This is a very rocky bay on the NE coast with a white house ashore and a small pier making identification easier. The rocks extend from the north side of the bay but the south side is relatively clean. There is 3 to 4m at the end of the pier but there is little room to manoeuvre because of the rocks.

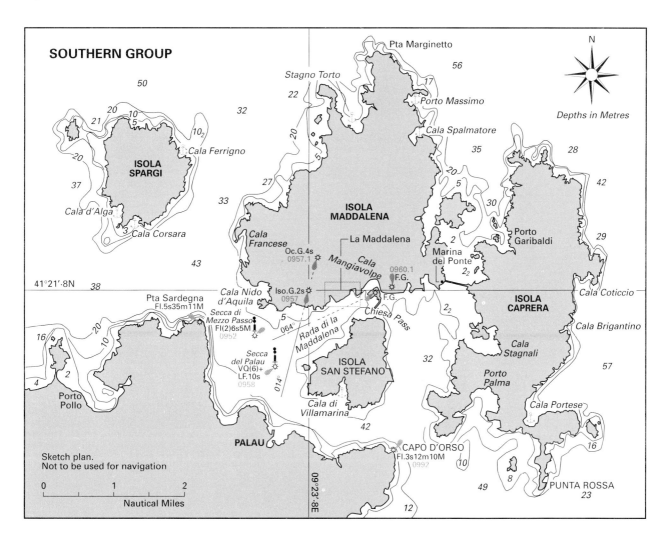

La Maddalena

This is the largest island of the entire group and the only one that supports a reasonable population, mainly clustered around the town of La Maddalena itself. It is fairly hilly at the south end (153m) and at the northern end (84m) with a much indented coast with a selection of anchorages that offer good shelter in almost any wind direction. The coast is fringed with rocks and great care is needed when navigating in and around the various bays.

From the main channel between the islands and the mainland there are three passages:

a. *North passage*

This is between Punta Tegge and Scoglio Bianco to the north and Secca di Mezzo Passo, a bank of rocks 3 cables south of Punta Tegge. Scoglio Bianco is painted white and has a 16m white obelisk on it. Secca di Mezzo Passo has a black and red daymark surmounted by two spheres. It is lit with Fl(2)6s5M. In the channel between these two beacons is a clear 20+m depth.

b. *Middle passage (Mezzo Passo)*

This is between the Secca di Mezzo Passo and a large reef 0·4 miles to the SE, Secca del Palau. On its S edge there is a S cardinal buoy, yellow and black with two cones point down as topmark, lit VQ(6)+LFl.10s5M. On the NE edge is a yellow cylindrical buoy with a topmark of an X lit by Fl.Y.5s. The leading lines on Forte Camicia and Chiesa lead through the centre of this passage on a course of 064° (very difficult to make out in daylight).

c. *South passage*

This is between the Secca del Palau and Santa Stefano – actually Isolotto Roma, a rocky islet just off the main island. Isolotto Roma has a column on its western extremity (in memory of the Italian navy personnel who perished at sea on the battleship *Roma* which was sunk by the Germans after the Italians had surrendered). Shoals exist for at least 1 cable to the west of Isolotto Roma and the channel is nearer to the Secca. There are leading lights for this passage on the hill to the west of La Maddalena town on 014° and this passage is used mainly by the ferry traffic plying between Palau and La Maddalena.

La Maddalena

General

The town is the main centre of habitation on the island and the harbour is used by commercial, military, fishing, ferry and pleasure vessels. It is a

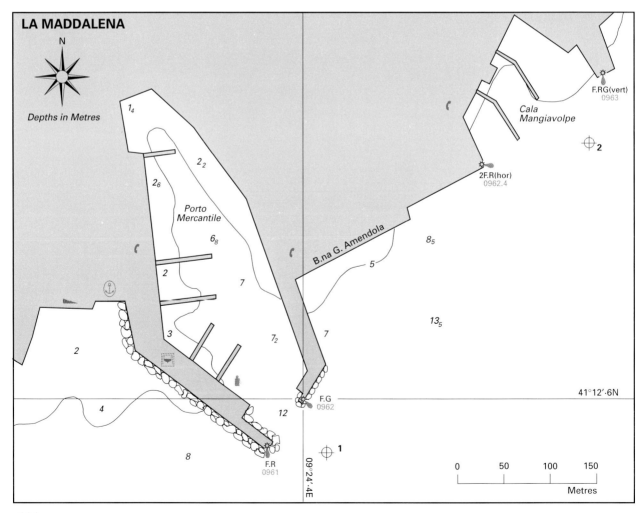

busy little place serving the Italian Naval base and the NATO base on Santo Stefano. In summer it attracts large numbers of day tourists from the hotels on the mainland.

There are three main harbours, the old Cala Gavetta, now renamed Porto Mercantile, the newer Cala Mangiavolpe and Cala Camicia. This latter is a military installation and is strictly out of bounds for private pleasure yachts. Just to the west of Porto Mercantile is a 100m long pontoon projecting south from the Scalo di Alaggio. It is very exposed to the washes from the ferries but in settled weather it is another possible berthing position with 3 to 5m depth at the outer end of the pontoon.

⊕1 (Porto Mercantile) 41°12'·55N 09°24'·46E
⊕2 (Cala Mangiavolpe) 41°12'·70N 09°24'·80E
Depth 0·5–5m
Number of berths 300
Maximum length 12m

Charts

Admiralty *1212*
Italian *42, 324, 325, 281, 282*

Port communications

VHF Ch 16 (or 11 between 0700-1900). ☎ 0789 79 06 00.

Lights

0961 Porto Mercantile W mole F.R.6m3M Red pole
0962 E mole F.G.7m3M Green pole
0962·4 Posto Pier 2F.R(hor)3M
0963 Ferry pier F.RG(vert)3M

Warnings

Berthing is under the orders of the harbourmaster who must be consulted before mooring.

Approach

By day Despite the many rocks fringing the approaches, once inside the approach is straightforward. The leading marks below Fort Camicia (on 064°) show the way but they are hardly necessary as the houses of the town are obvious and, if in any doubt, there are the many ferries to show you the way towards the harbour.

By night Follow the leading lights on the slopes to the west of the port which show the way through the south passage on 014° (Front Iso.G.2s8M Rear Oc.G.4s8M). Turn to 066° when the leading lights on Fort Camicio (two F.G.3M) come into line.

Entrance

There are no problems at either the Porto Mercantile or Cala Mangiavolpe.

Berths

Call on the VHF radio to get a berth before making fast.

Formalities

Customs and police are available.

Facilities

All.

Chiesa passage

If leaving and continuing south it is quicker to take the Chiesa Passage north of Santo Stefano Island. There are many off-lying rocks to the north of Santo Stefano and these are marked by 2 green buoys and a green conical beacon. To the north of this beacon a breakwater extends south from Chiesa Island. The passage is between the beacon and breakwater end and has a least depth of 3·3m. There is F.G on the beacon and F.R on the breakwater.

⚓ Marina del Ponte

41°13'·0N 09°26'·4E

Having passed through the Chiesa passage there is a new small marina at the root of the Caprera Bridge at the Maddelena end. It consists of a floating pontoon with 45 berths with plans for a larger extension to cater for a further 100 berths. Depths are from 1m to 6m and it is sheltered from all winds except southerlies. The local contact is Sig Cuneo Anselmo on ☎ 0368 55 38 58.

⚓ Cala Nido d'Aquila

Lies to the north of Punta Tegge. It is shallow and very rocky and not recommended.

⚓ Cala Francese

It is a bay on the west coast which is rocky and open at the south end but it is more sheltered from the north through east to south in the northern part. Anchor in 3 to 5m on a sand bottom. There is a small pier in the northwest corner to which a line can be taken if required.

⚓ Stagno Torto

A large bay on the north coast, fringed with rocks inshore but anchor in 6m in the centre of the bay.

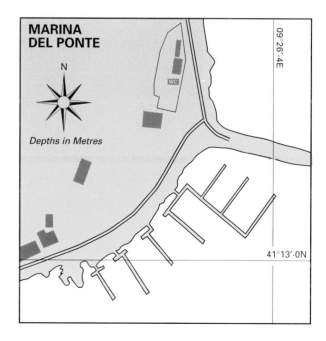

⚓ Porto Massimo

41°15'·4N 09°25'·7E

This is a private hotel complex on the NE coast. It is difficult to see when approaching from the north but when east of the entrance the hotel complex is clear. The entrance is lit by F.G and F.R. Go stern-to the outer mole as the inner pier is in shallow water. There is room for 200 craft, with water on the quay, a small shop, restaurant and bars.

⚓ Cala Spalmatore

This is just south of Porto Massimo. There are a number of above-water rocks to the north of the entrance so proceed in on the south side and anchor in 3m in the southern part of the bay. There is a pier running out from the west shore that has 4m of water at its end but there are rocks inshore and. Do not moor to the pier as it is part of the naval facilities. It has good holding and is only open to the east – there is a bar and restaurant ashore.

Isola Santa Stefano

A mainly barren island with a large military area on the north and east coasts. Anchoring and landing are prohibited in this area. There is only one good anchorage on the island.

⚓ Cala di Villamarina

⊕ 41°11'·25N 9°21'·80E

There is a green light structure (Fl.G.4s14m4M) on the eastern Punta Villamarina with an islet off. Take up a position at least 2 cables west of the point and steer north towards the ⊕. In the vicinity of the ⊕ alter to steer a course of about 020° towards the conspicuous white house near the head of the inlet. This avoids the extensive rocky outcrops both sides of the entrance. There is excellent shelter here in all

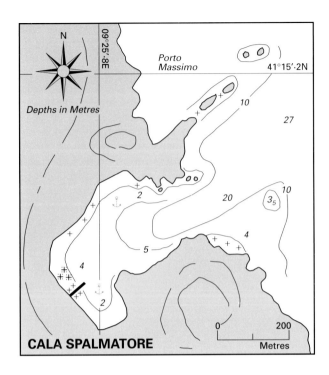

CALA SPALMATORE

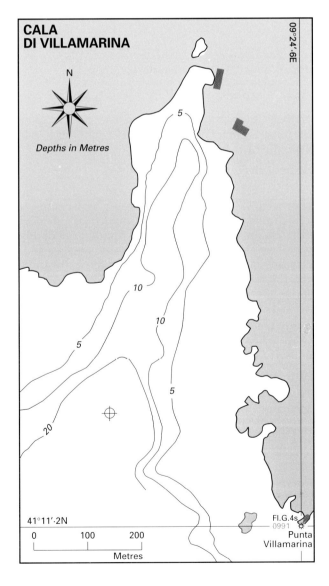

CALA DI VILLAMARINA

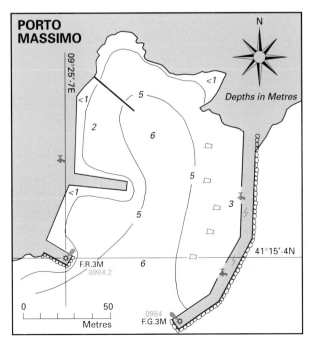

PORTO MASSIMO

but strong southerlies. Anchor off the quay in 5 to 6m and take a line ashore if required. No facilities.

Isola Caprera

The easternmost island of the group is hilly (212m) and sparsely populated. It is joined to La Maddalena by a causeway with a road bridge of only 4·8m clearance (from sea level) so yachts should not expect to use the Passo della Moneta between the islands. Most of the island is a nature reserve and there are areas off the south and east coasts where it is nominally prohibited to navigate, anchor or fish. Few seem to take notice of this, especially in the summer season.

⚓ **Cala Stagnali**

A large rocky inlet on the west coast of Caprera, just east of the north end of Santa Stefano. It has a buoy on the south side and a leading line (139°) of two daymarks on the shore in front of the village (these are both lit with F.G.3M). There are 2 piers here which are reserved exclusively for military use. To enter approach the outer buoy on an easterly course and follow the leading line into the inlet bearing to port after passing the port-hand headland to anchor in 2 to 3m on sand and rock in the middle of the inlet. Note the inlet to the north is extremely shallow.

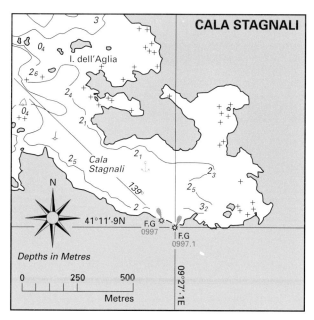

⚓ **Porto Palma**

This is a bay on the SW coast with many rocks on the eastern side of the entrance and two shallow patches on the eastern side of the inner bay. There are sailing schools on the shores but there are several places to anchor in 3 to 7m on sand with good holding in the bay. The small inlet on the west side of the bay is totally sheltered from any swell of the *maestrale*. There is a small pier at the north end with water adjacent but there are no other facilities.

⚓ **Cala Portese**

This is an anchorage north of Punta Rossa but is untenable with winds from the northeast.

⚓ **Cala Brigantino**

About a mile north of Portese is a small inlet with off-lying rocks on both sides of the entrance but you can go right in and anchor in 3m – so long as there is hardly anyone else there!

⚓ **Cala Coticcio (Tahiti Bay)**

This anchorage is really two coves and very popular in the season. The eastern cove is the more sheltered (and thus the more crowded). It is deep (8m) and holding is suspect. With strong westerlies there are the usual gusts that sweep down from various directions and can cause confusion in the anchorage. There are no facilities at all here.

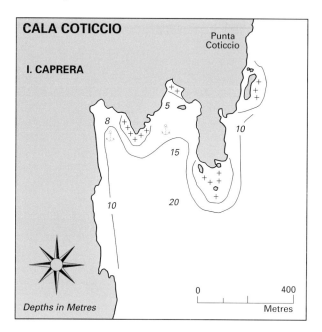

⚓ **Porto Garibaldi**

This anchorage is on the west side of Caprera and there are three small islets, called the Italian Isles. It is possible to anchor in 2·5 to 3m ESE or E of the southern islet. There is a small pier but with rocks off its west side which again is for military use only and a Club Med complex ashore. For those interested it is a short walk from here to see the house where Garibaldi spent his last years, which is now a museum to his memory.

Returning now to the Sardinian coast east of Palau, the channel between Caprera and Capo d'Orso is relatively clear. Capo d'Orso light Fl.3s12m10M is on the south side with a pole on a small islet of Fico with a green buoy off marking the edges of the half-mile-wide channel. Some 2 miles ahead, just south of Punta Rossa on Caprera is an isolated rock, Secca di Tre Monti, marked by a black single pole beacon with a red stripe, with two spherical topmarks. It is lit with Fl(2)8s5m5M.

⚓ Golfo di Saline

This bay lies one mile south of Capo d'Orso and gives good protection in westerly winds but is open to the east. Anchor near the head in 5m on sand.

Golfo di Arzachena

This is a large, 2-mile-deep bay. It has good shelter from all but north winds. There are 2 yacht harbours and a number of small bays with pontoons. It is recommended to keep to the centre of the entrance of the bay to avoid shoals on both sides.

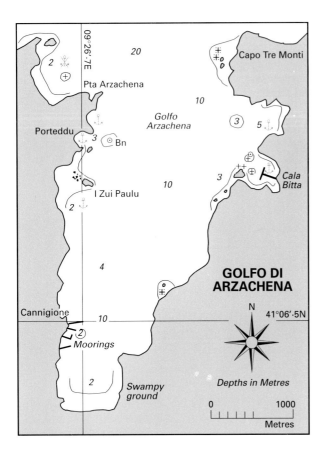

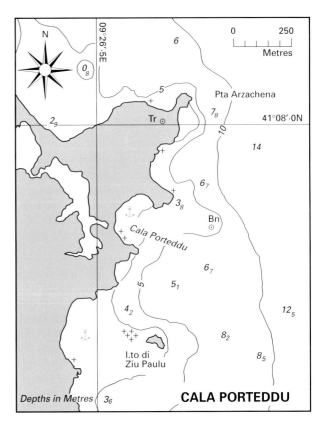

the jetty. During the season there are a number of floating pontoons available which can be used but take care that there is adequate water as depths do go down to less than 1m in places. There are 400 berths with 50 places for visitors but a call on VHF Ch 16 (11 from 0700–1900 or ☎ 0789 88422) may

⚓ Cala Porteddu

A small bay south of the day mark on Punta Arzachena with a small pier but it is very rocky and shallow – not recommended. There is a rock some 250m off the northern headland with a pole on it (occasionally).

⚓ La Conia (S of Ziu Paulu islet)

There is a pier and some floating pontoons on a small bay just inshore of Isloletto di Ziu Paulu. Anchor in 3 to 5m at least 1 cable south of the islet. There is a sailing school here so it may be rather busy – especially in school holiday time!

⛵ Cannigione

41°06'·5N 09°26'·7E

This harbour has a substantial breakwater, some 250m long on which you can go stern-to in depths of 3–5m. There is a F.G.7m3M light on the end of

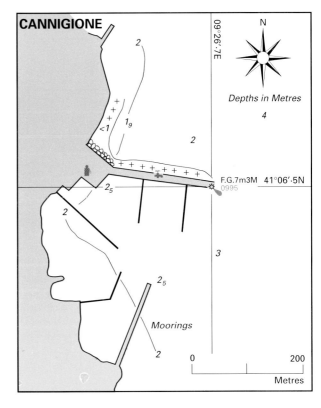

help to decide on a place for the night. It is possible to moor on the seaward side of the breakwater but the swell is much greater. Anchoring may be possible south of the jetty but the holding is poor and there are many laid moorings so a trip line is essential.

⚓ Cala Bitta

41°07'·5N 09°28'·1E

This is a small harbour built as an integral part of a plan for a large hotel and tourist complex ashore. Initial work has been completed but little has happened over the past 5 years and out of season the shoreside development is virtually derelict. It is a difficult approach, almost impossible in strong N to NW winds, but now there are red and green buoys showing a channel of 3m minimum depth in the summer season. There is a rock to the north side of the bay which is sometimes marked with a pole but this should not be relied on. Go stern-to inside the mole where there is excellent shelter but the place is usually completely crowded in the season. It is reputed that there are bars and restaurants ashore in July and August.

⚓ North Bay

If Cala Bitta is full you can anchor in the next bay to the north, under Capo Tre Monti. Anchor in 3 to 5m on sand and weed and apart from a northwesterly swell that can roll in the anchorage has reasonable shelter.

Capo Tre Monti & Secca di Tre Monti

Capo Tre Monti is the eastern headland of the Golfo Arzachena. It is a broad headland which only rises to 64m high at its centre. It has extensive reefs off its west coast which extend for up to 400m and a wide berth should be given to this point.

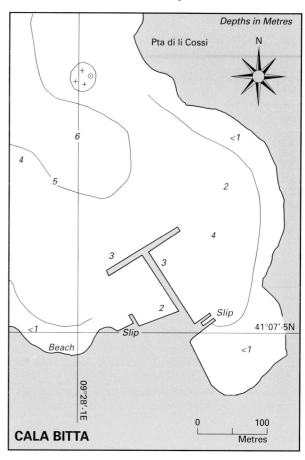

CALA BITTA

0·8 of a mile north of the point lies the Secca di Tre Monti, a large reef of rocks marked by an isolated danger pole, BRB with a topmark of 2 spheres and lit Fl(2)8s5M. There is a 20m deep, half-mile-wide channel both north and south of this reef.

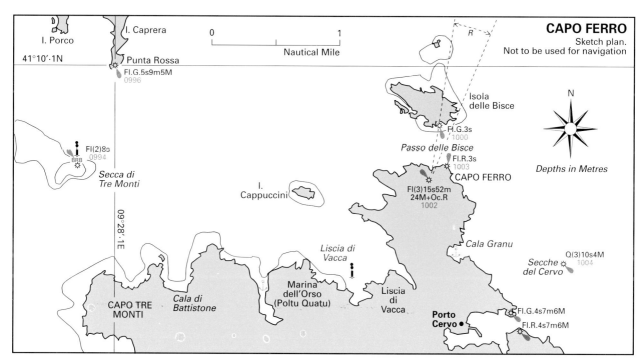

⚓ Marina dell'Orso (Poltu Quatu)

41°08'·6N 09°29'·7E

Rounding Capo Tre Monti and Capo Battistone look for a narrow fiord which has been dredged and converted to a yacht harbour for 500 yachts (50 for visitors) with nearly 2,000m of pontoons. Speed must be kept below 3 knots. Call on VHF Ch 9 for mooring assistance (or ☎ 0789 99477) before entering. At night there is Fl.R.5s4M on the eastern mole and Fl.G.5s4M on the western mole. The entrance is 60m wide, the depths inside are 2·5 to 3·5m and yachts up to a maximum length of 35m can be accommodated. There is water and electricity at all berths with some limited repair facilities ashore and fuel at the entrance. There is a small shop and a few cafés in the development but little else ashore.

⚓ Liscia di Vacca

This is quite a large bay just to the west of Capo Ferro. Pass to the south of Isola Cappuccini and make for the south of the bay. There is a small pier off a cluster of houses, but watch for an isolated rock marked, occasionally, by a black, red, black pole with topmarks some 250m off the western headland of the bay. The shore is ringed with rocks so care is needed in picking a position in 4–7m. The bottom is sand and weed but holding is reputed to be reasonable. There is good shelter here in all winds except for northwesterly. Ashore there is the Pitrizza Hotel which is the most expensive in this area, if not in the whole of Italy.

Isola Cappucini

Leaving to continue south there is a 7m deep passage between the mainland and Isola Cappuccini but it is not recommended if the sea is at all rough.

Capo Ferro & Isola delle Bisce

The passage between Isola delle Bisce and Capo Ferro is deep and clear of dangers in the fairway. Capo Ferro is steep-to while the rocks to the S and SE of the island are obvious in daylight.

By night there are lights Fl.G.3s8M and Fl.R.3s8M on the island and cape respectively. The main lighthouse of Capo Ferro is a white tower (52m high) on a two-storied building Fl(3)15s24M, with a red light Oc.R.5s8M on the same structure covering a sector of 189°–203° over 2 shoal patches, the Secca delle Bisce and the Secca dei Monaci to the north.

⚓ Cala Granu

A small cove, half a mile south of Capo Ferro, makes a pleasant stop before entering Porto Cervo. It is very popular with the small open-boat fraternity from Cervo and can get very crowded.

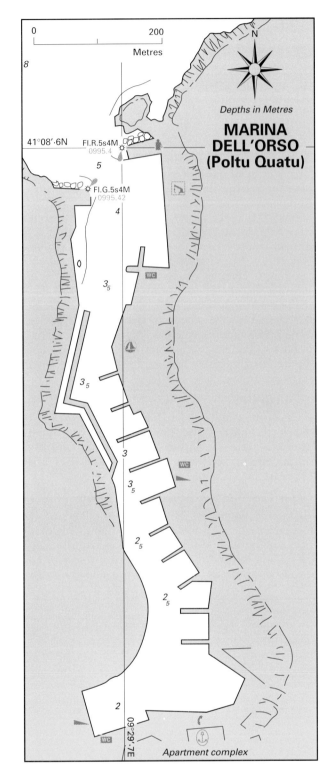

4·4 – Porto Cervo to Olbia

This section of coast consists of deeply indented gulfs and bays and a profusion of artificial yacht harbours, some of which have literally been dug out of the surrounding land. There are several off-shore islands and the whole coastline is dominated by Capo Figari and Isola Tavolara to the south.

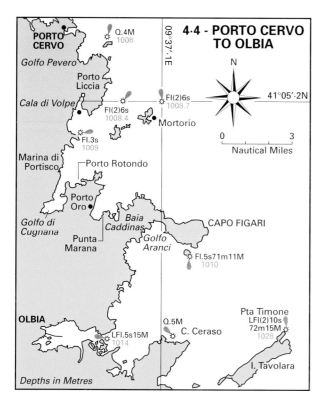

Porto Cervo

General

Porto Cervo is the yachting centre of the Consorzio Costa Smeralda and one of the first true marinas to be developed in this part of the world. It cost millions of dollars to build and is a real millionaire's playground. It has hotels, night-clubs etc. but they are all blended in skilfully with the landscape and it is quite difficult to see the place on first approaching. In July and August it is a popular place for the jet set but out of season it is just worth the exorbitant fee to say you have been there.

⊕ 41°08'·19N 09°32'·35E

Depth 1·7 to 7m in the marina
Number of berths 720 of which 80 are for visitors.

Charts

Admiralty *161B, 163*
Italian *42, 323, 319*

Port radio

VHF Ch 16 or 11 from 0700–1900. ☎ 0789 91100

Weather forecast

Posted daily at the office (available in English).

Lights

1004 Secche del Cervo 41°08'·6N 9°32'·8E
  Q(3)10s6m4M E card beacon
1005 North side of entrance Fl.G.4s7m6M Green tower 5m
1005·4 South side of entrance Fl.R.4s7m6M Red tower 5m
1006 Ldg Lts *Front* 41°07'·9N 9°31'·4E Iso.R.2s27m3M 247·4°-vis-252·4° White tower, black stripe 8m
1006·1 *Rear* (270m from front) Oc.R.4s47m3M 247·4°-vis-252·4° White tower, black stripe 3m
1007 Diga head F.7m3M Green pole 5m
1007·3 On coast 80m S of 1007 F.R.7m3M Red pole 5m

Warnings

Half a mile NE of the entrance there is the Secche del Cervo, a bank of rocks that are just awash. There is a pole at their eastern extremity with Q(3)10s4M light during the summer months. This is quite difficult to see and although there is a passage between the rocks and the mainland it is not recommended and the rocks should be left to starboard coming south.

Inside the entrance there is a free anchoring zone but be wary of the 1·6m patch in this area. In season the shallow areas are sometimes marked with small buoys with Fl.R.1s lights.

Porto Cervo runs many sailing regattas and there could be buoys laid outside the entrance which are not marked on any charts, they do not indicate dangers to navigation but the racing courses should be avoided if possible.

Approach

It is difficult to see the entrance to Porto Cervo when coming from the north although the passage of small vessels in and out will assist recognition.

By day Pick out the Secche del Corvo beacon and steer south until the entrance opens up and some buildings and masts may be seen. The leading line marks are difficult to see but steer in on 252°, keeping to the middle of the entrance.

By night The Secche del Cervo light may not be lit out of season so keep well clear until the leading lights can be picked up. Steer 252° through the entrance between the red and green flashing 4s lights at the entrance.

Entrance

There is no difficulty at the entrance except that gusts can sweep down, especially in northwest winds, and it is recommended to motor in.

Berths

The *capitano* (harbourmaster's office) is to port just inside the entrance and one can moor stern-to in the Porto Vecchio nearby if there is space. However it is better to have contacted the office by VHF prior to coming in and been given a berth. There is a free anchoring zone in the north of the harbour (marked by buoys) but there can be a nasty swell in easterly

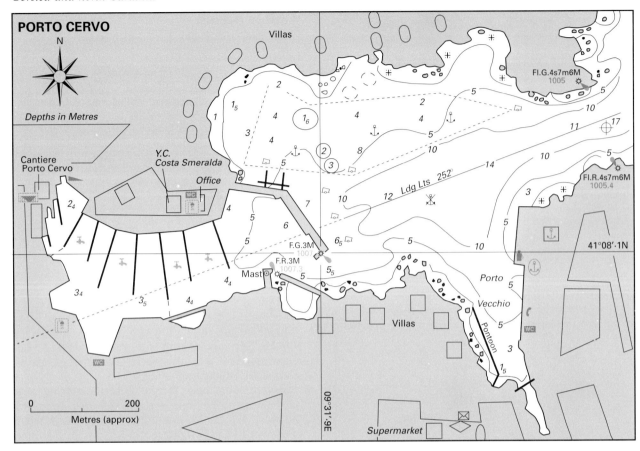

winds and washes from the general traffic make this somewhat uncomfortable (although the speed limit is 3 knots in the harbour!)

Formalities

All authorities available.

Facilities

All.

⚓ Golfo Pevero

This is a large bay just south of Porto Cervo with a rock (with a black beacon with a red stripe) off the eastern headland. There is a beach at the south end but it is very rocky so anchor well off. Also the holding is suspect on rock/sand/weed.

Isole di li Nibani and Passo delle Galera

These rocky islands have a 3m white conical structure on the northernmost islet which exhibits Q.21m4M from 1 June to 30 September. There is also a passage, the Passo delle Galera, between the islands and the mainland which had a beacon to the north which is now missing (1997) and has a depth of 5m. It is only recommended to use this in daylight and on calm days. On leaving this passage there are the Isole delle Rocche to the south with definitely no passage inside!

⚓ Porto Liccia

A small bay just to the north of Capo Capaccia with another one to the south of the cape. These are popular with the daytime/luncheon set from Cervo but watch for the isolated rock 1 cable SE of the cape. These bays are untenable in easterly winds.

Isole Poveri & Isole Mortorio and Soffi

Isole Poveri are a group of low islands southeast of Capo Capaccia with a light Fl(2)6s4M on a structure at the southern end. There is a black pole with a red stripe on an isolated rock at the northeastern end of the group. To seaward are a number of larger islands with Isola Soffi to the south and Isola Mortorio, the largest of the group, being 1 mile SE of the Isole Poveri. Another half mile to the NE is the Isolotto Mortoriotto which has a small white tower with light Fl(2)6s10m4M in the summer season.

⚓ Mortorio

Isola Mortorio has beautiful beaches on its western side and most craft anchor off these. However there is a fascinating anchorage on the eastern side. The charts do not do justice to the totally landlocked pool with 4m depth at the head of the inlet. There is only room for two or three yachts of 10m length but the swimming and the fish there should be sampled when passing.

Important note

The lights of Cervo, Isole Nibani, Poveri, Mortoriotto, Cala Volpe and Punta Ligata are maintained by local sources and are only lit from 1 June to 30 September. However in some cases they may not be lit and, in fact, may not even be there due to damage etc.

⚓ Cala di Volpe

This is a long, shallow bay with excellent holding in
sand but take care to avoid the even shallower
patches. There is a pier at the north end of the bay
with only 1m at the outer end and it leads to the
Hotel Cala Volpe – another of the Costa Smeralda
five-star hotels! The entrance lights are
Fl.G.4s6m1M and Fl.R.4s7m1M. The bay is
sheltered from all winds except southerlies.

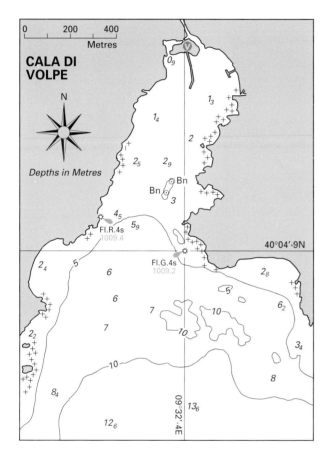

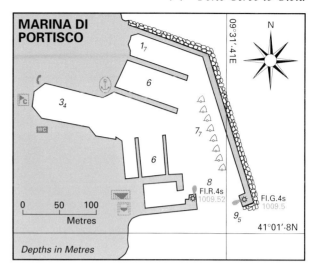

⛵ Marina di Portisco

41°01'·80N 09°31'·41E

A mile south of Cala di Volpe is Punta Ligata with
its light Fl.3s11m3M on a white conical tower.
Another 1·5 miles south of the point is an islet,
Isolotto Portisco, and just south of that is a new
yacht harbour with berths for 347 yachts. Plans are
in hand to increase this to about 600 berths in the
future. The entrance is marked by Fl.G.4s6m5M
and Fl.R.4s6m3M. Depths are 5 to 9m at the quays
and harbour authorities can be contacted on VHF
Ch 16, 9 and 69 as well as ☎ 0789 33520. Shelter
is good from all winds and there are all facilities
ashore. This is another example of the excellent new
marinas that are springing up around the coasts of
Sardinia and well worth a visit.

⚓ Golfo di Cugnana

A yacht can anchor in the gulf with good shelter and
little swell. There is a holiday development on the
east side with some private pontoons off Punta

Asfodeli to which you can moor (VHF Ch 9). At
Cugnana Verde in the southwestern corner of the
gulf there is a pier with some facilities for repair but
it is quite shallow and it is recommended to anchor
off and row ashore to seek advice before mooring.

⚓ Porto Rotondo

41°01'·7N 09°32'·6E

This is very sheltered marina complex a mile east of
Punta Volpe. The approach is fairly obvious because

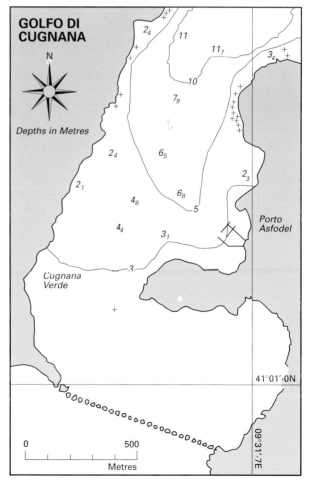

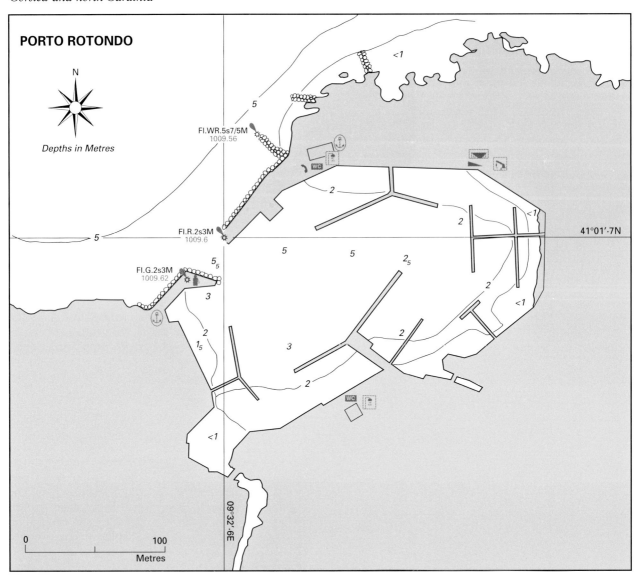

PORTO ROTONDO

N

Depths in Metres

Fl.WR.5s7/5M
1009.56

Fl.R.2s3M
1009.6

Fl.G.2s3M
1009.62

41°01'·7N

09°32'·6E

0   100
Metres

of all the buildings behind the marina but the entrance to the harbour itself is difficult to pick out until fairly close. At night there is a light on a short projecting mole Fl.WR.5s7m7/5M with a red sector visible 215°–240° which covers the dangers north of Punta Volpe. Approach in the white sector until the entrance lights become visible. These are Fl.G.2s5m3M on the western jetty and Fl.R.2s5m3M on the eastern.

As the entrance is quite narrow you should motor in – and note that sailing is prohibited in the harbour itself! There are berths for 633 yachts with 63 for visitors, in depths of 1·5 to 6m. Contact should be made with the authorities prior to entering on VHF Ch 9 (or ☎ 0789 34203). All facilities for yachtsmen are available.

Punta Volpe

From Porto Rotondo round Punta Volpe, keeping at least 3 cables clear as there are many off-lying dangers to this low, unlit headland and enter the Golfo di Marinella. There is an occasional daymark on the reef of rocks 3 cables to the north.

⚓ Porto Oro (Palumbalza)

41°00'·6N 09°33'·3E

This is a small private harbour, literally dug out of the ground, on the western side of the Gulf of Marinella about 1·5 miles south of Punta Volpe. There is a small rock jetty on the north side of the entrance with a F.G light. The southern side of the entrance (only 50m away) has a F.R light. Approach the berths up a 15m wide, 50m long channel 3m deep. There are 50 berths but call before entering on VHF Ch 9 (or ☎ 0789 32005). Yachts are restricted to 14m overall length and should proceed at less than 1kn. Water and electricity are available, as are minor repair facilities. There is no fixed fuel point but fuel can be delivered by tanker if required – check in the harbour office for this facility.

⚓ Punta Marana

41°00'·3N 09°33'·7E

On the opposite side of the bay there is another totally artificial yacht harbour with a buoyed

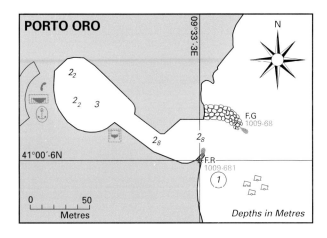

PORTO ORO

N

09°33'·3E

2₂

2₂   3

2₈   2₈

F.G
1009·68

41°00'·6N

F.R
1009·681

(1)

0   50
Metres

Depths in Metres

approach (watch for an isolated rock to the right of the entrance buoys) leading to 2 rocky jetties lit with Iso.R.3M and Iso.G.3M some 50m apart. There are berths for 300 yachts in depths of 1·5 to 2·5m with 18m maximum length. Call on VHF channels 9 or 16 before entering for berthing instructions.

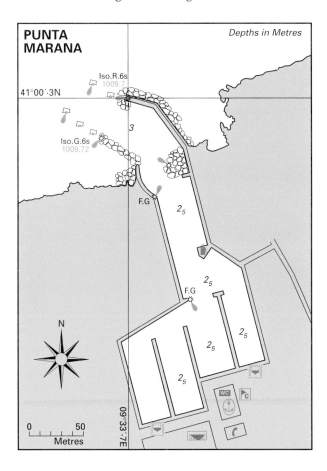

PUNTA MARANA

Depths in Metres

Iso.R.6s
1009.7

41°00'·3N

Iso.G.6s
1009.72

3

F.G

2₅

F.G

N

2₅

2₅

2₅

2₅

WC

0   50
Metres

09°33'·7E

⚓ **Marinelledda (or Marinella)**

At the southeast corner of this wide gulf there is the Isola Marinella. To the west and inshore of this island there is a tourist complex and there are a number of piers and floating pontoons run by the Circolo Nautico Marinella to which one can moor if there is space. There are 90 berths, contact the Circolo ☎ 0789 32592 for details of berthing.

There is water and electricity on the pontoons and there is a bar, restaurant and a small shop ashore.

To the east of the island there is a sailing school Vela Blu which has a floating pontoon with mooring buoys laid off. It is very rocky and shallow 1·5 to 2·5m with only limited facilities. Call on VHF Ch 9 for queries regarding berths.

It is also possible to anchor north of the island in 5m but it is a long way from the shore with reported poor holding and totally open to the NW–N winds.

Capo Figari

It is 5 miles to Capo Figari, passing Punta Sabina and Punta Cannigione. There are rocks some 2·5 cables off both these latter two headlands so they should be given a wide berth. There is an occasional daymark on the reef of rocks 2·5 cables to the north of Punta Cannigione.

Capo Figari is a high (340m) rocky cape that drops straight into the sea at its eastern edge. Watch for the very fluky winds that blow around these high headlands and be prepared to motor if the wind drops completely. This is the Golfo di Olbia. There is a small island, Isola Figarolo, to the south of the cape with a deep water channel between it and the land. There is a light on the island Fl.5s71m11M on a white hut with black bands.

Golfo Aranci

40°59'·6N 09°37'·3E

On the north shore, about 2 miles west of Capo Figari lies Golfo Aranci. This is a commercial port with many fishing boats and ferries coming and going at all times. There are 3 large quays for this traffic and there is a small harbour for 'minor vessels' which is usually completely full of small

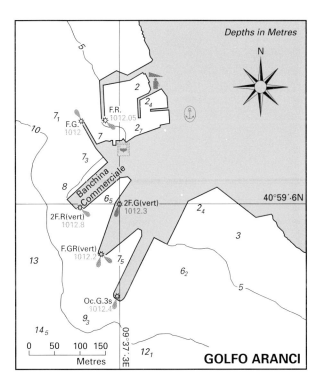

Depths in Metres

N

5

2

2₄

F.R.
1012.05

7₁

F.G.
1012

7

2₇

7₃

8

Banchina Commerciale

6₅   2F.G(vert)
1012.3

2F.R(vert)
1012.8

40°59'·6N

2₄

3

F.GR(vert)
1012.2

7₅

6₂

13

Oc.G.3s
1012.4

5

9₃

14₅

0   50   100 150
Metres

09°37'·3E

12₁

GOLFO ARANCI

fishing boats. There are lights on all the quays with the main light on the southeastern mole Oc.G.3s11m3M with a fog horn. There are plans to construct a port for pleasure boats on the north side of the harbour and work has started on this project. There is fuel and water at the quay with shops, restaurants etc. ashore and you can moor if you can find a space but with so many other delightful spots to visit this harbour is not recommended at present.

⚓ Baia Caddinas

40°59'·7N 09°36'·2E

A mile west of Golfo Aranci is a small yacht harbour with red and green buoys leading into an enclosed harbour with 100 berths (10 for visitors) with depths of 1–2·5m. There are lights on the entrance Fl.G.2s2M and Fl.R.2s2M, which appear to be in line on approaching but as the buoys of the fairway are not lit it is not recommended to enter at night. There is another light F.RG(vert)1M on the internal quay. There is water and electricity on the pontoons with fuel available and repairs can be undertaken but little else in the way of stores etc. These can be obtained in Golfo Aranci or Olbia.

⚓ Porri Island

Half way down the western coast of the gulf is a small island, Isola Porri, to the west of which is an anchorage sheltered from all but southerly winds. Anchor in 5m in excellent holding of sand and rock but take care of the Secca di Porri, a shallow rock (2m) at the south end of the bay.

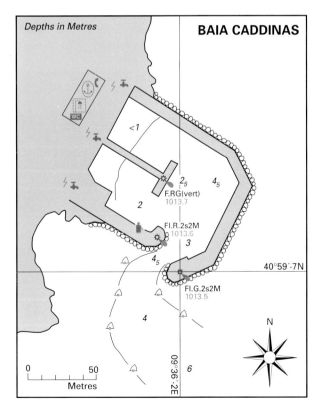

4·5 – Olbia to Capo Comino

South of Olbia and down to Capo Coda Cavallo the coast is indented with many small bays, many with a hotel complex at its head. The passage inside the islands of Tavolara and Molara are strewn with rocks and shallow patches as the scattered rusting wrecks testify. A large-scale chart is needed but the passages are of reasonable width and, with care, should not be too daunting a prospect. South of the Capo the coastal plain widens and the coast is reasonably flat with a small number of yacht harbours and more being developed each year. The area has many superb beaches – some sandy and others of pebbles – and is a favourite holiday area for local Sardinians and Italians who find the Costa Smeralda prices way above their budgets.

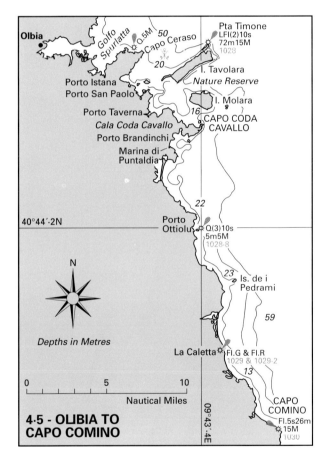

Olbia

General

Olbia is the main port for bringing commerce and tourists into Sardinia and does not really cater for yachtsmen. Having said that there is a small area, Darsena Bosazza, reserved for yachts just at the root of the long jetty on the south side. There is also a yacht club with some 150 private moorings to the south where it may be possible to moor if space is available. It is a busy town with all supplies and facilities available and it has excellent communications with the rest of the world (its airport and ferry terminals bring the majority of tourists to Sardinia).

⊕ (just SE of ferry terminal pier end) 40°55'·18N 09°31'·21E

Depth 7m in channel, 1 to 3m in darsena.
Number of berths 150 (all private and full) at YC, few in Darsena

Charts.

Admiralty *1210*
Italian *43, 322, 318*

Port radio

VHF Ch 16 or 11 for the *capitaneria*, VHF 12 or ☎ 26187 for YC.

Lights

1014 Isola della Bocca LFl.5s24m15M Two-storied white house 22m
1015 Buoy on N side of channel Fl.G.5s5m5M stbd hand triangle topmark
1015·2 Buoy on S side of channel Fl.R.5s5m5M port hand buoy can topmark
Buoys line the channel Fl.6s, 5s, 4s, 3s. as one enters
1019 Isola di Mezzo S end Fl.G.3s7m4M light on green tank 5m
1020 Quay Brin head F.G.6m3M Green pole 5m

Warnings

As stated above this is mainly a commercial harbour and commercial vessels must not be impeded, even in the approach channels but there is ample room. Work is continually going on in the harbour and buoys and beacons may disappear or be moved at any time – care is needed at all times.

Approach

From a position in the outer Gulf of Olbia the massive Capo Figari to the north and the unmistakable granite mass of Isola Tavolara to the south make for easy recognition.

By day Steer for the southwest corner of the gulf, but keeping well clear of Capo Ceraso which has rocks to the north (buoyed and with beacons), until the lighthouse on Isola della Bocca is identified (white square tower on a 2-storey building). Steer for that until the channel buoys are obvious then steer down the channel between the buoys on a course of 269°. When the large ferry terminal becomes obvious veer off to the left and pick up the second set of channel buoys that lead to the yacht moorings.

By night Identify the light on Isola della Bocca and steer for it until the ferry terminal light is clear

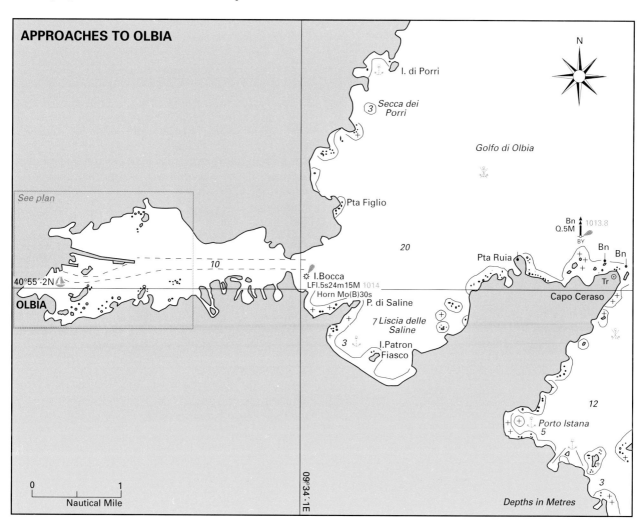

APPROACHES TO OLBIA

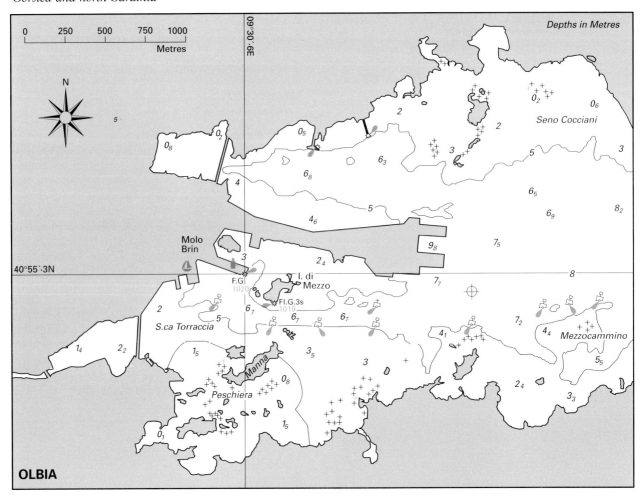

and/or the channel buoys can be picked up. Steer in towards the ferry terminal light on 269° and when close to the end of the jetty veer to the left and pick up the second channel buoys. Note that the lights of the yacht harbour can be difficult to pick out against the lights of the town.

Berths

Berthing is stern-to the quay wall at Molo Brin but contact should be made with harbourmaster or the yacht club (which does not have any visitors' moorings but may allow a short stay if there is space due to club yachts being away on cruises).

Formalities

As with all big ports there are police, customs and immigration authorities who may well wish to see the ship's, and possibly the crew's, papers.

Facilities

All.

⚓ Liscia delle Saline

Leaving Olbia there is a fair-sized bay just to the east of Isola della Bocca where you can anchor in 5m just to the west of the small island – there is just a salt marsh to the south and it is open to the north.

⚓ Porto Istana

Capo Ceraso has off-lying dangers to the north with a N cardinal buoy Q.5M some half a mile northwest of the point. Some 2 miles south of the point at the westernmost part of Golfo Spurlatta there is a small anchorage (with its usual large hotel complex ashore). There is a reef of rocks on the north side. Anchor in 3 to 5m on sand and rock but good holding.

Warning

Note that although Capo Ceraso falls steeply into the sea on its eastern side the waters from Porto Istana to Capo Coda Cavallo have numerous unmarked shallow reefs. The passage between the mainland and Tavolara is tricky and caution must be exercised when navigating in this area. It is recommended that a large-scale chart is available to show the many dangers in these waters.

⚓ Porto Spurlatta

Half-a-mile SE of Porto Istana is a small inlet with some wooden pontoons in shallow water for hotel guests' RIBs. One can anchor off in 3m on sand.

⚓ Porto San Paolo

A small bay where you can anchor in 3 to 5m on sand – care is needed in the approach as there is an unmarked rock just off the beach in front of the inevitable hotel complex. There may be up to 5 pontoons extending from the shore but the depths

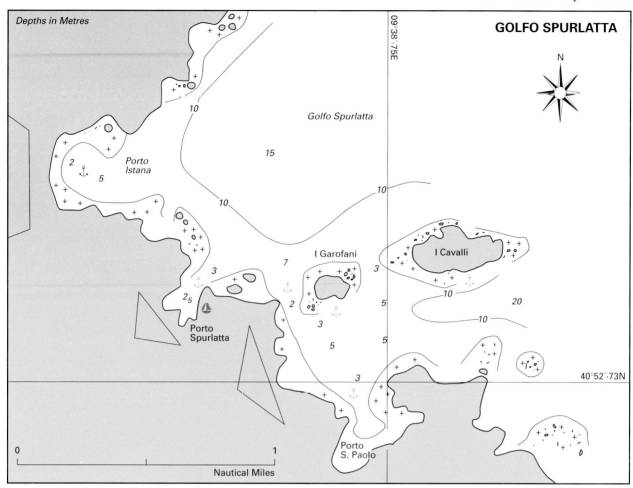

are only 1 to 2m and there is reputed to be berths for 150 boats but with maximum length of 8·5m.

⚓ Porto Taverna

This bay is a mile south of Isola Reulino (inshore of which is a shipwreck!). Anchor in 5m on sand and weed but the holding is good. There is a small quay ashore for use by the military but water can be obtained from it. There are many villas on the coast around the bay but no real facilities exist ashore.

⚓ Tavolara Island

This island is a steep-to granite plug rising to 565m (1,855ft) with a low-lying spit at the western corner. The eastern half of the island is a military base and a prohibited area. There is an anchorage on the south side of the spit off a beach in 3 to 6m on sand.

Isola Molara

Another steep-to granite island lying to the south of Tavolara – there is a small bay on the north shore which affords shelter from southerlies but there is nothing else on the island whatsoever.

⚓ Cala Coda Cavallo

Just to the west of the cape and south of Isola Proratora is a pleasant beach open only to northwesterly winds. There is some development ashore with a concrete jetty. Anchor in 3 to 5m with the better holding ground being in the west of the bay.

⚓ Porto Brandinchi

Immediately south of Capo Coda Cavallo is a large bay with Isola Rossa (or Ruia) at the north end. Approach should be made on a course of 270°, leaving the island 100m to starboard to avoid a bank of unmarked rocks, Scoglio Testa di Moro, situated at the centre of the entrance to the bay. Anchor in the bay WNW of the island in 4 to 8m on sand or off some shore development WSW of the island.

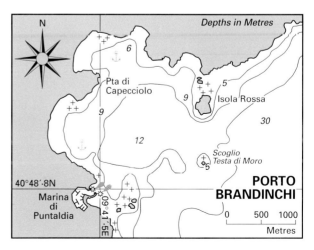

⚓ Marina di Puntaldia

40°48'·8N 09°41'·5E

This is a newly dredged marina some 2 miles south of Capo Coda Cavallo in the southwest corner of the above bay, just northwest of Punta Sabbatino. There are rocks on both sides of the entrance and entry is limited to daylight hours only. Buoys are laid in the season to mark the shallower patches and a sectored entry light is planned. At present there is a Fl.G.3s6m5M on the western mole with a Fl.R.3s6m5M on the eastern mole. Depths inside vary from 2·5 to 4·5m and there are 385 berths. Precedence in the entrance is given to departing yachts. VHF Ch 9 is available as is ☎ 0784 864390. All facilities are available.

⚓ Cala d'Ambra or La Cinta

Just south of Punta Sabbatino there is a very long (3kms) beach, La Cinta, on a spit of land that separates the Stagno di San Teodoro, an inland body of brackish water, from the sea. At the south end of the beach two breakwaters have been constructed. It appears a marina is being constructed and further news is being sought.

⚓ Porto Ottiolu

40°44'·3N 09°42'·9E

Some 6·5 miles south of Capo Coda Cavallo lies Punta d'Ottiolu with a small island, Isolotto d'Ottiolu, half a mile to the south again. Between these two lies the yacht harbour which has two stone moles projecting into the sea. The low-lying Isolotto d'Ottiolu is connected to the shore by a shallow (<1m) reef which extends for at least 200m

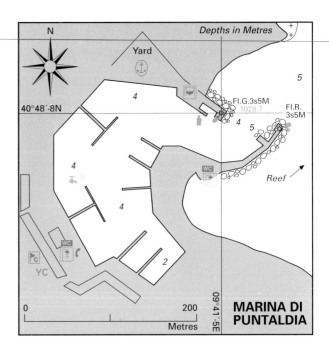

MARINA DI PUNTALDIA

northeast of the islet. Approaching from the north leave Punta Ottiolu at least 0·5 mile to starboard and steer south until the bearing of the outer mole is about 250° then it is clear to steer that course for the harbour entrance. From the south leave Isolotto d'Ottiolu at least ½ mile to port and steer north until the outer mole bears 250° and follow that course to the entrance. If leaving the harbour to continue southwards do NOT attempt to go between the islet and the mainland but keep well clear of the islet and reef.

The outer mole is lit with Fl.G.3s5m5M and the inner is Fl.R.3s5m5M – looking almost in line as the

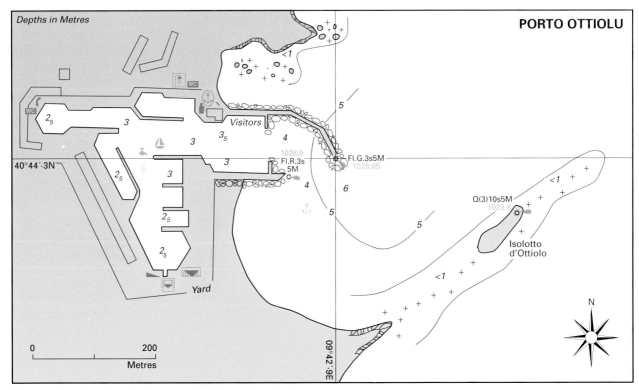

PORTO OTTIOLU

course of 250° is followed as the entrance faces southeast. Note there is also a light on the Isolotto d'Ottiolu Q(3)10s5m5M on a black mast with a yellow band with a topmark of two cones base-to-base (E cardinal). First time arrivals should call ahead on VHF Ch 16 or 9 to pass details of yacht to the harbour authorities. Inside there are berths for 400 yachts, of which 40 are for visitors, all in depths of 3m. There are several rules to be observed in this marina – all sensible – like no fishing, no ditching of anything from the yacht, 3-knot limit etc. All reasonable facilities are available here.

⛵ La Caletta

40°36'·6N 09°45'·3E

Some 9 miles south of Ottiolu lies the yacht harbour of La Caletta. Give Isola dei Pedrami half way down a good berth to seaward – the passage between the island and the shore is very rocky and shallow and is not recommended. This is another port with a southeast facing entrance with a long outer mole running southeast. The position of the entrance is difficult to make out from seaward but the WP position should be approached on a course of 270° to clear all dangers. Closer in the houses behind the harbour and the San Giovanni Tower, at the root of the long mole, become clear. The moles are lit Fl.G.3s11m1M and Fl.R.3s13m1M but note limited range of 1 mile. There are berths for 400 yachts with the southern mole being reserved solely for fishermen.

Capo Comino

5 miles south of La Caletta is Capo Comino, a bare headland lit Fl.5s26m15M which is housed in a white square tower and dwelling. For yachtsmen venturing further south they should be advised to remain at least one mile offshore to avoid (a) the worst of the gusts that may blow down the valleys suddenly and (b) the many unlit rocks that abound on this generally steep-to coast.

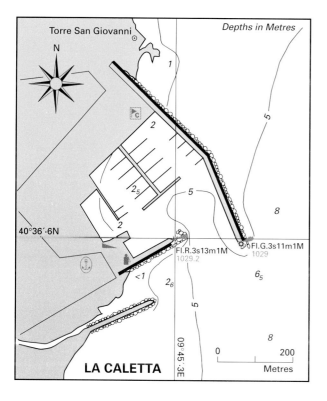

LA CALETTA

Appendix

The charts listed in this section are available from:

Imray Laurie Norie & Wilson Ltd
Wych House The Broadway St Ives
Cambridgeshire PE27 5BT England
+44(0)1480 462114 *Fax* +44(0)1480 496109
E-mail orders@imray.com
Payment can be made by credit card.

I. Charts
British Admiralty charts

Chart	Title	Scale
1202	Ports on the north and west coasts of Sardinia	
	Porto di Alghero	7,500
	Porto di Carloforte: Porto Vesme	12,500
	Porto Torres	15,000
	Approaches to Alghero	50,000
1204	Approaches to Porto Torres	60,000
1205	Oristano and approaches	40,000
	Oristano	20,000
1207	Canale di San Pietro and Golfo di Palmas	50,000
	Porto di Sant' Antioco (Pointe Romano)	10,000
1208	Approaches to Cagliari	30,000
	Porto di Cagliari	15,000
1210	Ports on the east coast of Sardinia	
	Porto di Arbatax	10,000
	Porto di Olbia	12,500
	Approaches to Arbatax	30,000
1211	Capo Ferro to Capo Coda Cavallo	50,000
1212	Approaches to La Maddalena	25,000
	La Maddalena	10,000
1213	Bonifacio strait	50,000
	Golfo di Arzachena	30,000
1424	Ports on the south and west coasts of Corse	
	Bonifacio	7,500
	Ajaccio: Propriano	10,000
	Golfe d'Ajaccio and Golfe de Valinco	60,000
1425	Ports on the north and east coasts of Corse	
	Macinaggio	10,000
	Bastia	15,000
	Calvi	17,500
	Porto-Vecchio	25,000
	Approaches to Calvi	50,000
1983	Capo Carbonara to Capo San Vito	300,000
1985	Ajaccio to Oristano including Bonifacio strait	300,000
1990	Oristano to Arbatax including Golfo di Cagliari	300,000
1992	Porto-Vecchio to Arbatax including Bonifacio Strait	300,000
1998	Nice to Livorno including Gulf of Genoa	300,000
1999	Livorno to Civitavecchia including Northern Corse	300,000

French charts (SHOM)

1461	Ile Capraja	20,000
3675	Carte générale de l'Île de Sardaigne	385,000
4212	Port Conte et Rade d'Alghero	30,000
4229	Golfe d'Asinara	94,600
	Cartouches: Passage dei Fornelli	15,000

Chart	Title	Scale
	Porto Torres	25,000
6713	Côte Nord-Est de la Corse, canal de Corse	152,000
6821	Côte Ouest de Corse – Du Cap Corse au golfe d'Ajaccio	152,000
6822	Abords Nord de Bastia	50,300
6823	Abords Sud de Bastia	50,300
6850	Saint-Florent, Centuri, Macinaggio	
	Cartouches: Golfe de Saint-Florent	15,000
	Baie de Centuri	10,000
	Baies de Macinaggio et de Tamarone	10,000
6851	Ports d'Ajaccio et de Propriano	
	Cartouches: Port d'Ajaccio	7,500
	Port de Propriano	10,000
6855	Du phare d'Alistro à Solenzara	51,000
6856	Abords et Port de Bastia	15,000
6911	Golfe de Porto-Vecchio	15,000
6929	Abords de Porto-Vecchio – De l'anse de Favone aux îles Lavezzi	50,000
6942	De Punta d'Orchina au Cap Muro – Abords d'Ajaccio	50,000
6969	Du Cap Corse à la Punta di l'Acciolu – Golfe de Saint-Florent	50,300
6970	De Punta di l'Acciolu à Capo Cavallo	50,500
6980	L'Ile Rousse – Sant'Ambrogio – Calvi	
	Cartouches: Abords de l'île Rousse	15,000
	Abords de la Marine de Sant'Ambrogio	15,000
	Abords de Calvi – De Punta Spano à La Revellata	15,000
7024	Bouches de Bonifacio	50,000
	Cartoches: Golfo di Arzachena	50,000
7025	Ile de Corse	250,000
7050	De Calvi à Cargèse	50,000
7096	Baie de Figari – Port de Bonifacio	
	Cartouches: Baie de Figari	10,000
	Port de Bonifacio	5,000
7162	Du Capo Muro au Capo Feno	50,000
	Cartouches: Mouillage de Porto Pollo	10,000
	Mouillage de Campomoro	10,000
7189	Golfes d'Olbia et d'Aranci – Iles Tavolara et Molara	25,000
7190	Golfe de Congianus – De Capo Ferro à Capo Figari	25,000
7191	Archipel de la Maddelena	25,000
7280	Golfe d'Ajaccio	25,000
7316	Golfe de Sagone	25,000

Italian charts

40	Da Capo Corso ad Alistro e all'isola d'Elba	100,000
41	Da Alistro alle Bocche di Bonifacio	100,000
42	Da Castelsardo a Olbia e Bocche di Bonifacio	100,000
43	Da Olbia a Capo de Monte Santu	100,000
44	Da Capo di Monte Santu a Capo Carbonara	100,000

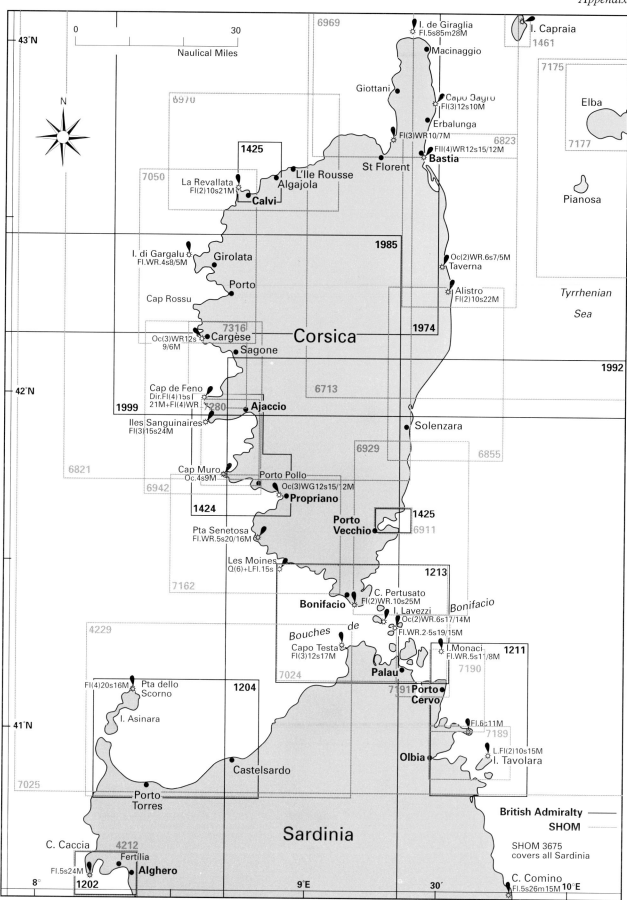

43°N

0   30
Nautical Miles

N

6969

I. de Giraglia
Fl.5s85m28M

I. Capraia
1461

Macinaggio

7175

Elba

Giottani

Capo Sagro
Fl(3)12s10M

7177

Erbalunga
Fl(3)WR10/7M

Pianosa

6823

Fll(4)WR12s15/12M
Bastia

St Florent

1425

L'Ile Rousse

7050

La Revallata
Fl(2)10s21M

Algajola

Calvi

1985

I. di Gargalu
Fl.WR.4s8/5M

Girolata

Oc(2)WR.6s7/5M
Taverna

Porto

Cap Rossu

Alistro
Fl(2)10s22M

Tyrrhenian

7316

Oc(3)WR12s
9/6M

Cargèse

Corsica

1974

Sea

Sagone

1992

42°N

Cap de Feno
Dir.Fl(4)1bs
21M+Fl(4)WR

6713

1999

7280

Ajaccio

Iles Sanguinaires
Fl(3)15s24M

Solenzara

6929

6855

6821

Cap Muro
Oc.4s9M

Porto Pollo
Oc(3)WG12s15/12M

6942

Propriano

1424

**Porto
Vecchio**

1425

6911

Pta Senetosa
Fl.WR.5s20/16M

Les Moines
Q(6)+LFl.15s

1213

7162

C. Pertusato
Fl(2)WR.10s25M

Bonifacio

Bonifacio

I. Lavezzi
Oc(2)WR.6s17/14M

4229

Bouches

de

Fl.WR.2·5s19/15M

Capo Testa
Fl(3)12s17M

I.Monaci
Fl.WR.5s11/8M

1211

7024

Palau

7190

Pta dello
Scorno
Fl(4)20s16M

1204

7191

**Porto
Cervo**

41°N

I. Asinara

Fl.6s11M

7189

Olbia

L.Fl(2)10s15M
I. Tavolara

Castelsardo

7025

Porto
Torres

Sardinia

British Admiralty ——
SHOM ‑‑‑‑‑‑

SHOM 3675
covers all Sardinia

C. Caccia

4212

Fertília

Fl.5s24M

Alghero

1202

8°

9°E

30′

C. Comino
Fl.5s26m15M **10°E**

BRITISH ADMIRALTY AND FRENCH (SHOM) CHARTS

Chart	Title	Scale
45	Da Capo Carbonara a Capo Spartivento	100,000
46	Da Capo Spartivento all'Isola S Pietro	100,000
47	Dall'isola S Pietro a Capo S Marco	100,000
48	Da Capo S Marco a Capo Caccia	100,000
49	Da Capo Caccia a Castel Sardo e isola Asinara	100,000
281	Rade di la Maddalena e di S Stefano	5,000
282	Ancoraggi tra La Maddalena e la costa nord della Sardegna	10,000
286	Porto Torres	10,000
289	Golfo dell'Asinara	50,000
	Passaggio del Fornelli	10,000
291	Porto di Oristano	10,000
292	Porto Conte e rada di Alghero	25,000
293	Golfo di Oristano	40,000
294	Canale di S Pietro	25,000
295	Porti di Porto Vesme e Portoscuso	5,000
296	Porto di S Antioco (Ponte Romano)	5,000
297	Porto di Carloforte	5,000
298	Golfo di Palmas	50,000
299	Litorale di Cagliari	30,000
311	Porto di Cagliari	10,000
315	Litorale di Arbatax	25,000
316	Porto di Arbatax	5,000
318	Porto di Olbia	10,000
319	Porti Minori a ancoraggi della Sardegna nord-orientale	
	Cala Volpe	5,000
	Iscia di Vacca	5,000
	Porto Cervo	5,000
322	Golfi di Oblia e degli Aranci – Isole Tavolara e Molara	25,000
	Porto di Golfo Aranci	5,000
323	Golfo di Congianus e Passo delle Bisce	25,000
324	Arcipelago di La Maddalena – Foglio est	25,000
325	Arcipelago di La Maddalena – Foglio ovest	25,000
326	Bocche di Bonifacio	50,000
	Golfo di Arzachena	50,000
911/05	Porto di Alghero	4,000
911/06	Porto di Bosa Marina	4,000
912/01	Porto di Santa Teresa di Gallura (Longosardo)	5,000
2140	Litorale e porto di Bastia	15,000
2143	Golfo di Porto Vecchio	15,000
2145	Baia di Figari – Porto de Bonifacio	
	Baia de Figari	10,000
	Porto de Bonifacio	5,000
2147	Porti de Ajaccio e di Propriano	
	Porto di Ajaccio	7,500
	Porto di Propriano	10,000
2150	Da Cap Corse a Punta di l'Acciolu - Golfo di Saint-Florent	50,300
2152	Da Punta di l'Acciolu a Capo Cavallo	50,500
2154	Da Calvi a Cargese	50,000
2156	Da Punta d'Orchina a Capo Muro – Paraggi di Ajaccio	50,000
2158	Da Cap Muro a Cap de Feno	50,000
	Ancoraggi di Porto Pollo	10,000
	Ancoraggi di Campomoro	10,000
2160	Litorale di Porto-Vecchio – Dall'anse de Favone alle Iles Lavezzi	50,000

Chart	Title	Scale
2162	Dal faro d'Alistro a Solenzara	51,000
2164	Litorale a sud di Bastia	50,600
2166	Litorale a nord di Bastia	50,300

Imray Charts

M6	La Corse	255,000
	Plans Macinaggio, Bastia, Calvi, Ajaccio, Bonifacio, Propriano	
M8	Sardegna (north)	250,000
	Plans Porto Brandinghi, Alghero, Porto Cervo, Palau, La Caletta, Porto Torres, Stintino, Passagio del Fornelli, Castelsardo	
M9	Sardegna (south)	250,000
	Plans Cagliari, Arbatax, Torre Grande, Carloforte, Calasetta, Capitana, Porto Seuso, Villasimius, Marina Piccola, Porto Carallo	

II. Bibliography

Navigational

Admiralty publications

Sailing Directions (NP 46), Mediterranean Pilot Vol. II and supplements

List of Lights, Vol. E, Mediterranean, Black and Red Seas

List of Radio Signals

Vol 1(1) Coast Radio Stations NP281(1)

Vol 2 Radio Navigation Aids, Electronic Position Fixing Systems and Radio Time Signals NP282

Vol3(1) Maritime Safety Information Services NP283(1)

Vol 5 Global Maritime Distress and Safety Systems NP285

Vol 6(3) Pilot Services, Traffic Services and Port Operations NP286(3)

Admiralty Maritime Communications NP289

French Naval publications

Instructions Nautiques Series D, Vol. II

Italian Naval Publications

Portolano del Mediterraneo, Vol. 1A (Istituto Idrografico N. 3148)

Elenco di Fari (Istituto Idrografico N. 3134)

The directions above are all for bigger craft than are catered for in this book but they are useful reference works however.

Other pilots and guides

Mediterranean France and Corsica Pilot Rod Heikell. Imray

Italian Waters Pilot Rod Heikell. Imray

Imray Mediterranean Almanac ed. Rod Heikell. A biennial almanac. Imray

Votre Livre de Bord, Bloc Marin, a type of almanac with many plans – published yearly

Pagine Azzurre Italian version of above – published yearly

Weather Forecasts RYA Handbook G5 – comprehensive weather data – updated yearly

Planning a Foreign Cruise Vol 2 RYA Handbook C2 – updated yearly

Guide Nautique de La Corse by La Fédération Corse des Ports de Plaisance (colour) in French

Pilot Côtiers Fenwick No. 3 Alain Rondeau, Editions du Pen Duick

Index